Introduction to UNIX®

Second Edition

David I. Schwartz

Department of Engineering
Cornell University
Ithaca, NY

PEARSON
Prentice
Hall

Upper Saddle River, NJ 07458

Library of Congress Cataloging-in-Publication Data

Schwartz, David I.
   Introduction to UNIX / David I. Schwartz.-- 2nd ed.
     p. cm.
   Includes bibliographical references and index.
   ISBN 0-13-061308-8
    1. UNIX (Computer file) 2. Operating systems (Computers I. Title.

   QA76.76.O63S439 2006
   005.4'32--dc22

                            2005050951

Editorial Director, ECS: *Marcia J. Horton*
Executive Editor: *Eric Svendsen*
Associate Editor: *Dee Bernhard*
Executive Managing Editor: *Vince O'Brien*
Managing Editor: *David A. George*
Production Editor: *Wendy Kopf*
Director of Creative Services: *Paul Belfanti*
Art Director: *Jayne Conte*
Cover Designer: *Bruce Kenselaar*
Art Editor: *Greg Dulles*
Manufacturing Manager: *Alexis Heydt-Long*
Manufacturing Buyer: *Lisa McDowell*
Senior Marketing Manager: *Holly Stark*

© 2006, 1999 by Pearson Education, Inc.
Upper Saddle River, New Jersey 07458

Pearson Prentice Hall™ is a trademark of Pearson Education, Inc.

Printed in the United States of America.

10 9 8 7 6 5 4 3 2 1

ISBN 0-13-061308-8

Pearson Education Ltd., *London*
Pearson Education Australia Pty.Ltd., *Sydney*
Pearson Education Singapore,Pte.Ltd.
Pearson Education North Asia Ltd., *Hong Kong*
Pearson Education Canada,Inc., *Toronto*
Pearson Educación de Mexico,S.A.de C.V.
Pearson Education—Japan, *Tokyo*
Pearson Education Malaysia,Pte.Ltd.
Pearson Education, *Upper Saddle River, New Jersey*

About ESource

ESource—The Prentice Hall Engineering Source—
www.prenhall.com/esource

ESource—The Prentice Hall Engineering Source gives professors the power to harness the full potential of their text and their first-year engineering course. More than just a collection of books, ESource is a unique publishing system revolving around the ESource website—www.prenhall.com/esource. ESource enables you to put your stamp on your book just as you do your course. It lets you:

Control   You choose exactly which chapters are in your book and in what order they appear. Of course, you can choose the entire book if you'd like and stay with the authors' original order.

Optimize   Get the most from your book and your course. ESource lets you produce the optimal text for your students needs.

Customize   You can add your own material anywhere in your text's presentation, and your final product will arrive at your bookstore as a professionally formatted text. Of course, all titles in this series are available as stand-alone texts, or as bundles of two or more books sold at a discount. Contact your PH sales rep for discount information.

ESource ACCESS

Professors who choose to bundle two or more texts from the ESource series for their class, or use an ESource custom book will be providing their students with an on-line library of intro engineering content—ESource Access. We've designed ESource ACCESS to provide students a flexible, searchable, on-line resource. Free access codes come in bundles and custom books are valid for one year after initial log-on. Contact your PH sales rep for more information.

ESource Content

All the content in ESource was written by educators specifically for freshman/first-year students. Authors tried to strike a balanced level of presentation, an approach that was neither formulaic nor trivial, and one that did not focus too heavily on advanced topics that most introductory students do not encounter until later classes. Because many professors do not have extensive time to cover these topics in the classroom, authors prepared each text with the idea that many students would use it for self-instruction and independent study. Students should be able to use this content to learn the software tool or subject on their own.

While authors had the freedom to write texts in a style appropriate to their particular subject, all followed certain guidelines created to promote a consistency that makes students comfortable. Namely, every chapter opens with a clear set of **Objectives**, includes **Practice Boxes** throughout the chapter, and ends with a number of **Problems**, and a list of **Key Terms**. **Applications Boxes** are spread throughout the book with the intent of giving students a real-world perspective of engineering. **Success Boxes** provide the student with advice about college study skills, and help students avoid the common pitfalls of first-year students. In addition, this series contains an entire book titled ***Engineering Success*** by Peter Schiavone of the University of Alberta intended to expose students quickly to what it takes to be an engineering student.

Creating Your Book

Using ESource is simple. You preview the content either on-line or through examination copies of the books you can request on-line, from your PH sales rep, or by calling 1-800-526-0485. Create an on-line outline of the content you want, in the order you want, using ESource's simple interface. Insert your own material into the text flow. If you are not ready to order, ESource will save your work. You can come back at any time and change, re-arrange, or add more material to your creation. Once you're finished you'll automatically receive an ISBN. Give it to your bookstore and your book will arrive on their shelves four to six weeks after they order. Your custom desk copies with their instructor supplements will arrive at your address at the same time.

To learn more about this new system for creating the perfect textbook, go to www.prenhall.com/esource. You can either go through the on-line walkthrough of how to create a book, or experiment yourself.

Titles in the ESource Series

Design Concepts for Engineers, 3/e
0-13-146499-X
Mark N. Horenstein

Engineering Success, 2/e
0-13-041827-7
Peter Schiavone

Engineering Design and Problem Solving, 2E
0-13-093399-6
Steven K. Howell

Exploring Engineering
0-13-093442-9
Joe King

Engineering Ethics
0-13-784224-4
Charles B. Fleddermann

Introduction to Engineering Analysis, 2/e
0-13-145332-7
Kirk D. Hagen

Introduction to Engineering Communication
0-13-146102-8
Hillary Hart

Introduction to Engineering Experimentation
0-13-032835-9
Ronald W. Larsen, John T. Sears, and Royce Wilkinson

Introduction to Mechanical Engineering
0-13-019640-1
Robert Rizza

Introduction to Electrical and Computer Engineering
0-13-033363-8
Charles B. Fleddermann and Martin Bradshaw

Introduction to MATLAB 7
0-13-147492-8
Delores Etter and David C. Kuncicky with Holly Moore

MATLAB Programming
0-13-035127-X
David C. Kuncicky

Introduction to Mathcad 2000
0-13-020007-7
Ronald W. Larsen

Introduction to Mathcad 11
0-13-008177-9
Ronald W. Larsen

Introduction to Maple 8
0-13-032844-8
David I. Schwartz

Mathematics Review
0-13-011501-0
Peter Schiavone

Power Programming with VBA/Excel
0-13-047377-4
Steven C. Chapra

Introduction to Excel 2002
0-13-008175-2
David C. Kuncicky

Introduction to Excel, 3/e
0-13-146470-1
David C. Kuncicky and Ronald W. Larsen

About the Authors

No project could ever come to pass without a group of authors who have the vision and the courage to turn a stack of blank paper into a book. The authors in this series, who worked diligently to produce their books, provide the building blocks of the series.

Martin D. Bradshaw was born in Pittsburg, KS in 1936, grew up in Kansas and the surrounding states of Arkansas and Missouri, graduating from Newton High School, Newton, KS in 1954. He received the B.S.E.E. and M.S.E.E. degrees from the University of Wichita in 1958 and 1961, respectively. A Ford Foundation fellowship at Carnegie Institute of Technology followed from 1961 to 1963 and he received the Ph.D. degree in electrical engineering in 1964. He spent his entire academic career with the Department of Electrical and Computer Engineering at the University of New Mexico (1961-1963 and 1991-1996). He served as the Assistant Dean for Special Programs with the UNM College of Engineering from 1974 to 1976 and as the Associate Chairman for the EECE Department from 1993 to 1996. During the period 1987-1991 he was a consultant with his own company, EE Problem Solvers. During 1978 he spent a sabbatical year with the State Electricity Commission of Victoria, Melbourne, Australia. From 1979 to 1981 he served an IPA assignment as a Project Officer at the U.S. Air Force Weapons Laboratory, Kirkland AFB, Albuquerque, NM. He has won numerous local, regional, and national teaching awards, including the George Westinghouse Award from the ASEE in 1973. He was awarded the IEEE Centennial Medal in 2000.

Acknowledgments: Dr. Bradshaw would like to acknowledge his late mother, who gave him a great love of reading and learning, and his father, who taught him to persist until the job is finished. The encouragement of his wife, Jo, and his six children is a never-ending inspiration.

Stephen J. Chapman received a B.S. degree in Electrical Engineering from Louisiana State University (1975), the M.S.E. degree in Electrical Engineering from the University of Central Florida (1979), and pursued further graduate studies at Rice University. Mr. Chapman is currently Manager of Technical Systems for British Aerospace Australia, in Melbourne, Australia. In this position, he provides technical direction and design authority for the work of younger engineers within the company. He also continues to teach at local universities on a part-time basis.

Mr. Chapman is a Senior Member of the Institute of Electrical and Electronics Engineers (and several of its component societies). He is also a member of the Association for Computing Machinery and the Institution of Engineers (Australia).

Steven C. Chapra presently holds the Louis Berger Chair for Computing and Engineering in the Civil and Environmental Engineering Department at Tufts University. Dr. Chapra received engineering degrees from Manhattan College and the University of Michigan. Before joining the faculty at Tufts, he taught at Texas A&M University, the University of Colorado, and Imperial College, London. His research interests focus on surface water-quality modeling and advanced computer applications in environmental engineering. He has published over 50 refereed journal articles, 20 software packages and 6 books. He has received a number of awards including the 1987 ASEE Merriam/Wiley Distinguished Author Award, the 1993 Rudolph Hering Medal, and teaching awards from Texas A&M, the University of Colorado, and the Association of Environmental Engineering and Science Professors.

Acknowledgments: To the Berger Family for their many contributions to engineering education. I would also like to thank David Clough for his friendship and insights, John Walkenbach for his wonderful books, and my colleague Lee Minardi and my students Kenny William, Robert Viesca and Jennifer Edelmann for their suggestions.

Mark Dix began working with AutoCAD in 1985 as a programmer for CAD Support Associates, Inc. He helped design a system for creating estimates and bills of material directly from AutoCAD drawing databases for use in the automated conveyor industry. This system became the basis for systems still widely in use today. In 1986 he began collaborating with Paul Riley to create AutoCAD training materials, combining Riley's background in industrial design and training with Dix's background in writing, curriculum development, and programming. Mr. Dix received the M.S. degree in education from the University of Massachusetts. He is currently the Director of Dearborn Academy High School in Arlington, Massachusetts.

Delores M. Etter is a Professor of Electrical and Computer Engineering at the University of Colorado. Dr. Etter was a faculty member at the University of New Mexico and also a Visiting Professor at Stanford University. Dr. Etter was responsible for the Freshman Engineering Program at the University of New Mexico and is active in the Integrated Teaching Laboratory at the University of Colorado. She was elected a Fellow of the Institute of Electrical and Electronics Engineers for her contributions to education and for her technical leadership in digital signal processing.

Charles B. Fleddermann is a professor in the Department of Electrical and Computer Engineering at the University of New Mexico in Albuquerque, New Mexico. All of his degrees are in electrical engineering: his Bachelor's degree from the University of Notre Dame, and the Master's and Ph.D. from the University of Illinois at Urbana-Champaign. Prof. Fleddermann developed an engineering ethics course for his department in response to the ABET requirement to incorporate ethics topics into the undergraduate engineering curriculum. *Engineering Ethics* was written as a vehicle for presenting ethical theory, analysis, and problem solving to engineering undergraduates in a concise and readily accessible way.

Acknowledgments: I would like to thank Profs. Charles Harris and Michael Rabins of Texas A & M University whose NSF sponsored workshops on engineering ethics got me started thinking in this field. Special thanks to my wife Liz, who proofread the manuscript for this book, provided many useful suggestions, and who helped me learn how to teach "soft" topics to engineers.

Kirk D. Hagen is a professor at Weber State University in Ogden, Utah. He has taught introductory-level engineering courses and upper-division thermal science courses at WSU since 1993. He received his B.S. degree in physics from Weber State College and his M.S. degree in mechanical engineering from Utah State University, after which he worked as a thermal designer/analyst in the aerospace and electronics industries. After several years of engineering practice, he resumed his formal education, earning his Ph.D. in mechanical engineering at the University of Utah. Hagen is the author of an undergraduate heat transfer text.

Mark N. Horenstein is a Professor in the Department of Electrical and Computer Engineering at Boston University. He has degrees in Electrical Engineering from M.I.T. and U.C. Berkeley and has been involved in teaching engineering design for the greater part of his academic career. He devised and developed the senior design project class taken by all electrical and computer engineering students at Boston University. In this class, the students work for a virtual engineering company developing products and systems for real-world engineering and social-service clients.

Acknowledgments: I would like to thank Prof. James Bethune, the architect of the Peak Performance event at Boston University, for his permission to highlight the competition in my text. Several of the ideas relating to brainstorming and teamwork were derived from a workshop on engineering design offered by Prof. Charles Lovas of Southern Methodist University. The principles of estimation were derived in part from a freshman engineering problem posed by Prof. Thomas Kincaid of Boston University.

 **Steven Howell** is the Chairman and a Professor of Mechanical Engineering at Lawrence Technological University. Prior to joining LTU in 2001, Dr. Howell led a knowledge-based engineering project for Visteon Automotive Systems and taught computer-aided design classes for Ford Motor Company engineers. Dr. Howell also has a total of 15 years experience as an engineering faculty member at Northern Arizona University, the University of the Pacific, and the University of Zimbabwe. While at Northern Arizona University, he helped develop and implement an award-winning interdisciplinary series of design courses simulating a corporate engineering-design environment.

 **Douglas W. Hull** is a graduate student in the Department of Mechanical Engineering at Carnegie Mellon University in Pittsburgh, Pennsylvania. He is the author of *Mastering Mechanics I Using Matlab 5*, and contributed to *Mechanics of Materials* by Bedford and Liechti. His research in the Sensor Based Planning lab involves motion planning for hyper-redundant manipulators, also known as serpentine robots.

 **Scott D. James** is a staff lecturer at Kettering University (formerly GMI Engineering & Management Institute) in Flint, Michigan. He is currently pursuing a Ph.D. in Systems Engineering with an emphasis on software engineering and computer-integrated manufacturing. He chose teaching as a profession after several years in the computer industry. "I thought that it was really important to know what it was like outside of academia. I wanted to provide students with classes that were up to date and provide the information that is really used and needed."

Acknowledgments: Scott would like to acknowledge his family for the time to work on the text and his students and peers at Kettering who offered helpful critiques of the materials that eventually became the book.

 **Joe King** received the B.S. and M.S. degrees from the University of California at Davis. He is a Professor of Computer Engineering at the University of the Pacific, Stockton, CA, where he teaches courses in digital design, computer design, artificial intelligence, and computer networking. Since joining the UOP faculty, Professor King has spent yearlong sabbaticals teaching in Zimbabwe, Singapore, and Finland. A licensed engineer in the state of California, King's industrial experience includes major design projects with Lawrence Livermore National Laboratory, as well as independent consulting projects. Prof. King has had a number of books published with titles including *Matlab*, MathCAD, *Exploring Engineering*, and *Engineering and Society*.

 **David C. Kuncicky** is a native Floridian. He earned his Baccalaureate in psychology, Master's in computer science, and Ph.D. in computer science from Florida State University. He has served as a faculty member in the Department of Electrical Engineering at the FAMU–FSU College of Engineering and the Department of Computer Science at Florida State University. He has taught computer science and computer engineering courses for over 15 years. He has published research in the areas of intelligent hybrid systems and neural networks. He is currently the Director of Engineering at Bioreason, Inc. in Sante Fe, New Mexico.

Acknowledgments: Thanks to Steffie and Helen for putting up with my late nights and long weekends at the computer. Finally, thanks to Susan Bassett for having faith in my abilities, and for providing continued tutelage and support.

Ron Larsen is a Professor of Chemical Engineering at Montana State University, and received his Ph.D. from the Pennsylvania State University. He was initially attracted to engineering by the challenges the profession offers, but also appreciates that engineering is a serving profession. Some of the greatest challenges he has faced while teaching have involved non-traditional teaching methods, including evening courses for practicing engineers and teaching through an interpreter at the Mongolian National University. These experiences have provided tremendous opportunities to learn new ways to communicate technical material. Dr. Larsen views modern software as one of the new tools that will radically alter the way engineers work, and his book *Introduction to MathCAD* was written to help young engineers prepare to meet the challenges of an ever-changing workplace.

Acknowledgments: To my students at Montana State University who have endured the rough drafts and typos, and who still allow me to experiment with their classes—my sincere thanks.

Sanford Leestma is a Professor of Mathematics and Computer Science at Calvin College, and received his Ph.D. from New Mexico State University. He has been the long-time co-author of successful textbooks on Fortran, Pascal, and data structures in Pascal. His current research interest are in the areas of algorithms and numerical computation.

Jack Leifer is an Assistant Professor in the Department of Mechanical Engineering at the University of Kentucky Extended Campus Program in Paducah, and was previously with the Department of Mathematical Sciences and Engineering at the University of South Carolina–Aiken. He received his Ph.D. in Mechanical Engineering from the University of Texas at Austin in December 1995. His current research interests include the analysis of ultra-light and inflatable (Gossamer) space structures.

Acknowledgments: I'd like to thank my colleagues at USC–Aiken, especially Professors Mike May and Laurene Fausett, for their encouragement and feedback; and my parents, Felice and Morton Leifer, for being there and providing support (as always) as I completed this book.

Richard M. Lueptow is the Charles Deering McCormick Professor of Teaching Excellence and Associate Professor of Mechanical Engineering at Northwestern University. He is a native of Wisconsin and received his doctorate from the Massachusetts Institute of Technology in 1986. He teaches design, fluid mechanics, an spectral analysis techniques. Rich has an active research program on rotating filtration, Taylor Couette flow, granular flow, fire suppression, and acoustics. He has five patents and over 40 refereed journal and proceedings papers along with many other articles, abstracts, and presentations.

Acknowledgments: Thanks to my talented and hard-working co-authors as well as the many colleagues and students who took the tutorial for a "test drive." Special thanks to Mike Minbiole for his major contributions to Graphics Concepts with SolidWorks. Thanks also to Northwestern University for the time to work on a book. Most of all, thanks to my loving wife, Maiya, and my children, Hannah and Kyle, for supporting me in this endeavor. (Photo courtesy of Evanston Photographic Studios, Inc.)

Holly Moore is a professor of engineering at Salt Lake Community College, where she teaches courses in thermal science, materials science engineering, and engineering computing. Dr. Moore received the B.S. degree in chemistry, the M.S. degree in chemical engineering from South Dakota School of Mines and Technology, and the Ph.D. degree in chemical engineering from the University of Utah. She spent 10 years working in the aerospace industry, designing and analyzing solid rocket boosters for both defense and space programs. She has also been active in the development of hands-on elementary science materials for the state of Utah.

Acknowledgments: Holly would like to recognize the tremendous influence of her father, Professor George

Moore, who taught in the Department of Electrical Engineering at the South Dakota School of Mines and Technology for almost 20 years. Professor Moore earned his college education after a successful career in the United States Air Force, and was a living reminder that you are never too old to learn.

Larry Nyhoff is a Professor of Mathematics and Computer Science at Calvin College. After doing bachelor's work at Calvin, and Master's work at Michigan, he received a Ph.D. from Michigan State and also did graduate work in computer science at Western Michigan. Dr. Nyhoff has taught at Calvin for the past 34 years—mathematics at first and computer science for the past several years.

Paul Riley is an author, instructor, and designer specializing in graphics and design for multimedia. He is a founding partner of CAD Support Associates, a contract service and professional training organization for computer-aided design. His 15 years of business experience and 20 years of teaching experience are supported by degrees in education and computer science. Paul has taught AutoCAD at the University of Massachusetts at Lowell and is presently teaching AutoCAD at Mt. Ida College in Newton, Massachusetts. He has developed a program, Computer-aided Design for Professionals that is highly regarded by corporate clients and has been an ongoing success since 1982.

Robert Rizza is an Assistant Professor of Mechanical Engineering at North Dakota State University, where he teaches courses in mechanics and computer-aided design. A native of Chicago, he received the Ph.D. degree from the Illinois Institute of Technology. He is also the author of *Getting Started with Pro/ENGINEER*. Dr. Rizza has worked on a diverse range of engineering projects including projects from the railroad, bioengineering, and aerospace industries. His current research interests include the fracture of composite materials, repair of cracked aircraft components, and loosening of prostheses.

Peter Schiavone is a professor and student advisor in the Department of Mechanical Engineering at the University of Alberta, Canada. He received his Ph.D. from the University of Strathclyde, U.K. in 1988. He has authored several books in the area of student academic success as well as numerous papers in international scientific research journals. Dr. Schiavone has worked in private industry in several different areas of engineering including aerospace and systems engineering. He founded the first Mathematics Resource Center at the University of Alberta, a unit designed specifically to teach new students the necessary *survival skills* in mathematics and the physical sciences required for success in first-year engineering. This led to the Students' Union Gold Key Award for outstanding contributions to the university. Dr. Schiavone lectures regularly to freshman engineering students and to new engineering professors on engineering success, in particular about maximizing students' academic performance.

Acknowledgments: Thanks to Richard Felder for being such an inspiration; to my wife Linda for sharing my dreams and believing in me; and to Francesca and Antonio for putting up with Dad when working on the text.

David I. Schneider holds an A.B. degree from Oberlin College and a Ph.D. degree in Mathematics from MIT. He has taught for 34 years, primarily at the University of Maryland. Dr. Schneider has authored 28 books, with one-half of them computer programming books. He has developed three customized software packages that are supplied as supplements to over 55 mathematics textbooks. His involvement with computers dates back to 1962, when he programmed a special purpose computer at MIT's Lincoln Laboratory to correct errors in a communications system.

David I. Schwartz is an Assistant Professor in the Computer Science Department at Cornell University and earned his B.S., M.S., and Ph.D. degrees in Civil Engineering from State University of New York at Buffalo. Throughout his graduate studies, Schwartz combined principles of computer science to applications of civil engineering. He became interested in helping students learn how to apply software tools for solving a variety of engineering problems. He teaches his students to learn incrementally and practice frequently to gain the maturity to tackle other subjects. In his spare time, Schwartz plays drums in a variety of bands.

Acknowledgments: I dedicate my books to my family, friends, and students who all helped in so many ways.

Many thanks go to the schools of Civil Engineering and Engineering & Applied Science at State University of New York at Buffalo where I originally developed and tested my UNIX and Maple books. I greatly appreciate the opportunity to explore my goals and all the help from everyone at the Computer Science Department at Cornell.

John T. Sears received the Ph.D. degree from Princeton University. Currently, he is a Professor and the head of the Department of Chemical Engineering at Montana State University. After leaving Princeton he worked in research at Brookhaven National Laboratory and Esso Research and Engineering, until he took a position at West Virginia University. He came to MSU in 1982, where he has served as the Director of the College of Engineering Minority Program and Interim Director for BioFilm Engineering. Prof. Sears has written a book on air pollution and economic development, and over 45 articles in engineering and engineering education.

Michael T. Snyder is President of Internet startup company Appointments 123.com. He is a native of Chicago, and he received his Bachelor of Science degree in Mechanical Engineering from the University of Notre Dame. Mike

also graduated with honors from Northwestern University's Kellogg Graduate School of Management in 1999 with his Masters of Management degree. Before Appointments123.com, Mike was a mechanical engineer in new product development for Motorola Cellular and Acco Office Products. He has received four patents for his mechanical design work. "Pro/ENGINEER was an invaluable design tool for me, and I am glad to help students learn the basics of Pro/ENGINEER."

Acknowledgments: Thanks to Rich Lueptow and Jim Steger for inviting me to be a part of this great project. Of course, thanks to my wife Gretchen for her support in my various projects.

Jim Steger is currently Chief Technical Officer and cofounder of an Internet applications company. He graduated with a Bachelor of Science degree in Mechanical Engineering from Northwestern University. His prior work included mechanical engineering assignments at Motorola and Acco Brands. At Motorola, Jim worked on part design for two-way radios and was one of the lead mechanical engineers on a cellular phone product line. At Acco Brands, Jim was the sole engineer on numerous office product designs. His Worx stapler has won design awards in the United States and in Europe. Jim has been a Pro/ENGINEER user for over six years.

Acknowledgments: Many thanks to my co-authors, especially Rich Lueptow for his leadership on this project. I would also like to thank my family for their continuous support.

Royce Wilkinson received his undergraduate degree in chemistry from Rose-Hulman Institute of Technology in 1991 and the Ph.D. degree in chemistry from Montana State University in 1998 with research in natural product isolation from fungi. He currently resides in Bozeman, MT and is involved in HIV drug research. His research interests center on biological molecules and their interactions in the search for pharmaceutical advances.

Reviewers

We would like to thank everyone who has reviewed texts in this series.

Christopher Rowe, *Vanderbilt University*
Steve Yurgartis, *Clarkson University*
Heidi A. Diefes-Dux, *Purdue University*
Howard Silver, *Fairleigh Dickenson University*
Jean C. Malzahn Kampe, *Virginia Polytechnic Institute and State University*
Malcolm Heimer, *Florida International University*
Stanley Reeves, *Auburn University*
John Demel, *Ohio State University*
Shahnam Navee, *Georgia Southern University*
Heshem Shaalem, *Georgia Southern University*
Terry L. Kohutek, *Texas A & M University*
Liz Rozell, *Bakersfield College*
Mary C. Lynch, *University of Florida*
Ted Pawlicki, *University of Rochester*
James N. Jensen, *SUNY at Buffalo*
Tom Horton, *University of Virginia*
Eileen Young, *Bristol Community College*
James D. Nelson, *Louisiana Tech University*
Jerry Dunn, *Texas Tech University*
Howard M. Fulmer, *Villanova University*
Naeem Abdurrahman, *University of Texas, Austin*
Stephen Allan, *Utah State University*
Anil Bajaj, *Purdue University*
Grant Baker, *University of Alaska–Anchorage*
William Beckwith, *Clemson University*
Haym Benaroya, *Rutgers University*
John Biddle, *California State Polytechnic University*
Tom Bledsaw, *ITT Technical Institute*
Fred Boadu, *Duke University*
Tom Bryson, *University of Missouri, Rolla*
Ramzi Bualuan, *University of Notre Dame*
Dan Budny, *Purdue University*
Betty Burr, *University of Houston*
Dale Calkins, *University of Washington*
Harish Cherukuri, *University of North Carolina –Charlotte*
Arthur Clausing, *University of Illinois*
Barry Crittendon, *Virginia Polytechnic and State University*
James Devine, *University of South Florida*

Ron Eaglin, *University of Central Florida*
Dale Elifrits, *University of Missouri, Rolla*
Patrick Fitzhorn, *Colorado State University*
Susan Freeman, *Northeastern University*
Frank Gerlitz, *Washtenaw College*
Frank Gerlitz, *Washtenaw Community College*
John Glover, *University of Houston*
John Graham, *University of North Carolina–Charlotte*
Ashish Gupta, *SUNY at Buffalo*
Otto Gygax, *Oregon State University*
Malcom Heimer, *Florida International University*
Donald Herling, *Oregon State University*
Thomas Hill, *SUNY at Buffalo*
A.S. Hodel, *Auburn University*
James N. Jensen, *SUNY at Buffalo*
Vern Johnson, *University of Arizona*
Autar Kaw, *University of South Florida*
Kathleen Kitto, *Western Washington University*
Kenneth Klika, *University of Akron*
Terry L. Kohutek, *Texas A&M University*
Melvin J. Maron, *University of Louisville*
Robert Montgomery, *Purdue University*
Mark Nagurka, *Marquette University*
Romarathnam Narasimhan, *University of Miami*
Soronadi Nnaji, *Florida A&M University*
Sheila O'Connor, *Wichita State University*
Michael Peshkin, *Northwestern University*
Dr. John Ray, *University of Memphis*
Larry Richards, *University of Virginia*
Marc H. Richman, *Brown University*
Randy Shih, *Oregon Institute of Technology*
Avi Singhal, *Arizona State University*
Tim Sykes, *Houston Community College*
Neil R. Thompson, *University of Waterloo*
Dr. Raman Menon Unnikrishnan, *Rochester Institute of Technology*
Michael S. Wells, *Tennessee Tech University*
Joseph Wujek, *University of California, Berkeley*
Edward Young, *University of South Carolina*
Garry Young, *Oklahoma State University*
Mandochehr Zoghi, *University of Dayton*

Contents

3   FILE EDITING 26

7   PROCESSES   160

8   SHELLS   180

1

Computing with Unix

1.1 COMPUTER BASICS

What is a computer? Why do we need computers? How do we use them? This section provides some answers to these questions, as well as a bit of background on computing and computers.

1.1.1 Computers Are Tools

Computers are tools—devices that assist and ease cumbersome and seemingly impossible tasks. Do not think that all tools are physical devices; some are instructions and methods. Such abstract tools instruct us in how to accomplish a goal—solving mathematical problems, for example—and often, no physical tools other than a human brain, some paper, and a pencil are necessary. So, do we need computers?

Some people still insist that a dependency on computers turns our brains into mush. Without computers, though, many tasks would require countless hours of hand calculations, and in any case, no one should depend completely on computers. Never blindly trust a computer's output. Always check your input. Have you heard of *GIGO*? It stands for *garbage in, garbage out*. So, to check your computer software's results, use traditional pencil-and-paper analysis on simplified engineering models. Always remember that computers are incredibly useful tools that require diligence and understanding.

OBJECTIVES

After reading this chapter, you should be able to:

- Discuss the background and philosophy underlying the use of computers.
- Overview the basics of computer hardware and software.
- Explain why you are learning about Unix.
- Illustrate features and advantages of using the Unix operating system.

1.2.3 Bits, Bytes, and All That

Often, movies glorify computers. How many times have you seen a character enter a command like "Find password" and, after a few moments, have the computer report, "Secret password found"? Be glad that cracking into someone's account is not so simple. How *do* real computers understand instructions? Most computers today are *digital*, converting and storing information with the digits 0 and 1—binary digits, or just *bits*. Bits form the smallest component of computer memory. A group of eight bits makes up a **byte**. Jargon such as "megs" or "gigs" refers to larger chunks of memory, as shown in Table 1.1.

1.2.4 Programs

Everyone follows instructions every day. Baking a cake requires following a recipe to produce a tasty dessert. Starting a car requires a sequence of steps, without which you would be seeking other modes of transportation. Computer **programs** are also instructions, written in a programming language that the CPU understands. Some programs, such as file management software, are stored internally in the computer. Others are loaded into memory from external storage devices.

Common programs that perform tasks, such as word processing, financial analysis, and number crunching, are called application software or just *applications*. Typically, applications are purchased from independent vendors. Many software engineers even develop in-house programs for companies to use.

Programs designed to help people use computers and applications are called *system software*. There programs include utilities for common tasks, such as file management and electronic mail. System software that specifically controls the internal workings of the computer is called an *operating system* (OS).

1.2.5 Operating Systems

The CPU uses the operating system to control all computer functions. When you turn on a computer, the OS is loaded into main memory. The OS is typically activated with typed commands or graphical interfaces, and all instructions from input are then interpreted and acted upon by the OS. Because different processes require different memory demands, the OS must act as referee and allocate resources properly. The OS also controls how applications transfer data between main memory and output.

1.2.6 Graphical User Interface

Originally, computers had unfriendly interfaces, such as monochrome monitors and teletype machines. Programming even required punch cards for input! Eventually, windows-based **graphical user interfaces** (GUIs, pronounced *goo-ees*) for computers were developed. GUI-oriented software presents an interface of pull-down menus and point-and-click mouse operations inside windows, which together activate the actual operating system. GUIs tend to avoid text-based command entry in order to provide a friendlier environment. Refer to Appendix B for more information on Unix GUIs.

TABLE 1.1 Computer Memory Sizes

Jargon	Bits	Bytes
K = kilobyte	2^{10}	1,024
M = megabyte	2^{20}	1,048,576
G = gigabyte	2^{30}	1,073,741,824
T = terabyte	2^{40}	1,099,511,627,776

1.3   THE UNIX OPERATING SYSTEM

Unix[1] (pronounced *you-nix*) is an operating system typically used by academic and scientific researchers. However, "flavors" of Unix, like Linux, have become popular with a variety of users. Even the Internet and Unix share a common background. This section presents a brief history of Unix and some reasons for using the system.

1.3.1   History of Unix

Unix did not start as a multimillion-dollar research project sponsored by some large multinational corporation. Nor did Unix hide from prying eyes as a supersecret military project. Rather, Unix was born in 1969 in Bell Labs as a better way to run *Space Travel*, an astronomical-simulation program. (Yes, Unix was developed to play a computer game!)

Ken Thompson, a developer of Unix, had become frustrated with running *Space Travel* on a *Multics* (multiplexed information and computing system) computer. He eventually moved the program to another computer in the corner of his lab so that he could experiment with it. By 1973, after many revisions in assembly code, Ken Thompson and Dennis Ritchie rewrote Unix in C, a language specifically developed for just that task. (Unix, in fact, is a pun on Multics: Just replace "multiplexed" with "uniplexed.")

Eventually, AT&T, the owner of Bell Labs, released Unix to educational institutions, but without any support. Since the source code was publicly available, computer programmers began enhancing Unix's capabilities. For example, programmers at the University of California at Berkeley added many features that eventually became standardized in Berkeley Software Distribution (BSD) and other versions of Unix. AT&T retained its own version, too, one that incorporated features developed by others and was eventually released as System V, Release 4 (SVR4). Several variants have subsequently been developed.

1.3.2   Unix Variants

At press time, The Open Group owns the UNIX® trademark and published a specification of the system. Since the inception of Unix, different versions, both commercial and free, have cropped up. For example, *Linux (www.linux.org)* is freely available for virtually every computer in the world. So, if you own your own computer, you do not have to use your school's computer labs for your Unix work! If you are a Mac user, you already have Unix! (See *www.apple.com/macosx/features/unix.*) For more information about Unix and its variants, visit *www.unix.org.*

If you prefer not to install a new operating system, you might wish to try *Cygwin (www.cygwin.com)*, which is a Linux emulator. Cygwin is a collection of programs that provide a Unix-like environment that runs on top of Microsoft® Windows. I recommend you download the default configuration. After learning more Unix, you will discover several additional programs that mimic almost every Unix command you need.

1.3.3   Why Unix?

Students often ask why they need to learn Unix. After all, what about those "other" operating systems? There is, of course, the simple answer: "because that's what we use here." However, this answer begs the question of *why* Unix in the first place.

---

[1]Technically, I should use the spelling *UNIX* (all capital letters). See *A Quarter Century of Unix* by P. H. Salus in the bibliography.

First, forget the notion that any GUI environment is an OS. GUIs shield users from the OS. Unfortunately, an inexperienced or unknowledgeable user can still get burned if a GUI crashes[2], and knowing text-based commands helps the user diagnose and fix computer problems. Even with well-oiled GUIs, experienced users eventually tire of tedious point-and-click mouse operations. Have you ever wondered why most GUI programs include keyboard shortcuts? Text-based command entry often improves efficiency.

Originally, Unix was designed for computers with limited internal memory. Every character counted. For example, why use "copy" when "cp" suffices? Unix commands were created to be "lean and mean" to quickly perform a wide variety of tasks. Granted, many commands appear somewhat cryptic. But despite the learning curve, in rating an OS, look beneath glittery window interfaces. Unix has many advantages to offer:

- *Openness*: The source code for Unix is publicly available. Developers can readily adapt utilities to suit their needs. Often, standard releases globally adapt Unix variants.
- *Utilities*: A multitude of programs arrive standard, or bundled, with most versions of Unix. A variety of commercial and public-domain software is also available.
- *Portability*: Virtually every kind of computer supports Unix.
- *Multiuser*: Unix can simultaneously handle many users running different programs.
- *Multitasking*: A user can run different programs simultaneously in Unix.
- *Networking*: Unix allows computers to connect and share information. In fact, Unix protocols, or methods of transferring information, form the basis of the Internet.
- *Prevalence*: Workstations that employ Unix help solve many complicated engineering and science problems.

1.3.4 Window Systems and Other Operating Systems

Although I assume little to no prior computer experience in this text, most students will likely have had some experience using Microsoft Windows or Macintosh operating systems. The windows used in these operating systems essentially shield the user from the text-based commands that were required many years ago. However, personal computers still support text input. In my programming courses, I often discover students hesitating to use the command window and the DOS prompt. So, a great side effect of learning Unix is reducing the fear of DOS. In fact, Windows users will occasionally discover that some Unix and DOS commands have the same names. Mac users have an additional benefit: The Mac operating system is now based on Unix!

Although Unix is typically taught and used as a text-based OS, many type of Unix GUIs are available, including *X Windows*, *Common Desktop Environment*, and others. These GUIs contain essentially the same features other GUIs have for other operating systems. But before rushing to use a GUI, consider that a good engineer or scientist strives to understand the theory behind his or her tools. Knowing the "guts" of Unix will help you customize your commands later on and better understand a GUI. Granted, using a cryptic text-based OS might seem like taking a step backward, but in light of the power that Unix offers, moving backward will help you leap forward. Refer to Appendix B for an explanation of Unix GUIs.

[2]There are even more colorful expressions for computer software failures. Such vulgar—and often humorous—terminology shall be left for the reader to discover in the course of their career.

1.4   UNIX BASICS

Even today, software developers try to abide by the original Unix philosophy, which dictates that commands should be simple, general, and adaptable. Not all Unix commands and utilities follow this principle exactly, but Unix has retained the general nature of its origins. This section provides an overview of the main components of Unix.

1.4.1   Software Layers

Figure 1.3 depicts the kinds of layers between the user and the computer hardware in Unix. The outermost layer, the **shell**, reads and interprets your commands. Not all versions of Unix use the same shells, and often, a few different shells may be available on any given system. Furthermore, some commands even differ from shell to shell. **Utilities** and programs created by the user can be called by the shell to do a variety of tasks. The **resident modules** compose the next layer and perform important services, such as input/output and process control. The innermost layer, the **kernel**, directs the hardware to perform your commands.

1.4.2   File System

Scientists and engineers are frequently concerned with managing data—how to enter data, where to put data, and how to use data are crucial tasks. A file system provides methods for doing so. Common tasks such as report writing, programming, and analysis, generate electronic information that **files** store. In time, storing groups of related files inside directories will better organize your data. Directories, in turn, are arranged in a hierarchical structure often known as a **directory tree**, as illustrated in Figure 1.4. Think of a directory tree as a filing cabinet: Directories would be drawers containing files as their contents. But Unix would be a very large filing cabinet! With Unix, very many directories may store other directories, and all may house their own files as well.

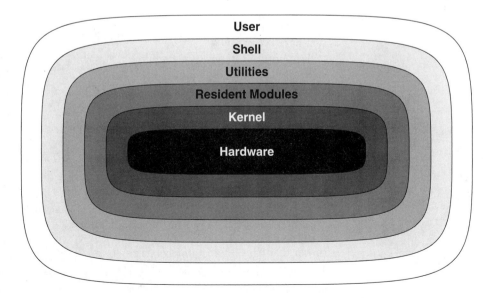

Figure 1.3   Unix Software Layers

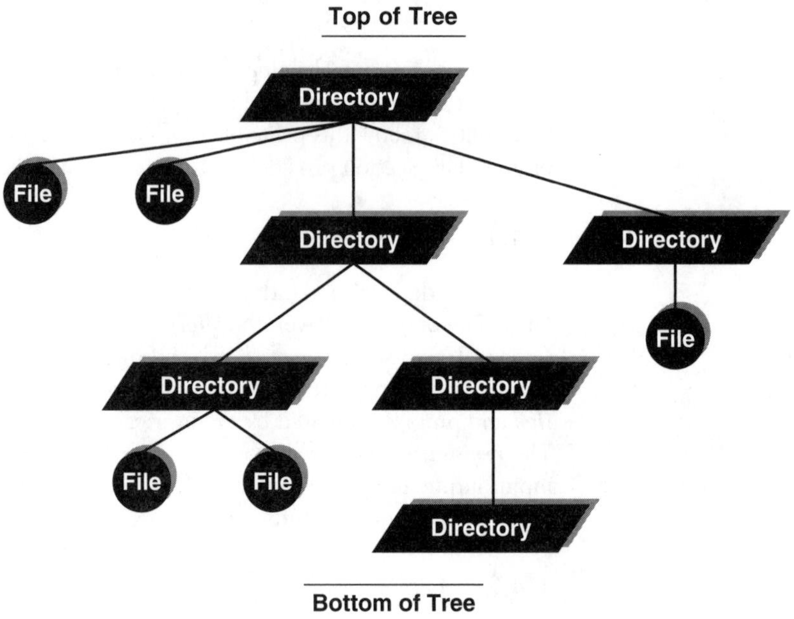

Top of Tree

Bottom of Tree

Figure 1.4 Directory Tree

1.4.3 Utilities

Hundreds of separate Unix programs arrive built in with the OS. Many system administrators further enhance their computing environments with public-domain freeware—programs that are freely (or at least cheaply) distributed. Just about every possible task is covered by one, if not more, programs. Moreover, additional commercial software is available. After you become familiar with Unix, you may wish to learn how to write programs called *shell scripts,* which perform customized tasks that you devise.

1.4.4 Unix GUIs

As discussed in Sections 1.2.6 and 1.3.4, Unix is primarily text based, but GUIs are available for it. The X Windows system developed by Xerox Park is a common Unix-based window system. In addition to this GUI, a consortium of computer companies has produced the Common Desktop Environment that is now very popular

---

PROFESSIONAL SUCCESS: UNIX AND YOUR CAREER

How will learning Unix help your career? I asked four engineering and science professionals about their Unix experience. Here's some advice they have for students:

- Jeffrey Chottiner, Ford product-design engineer, designs engines. Some of his recent projects are a crank train for a highly efficient all-aluminum diesel engine in a hybrid electric vehicle. Jeff says

that "Unix is like coffee. Without it, I'm useless." Besides using Unix to edit "finite-element decks" (structural-analysis input-data files) and organize his many project files, he uses FTP (File Transfer Protocol, a Unix Internet program) to immediately obtain "vital engine-performance data from Germany." Unix features such as multitasking have improved his efficiency. "Unix saves me and Ford time and money."

- Anthony Dalessio, radio-frequency (RF)/microwave engineer, designs circuits such as filters, amplifiers, and power dividers for use in cellular, paging, and public-safety communication systems. Tony has used Unix for several years. When he worked at Wright Patterson Air Force Base, "all the microwave-design tools in the avionics directorate were running on Unix workstations." He is also a Linux expert and suggests that students download Linux for their PCs. "Several programs for electrical engineering, such as Spice [a circuit simulator] and Magic [for very large scale integration—VLSI—design] have been ported to Linux." Better yet, "using Linux sure beats going to a computer lab at 2 a.m. to get an open terminal."

- Forrest Hoffman, computer specialist, designs and implements scientific computer models. Forrest uses Unix for scientific software development, visualization, and communications. His familiarity with the Unix operating system allowed him to develop a World Wide Web site and a commodity parallel-computer cluster built from PCs running Linux at Oak Ridge National Laboratory. "Unix is the perfect environment for scientific computing," he states. Most of the best scientific analysis and prediction software runs under Unix, "and the source code is usually available, so anyone can modify it for his or her own use." For parallel computing, Linux, GNU compilers and tools, and the Parallel Virtual Machine (PVM) and Message Passing Interface (MPI) message-passing libraries running on PCs offer the lowest-cost solutions, because "All the software is free."

- Michael Lamanna, civil and software engineer, is currently involved in software development for civil-engineering applications. Mike has used Unix for school, work, and research. His projects include remote structural-monitoring applications, as well as blowing snow mitigation for roads and highways. He prefers to use Unix for e-mail and reminds us that the world's greatest editor/environment/everything is Emacs, a popular Unix text editor and programming-development environment!

CHAPTER SUMMARY

- Computers are tools that assist people in a multitude of tasks.
- Users should still check their work in fear of GIGO: "garbage in, garbage out."
- Computers are essentially lifeless, inert chunks of circuits and chips until they are activated and "brought to life" by software.
- Software programs perform instructions usually entered by users.
- System software, or the operating system (OS), controls the interaction between hardware and software.
- Unix is an operating system that is available for virtually all computers.
- Unix has many advantages, such as multitasking, networking, and portability.
- Files store data; directories store files.
- Unix uses a hierarchical directory tree to store files.

KEY TERMS

bit	graphical user interface (GUI)	shell
byte	hardware	software
computer	kernel	Unix
directory tree	operating system (OS)	unilities
file	program	
file system	resident module	

Problems

1. What is Unix?
2. Which version(s) of Unix does your school provide?

3. What is a file?

4. What is a directory? In particular, what role does a directory serve in terms of managing files?

5. Review Appendix B. Explain these terms: *mouse*, *mouse click*, *window*, and *GUI*.

6. For Microsoft Windows users: Pick a free Unix variant, such as Linux (*www.linux.org*), FreeBSD (*www.freebsd.org*), or Cygwin (*www.cygwin.com*), and install it.

7. For Macintosh users: How do you access a command window to enter Unix commands?

2

Getting Started

2.1 NOTATION

Table 2.1 summarizes the notation used throughout this text. I strongly recommend that you do not gloss over this table. At the very least, you should remember that it is here.

TABLE 2.1 Summary of Notation

Notation	Meaning
keyterm	Key term in this text.
`input`	Literal Unix commands and other input—this font indicates what you need to type.
`value`	General Unix input: Type the name or value called for by this input. For example, if I instruct you to enter **`finger yourlastname`**, you would type **`finger`** followed by *your* last name, not the word "yourlastname." You might be amazed how many people will type that atrocity.
Key **Menu**	Press a specific key on your keyboard or select a menu action for a GUI. Select a menu item in a GUI.
`^K`	This notation represents pressing **Control** and then another key. For example, `^C` means that you press and hold **Control** and then press the **C** key. Do not press the caret (^) key! Note also that your particular **Control** key might have a different, but similar, name, such as **Ctrl**.
output	Results of a Unix command (or commands) or general Unix information.
comment	Commentary on a Unix command sequence or output.

OBJECTIVES

After reading this chapter, you should be able to:

- Recognize important notation employed throughout the text.
- Understand the computing environment in which you will practice.
- Practice your first Unix session by logging on and off your computer network.
- Experiment with a few Unix commands to develop a "feel" for Unix.
- Acknowledge responsibilities and concerns of computer use.

Without a doubt, reading a computer manual, let alone any manual, can be quite boring. Have you ever tried reading recipes for fun? For myself, I tend to learn best through examples rather than just conversation. I have tried to structure this textbook in such a fashion. But not all books may suit your particular learning style, so I offer the following advice:

- *Open the book!* I am continually amazed when students tell me that they haven't even *opened* their books. Little do they realize that many of their answers lie within that mysterious thing with pages. If you know someone in your classes who doesn't follow this advice, please nudge him or her to at least read this section.

- *Familiarize yourself with the book.* Successful professionals don't know everything; they just know where to look. With any book, you should first review the table of contents and quickly flip though all of the chapters and appendices. Ask yourself, "What information has the author provided to help you learn?"

- *Review the book's organization.* Consider the table of contents as your guide. Each section and subsection represents the portion of knowledge you must obtain and retain. Sorting out important material before class will also help save time. The author(s) will typically provide suggestions on how to use the book in a preface or foreword. For this book, I have scattered the advice in each section,

knowing that students generally don't read the preface.

- *Learn the notation.* All manuals and technical materials employ *notation*, usually in distrinct fonts, that alerts you to particular items, such as the computer commands in this text. Be patient: As boring as it might seem, understanding the author's notation will prevent you from getting stuck.

- *Set small goals.* If you are taking a class, read your assignment carefully. Knowing your objectives will improve your motivation to slug through boring reading. If the goals seem unclear, review the beginning of the assigned section of the text. Never try to learn everything at once! Follow the author's suggested course outline, or perhaps attempt one section at a time.

- *Practice.* Learning comes from both understanding and *practice*. Study the text and practice the commands! Having first reviewed the notation, skim a portion of the text a few times. Periodically remind yourself of chapter objectives. Knowing what happens and why it happens will help you retain the material.

- *Implement what you are learning.* Attempting and practicing commands will ease your memorization. Follow the suggested commands and exercises in the book. Understand why you are trying a command. Also, guess the result ahead of time. Read the text above and below each command for explanations of syntax and behavior.

PRACTICE!

1. This practice problem is your first *exercise*. Find the solution to this problem somewhere in the book. *Hint*: See the appendices.
2. In this text, if you see me instruct you to enter **more filename**, do you literally type **filename**?
3. If I instruct you to press **^S**, what should you do?

2.2 THE "UNIX LANGUAGE"

To be safe, I am assuming that you, the reader, have barely touched a computer. Although I realize that many students have significant experience, I have found that few have experience entering commands in a command window. So we will start at the beginning.

2.2.1 ASCII

Just as English has an alphabet, so does Unix. The Unix alphabet is composed of the letters, numbers, and symbols you can type at a computer keyboard. More formally, Unix uses ***ASCII*** (American Standard Code for Information Interchange), which is a universally agreed upon set of numerical codes for a variety of characters. Originally, ASCII used only 7 bits (0's and 1's) providing for 128 characters (keyboard characters plus nonprinting characters, such as the backspace and the bell). Extended ASCII uses 8 bits to store 256 characters. For example, the English letter H has the decimal code 72. In terms of bits, H is 01001000. Given the need to represent other languages and a variety of other symbols, the Unicode standard has been developed. (Visit *www.unicode.org* for more information.) Do you need to type bit patterns? See below.

2.2.2 Keyboard Characters and Keys

For introductory Unix, you do not need to work at the bit level of understanding. Instead, you should realize that the instructions you type are plain text—all the letters, numbers, and symbols on your keyboard. Although it might seem silly to show an example of a keyboard in Figure 2.1, students often ask me about the names of the characters ~ and & . (No, ~ is not called *twiddle*!) The names of all the characters are given in Appendix A and categorized in Table 2.2.

2.2.3 Case Sensitivity

Beware of inadvertently using **Shift** and **CapsLock**. Unix is ***case sensitive***, which means that you must you must not interchange upper- or lowercase letters because a specific case is required.

2.2.4 Control Characters

Many commands employ ***control characters***. The beep, or bell, sound that the computer can make, is signified as `^G` and provides a common example. Activate `^G` by *holding down* **Control** and then pressing the **G** key. Do not actually type the caret (^)! In general, you can enter either `^g` or `^G`, though some applications rely on the difference. Lest you think these characters are a needless irritation, a useful control character is `^L`, which usually clears your window.

2.2.5 Syntax and Semantics

Although it isn't quite accurate to call Unix a language, I find it helpful to make a comparison to written languages. Why? You will ultimately learn how to type various commands,

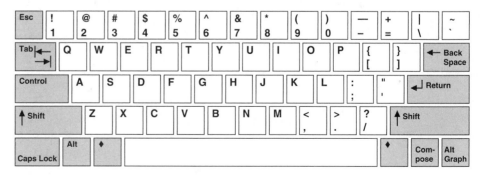

Figure 2.1 Keyboard

TABLE 2.2 Typical Keyboard Keys

Keys	Description
Uppercase English letters	`ABCDEFGHIJKLMNOPQRSTUVWXYZ` Hold down **Shift** and press the key with the appropriate letter.
Lowercase English Letters	`abcdefghijklmnopqrstuvwxyz` Press the key with the appropriate letter.
Digits	`1234567890` Common typing mistakes to avoid: confusing the letter **O** ("oh") and the number **0** (zero); confusing the number one (**1**) and the lowercase letter L (**l**).
Symbols	`!"#$%&'()*+,-./:;<=>?@[\]^_`{|}~` To create a blank space, press the **Spacebar** at the bottom of the keyboard.
Special keys	**Esc**, **Tab**, **Control**, **Shift**, **CapsLock**, **Alt**, **Meta** (♦), **Backspace**, **Return**, **Enter** **Alt** and **Meta** are sometimes interchanged on keyboards. These keys are often used as keyboard shortcuts for menu-driven options.
Function keys	**F1**, **F2**, **F3**, **F4**, etc. These keys are typically assigned to various commands or functions for operating systems and particular software.
Arrow keys	→, ←, ↓, ↑
Miscellaneous	These keys often have uses specific to software packages, such as editors and word processors.

and those commands and their options require a very specific spelling and order (*syntax*), and choice of usage and meaning (*semantics*). For example, the English command *Do your homework!* is spelled correctly, follows grammatical rules, and has a coherent message. However, *Blargle koopsy wu#* has all kinds of problems. Unix works in a similar fashion. If you ask it to view the contents of a file with `more filename`, you should not spell `more` as `mroe` (syntax), and the `filename` has to be viewable (semantics).[1]

PRACTICE!

4. What are two names for the character ^?
5. What is a correct name for the character ~?
6. Draw an ampersand (Appendix A) by hand. (Students *do* ask me how to do this.)

2.3   LOGGING IN

Now, it's time for your first Unix session. You will log in, play around, and log out. Of course, the "playing around" portion requires some work. You should try all of the steps that follow.

2.3.1   Obtain a Computer Account

Your site should supply you with an *account*, which provides space and privileges for using the site's computer system. Make sure that you learn how to access your account, too, because access methods differ from system to system. A unique username identifies your account. The *username*, also referred to as a *login name*, *user account*, or *user ID*, is typically chosen for you and is usually abstracted from your real name. Throughout this text, I use my initials `dis` for my system's user ID.

---

[1] Technically, Unix allows you to rename various commands. After you learn more about Unix, look up the **alias** command.

2.3.2   Accessing Your Account

Before doing anything, you must obtain a username and temporary password from a system administrator. Locate a Unix computer site. Do not worry about remote access yet, because, although it's convenient, your first session should take place where you can seek help. You commence a session when you *log in*, or as some say, *log on*. There will be two prompts:

- The *login prompt* is where you enter your user ID. Where the screen says `login:`, type your user ID and then press **Return** or **Enter**. For GUIs, you might have to point your mouse cursor to the prompt. If you want to be safer, press **^C** before entering anything. (Perhaps someone has a malicious program running to harvest account information!)
- Assuming that Unix accepts your user ID, type your password at the password prompt and then press **Return** or **Enter**.

In this text, I try to encourage students to practice concepts immediately, so the following step summarizes the process I have just described and should resemble what you see on your screen:

Step 2.1:   Logging In

```
login: dis
password:
```
Enter your user ID.
Enter your password. Unix will not display what you type.

If accepted, Unix should be ready to work, as shown in Figure 2.2. The computer system might "hang" for a moment while checking your account. Next, you might receive a welcome message or, alternatively, be prompted to create a different password.

2.3.3   More about Your Password

Your **password** is a special combination of characters, numbers, and symbols that you create to protect your account. No one else should know your password! If your system prompts you to create a password, review Section 2.6 before continuing. You will not actually see the characters of your password as you type them; after all, the password is supposed to be secret, and maybe that person sitting near you is peeking.

Figure 2.2   Unix Ready for Work!

2.3.4 What if You Make a Mistake?

Did you make a mistake while typing? If so, press either **Backspace** or **Delete** to erase your mistake. If neither key works, try **^H**, the control sequence for **Backspace**. Pressing **^C** usually cancels a login attempt, too. If you get the error message `incorrect password`, your login attempt failed. Try logging in and out again; perhaps you typed something wrong. A common mistake is not realizing that **Caps Lock** is on.

2.4 ELEMENTS OF YOUR COMMAND WINDOW

If you have never used a GUI before, please review Appendix B. You might need to navigate around various windows after logging on. This section reviews the fundamental elements of a Unix command window, which is depicted in Figure 2.3.

2.4.1 Command Prompt

Assuming that you have succeeded in logging in, Unix awaits your instructions. At this point, some new users erroneously think, "I've logged into Unix," but that is not so. In reality, you've logged onto your computer network *using* Unix. You are running a shell, which is a program that will interpret your instructions for Unix.

The shell prompts you for command entry. Unix often comes with three main shells, each with different default prompts. The Bourne and Korn shells use the dollar sign (\$), while the C shell uses the percent symbol (%). Your system might even be customized with an entirely different prompt. Sometimes the prompt provides a date or a computer name, such as `(11:00pm)dis@jarvik>`. Throughout this book, I will use a rather bland prompt: `unix>`. Note that you do *not* type the prompt!

2.4.2 Cursor

Cursors are symbols that indicate where to type commands after the prompt. With GUIs, your cursor might appear as a rectangle. To enable text entry, just point and click inside the desired window, which is called setting the *focus*. For clarity, the cursor is usually not shown in examples throughout this text.

2.4.3 Command Line

In Unix, commands activate the shell to perform various tasks. Look at the sample command input and output in Figure 2.3. Everything that follows the prompt (`unix>`) forms the **command line**—your input to Unix. Using the language analogy, you can think of a command line as a sentence of instructions. But instead of ending your "Unix sentence" with punctuation, you terminate command-line input by pressing **Return** or **Enter**. After entering the command line, Unix processes your instructions, sometimes reporting the results of its actions as output.

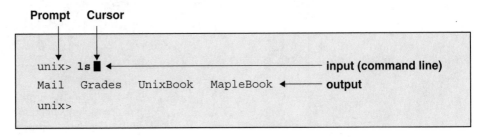

Figure 2.3 Command Window Elements

2.4.4   Editing the Command Line

Before pressing **Return** or **Enter**, you can edit the command line. Sometimes computers are configured differently, so you may occasionally need to swap **Delete** with **Backspace**. Sometimes keyboards allow for the arrow keys. If you feel even more adventurous, you may have several control-key shortcuts available to you. For example, **^C** usually cancels your input. I typically use **^A** and **^E**, which put you at the beginning and ending, respectively, of the command line.

2.4.5   Command-Line Syntax

Unix has some general rules that you should heed:

- *Unix is case sensitive!* It matters whether you use upper- or lowercase letters. For example, never type the command **ls** as **Ls**, **lS**, or even **LS**.
- *Separate command-line elements with spaces!* Enter spaces with **Spacebar**. Use as many spaces as you wish. For example, to enter **ls ~dis**, do not enter **ls~dis**. Sometimes, however, you do not need spaces; we will encounter such cases later on.
- *Dashes and underscores are different!* The underline, or underscore, symbol (_), is not the same as the dash (-) or a blank space.

2.4.6   Command Options

Pretend that you have a momentary identity crisis. You could try the **who** command, but Unix needs you to be more specific. The command line **who am i** modifies the behavior of **who** to find out your username. Give it a try:

Step 2.2:   Modifying a Command

```
unix> who am i                                    See if Unix knows who you are.
                                       Be sure to type spaces between each word.

dis    pts/16    Mar 1 16:47    (000.00.00.00)           Unix reports your user ID,
                                      terminal ID, login time, and location, which I have hidden
```

This input **who am i** has two distinct components:

- The primary command **who**. (What does an unmodified **who** do?)
- The command options **am i**, which modify the behavior of **who**, restricting its report to only your identity.

In general, a Unix command has the form **command options arguments**, as shown in Figure 2.4. In this example, the print command **lp** (I remember it as "laser print") has one option, **d** (for destination), which has it's own argument, the printer name **arcturus** (your printer will likely have a different name). If the command seems complicated, note the following rules:

- Unix reads the command line from left to right.
- The hyphen (-) indicates to Unix that an option appears in the command line. Do not seperate the hyphen and the option.
- Option arguments follow the option.
- The command argument is the last item in the command line.

So, you could read the command in Figure 2.4 as "print to destination **arcturus** a file called **data.txt**." At this point, we haven't created any ASCII files (files composed of text), but perhaps your instructors will provide some for you to test.

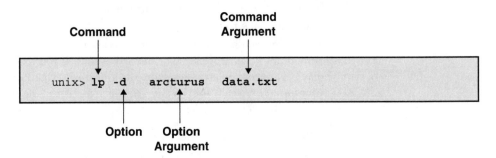

Figure 2.4 Command Options

PRACTICE!

7. Do the command lines `ls -aF`, `ls -a -F`, and `ls -Fa` provide the same output? What rules for command options have you stumbled upon?
8. Is `LS -AF` a valid command? Why or why not?

2.4.7 Finding Help

You might be curious how on earth you could have known about the command options I have demonstrated so far. There's a special Unix command called **man**, which means *manual*. To find help on a particular ***command***, enter **man *command***:

Step 2.3: Manual

> unix> **man lp**   *Find help on the print command. See also **man lpr**.*
> *Upon processing this command, Unix will report a bewildering set of options. Reproducing the output would consume the rest of this chapter.*

A well-known irony of Unix is that to learn a command, you need to use **man**. But how do you learn how to use **man**? Well, (not so) obviously—it's **man man**! To avoid this circular nightmare for you, we will gradually explore essential commands a few at a time. The use of **man** is reviewed in much greater detail in Appendix C. One thing to note: if **man *command*** starts off with Standard C++, use **man -s1** (or **s2** or **s5**) instead. (Appendix C contains the reason.)

PRACTICE!

9. What does **who** do?
10. Is **am i** a valid Unix command line? Try entering **am i** to find out.
11. Does your system support the command **dis**? If so, what does that command do?

2.4.8 What's Your Shell?

The shell is a special Unix program that helps you to communicate with Unix's core programs. The shell is effectively a program that runs on top of Unix's core. You might now be wondering why you need to know this fact. Well, you will eventually discover that not all systems run the same shells. In fact, you can usually change your shell. To determine your current shell, enter **echo $SHELL**. The dollar sign ($) tells Unix to look at the value of **SHELL**, which is an ***environment variable***—a special value that customizes your Unix session.

Step 2.4:   Show Default Shell

```
unix> echo $SHELL                              Report the value of SHELL.
/usr/local/bin/tcsh              I am using a T-shell. Your shell might be different.
```

Unix sets **SHELL** and other environment variables each time you log on. You can set and change these values, although I do not recommend doing so until you have become comfortable with Unix. I explain this concept in Chapter 8.

PRACTICE!

> 12.   What is your default system shell?
>
> 13.   Try the command line **echo SHELL**. What happens?

2.4.9   Logging Out

When you finish your work, you must end your session. You must remember to log out, or, as is sometimes said, log off. Use the command exit to log out:

Step 2.5:   Logout

```
unix> exit           If you are using a GUI, you might need to exit the entire system.
login:         If you are using a command window, the login prompt should reappear.
```

With C–shells, the command **log out** will end your session. Note that with a GUI, logging out of a single window alone usually does not end your session! Typically, you must choose a menu option such as **exit**, **log out**, or **Kill TWM**. But regardless, whether using a GUI or not, wait until you see the same screen or message that appeared before you logged on. Only when the login prompt reappears is your session over. Do not leave your computer until you have logged out!

PRACTICE!

> 14.   End your computer session if you have not done so already.
>
> 15.   Log in again.
>
> 16.   Try logging out with the command logout. If the command fails, log off with exit. Why might the command have failed?

2.5   GENERAL ADVICE

This section addresses some Unix problems that inexperienced users often encounter. If you get stuck while learning Unix, refer back to this section.

2.5.1   Error Messages

If you make a mistake, Unix will usually respond with an error message:

Step 2.6:   Making Mistakes

```
unix> sl                              Mess up the ls command, which lists files.
sl: command not found              Unix warns you about the syntax mistake
```

Pay attention to Unix's warning messages, even though they might sometimes be cryptic. The computer cannot actually read your mind! Although Unix might not fathom what you are trying to do, it might at least provide a clue to your mistake.

2.5.2 Something's Wrong?

Other things go wrong besides typing errors. Computers sometimes crash for their own reasons: Too many users, too many processes, a software glitch, and system "hiccups" can all cause networkwide grief. Also, beware that not all versions of Unix produce the same results, so what suits one system may not work on another. To help avoid incompatibilities, you should consult a local user guide specific to your system when studying this text.

Most problems, though, are user related. Typing "bad" command lines, for instance, can often "freeze" or "hang" the computer. If this happens, try pressing ^C, the "kill" control sequence. Should that not help, try ^Z as a last-ditch attempt to suspend your command. Out of courtesy, avoid suspending processes: Suspended processes linger and thus consume system memory. Freezing and other common problems are diagnosed in Table 2.3.

2.5.3 Security

Always remember to log out! Never remain logged on if you leave your computer. Unscrupulous users could wreak havoc in your account and, perhaps, your life. Even when you log off, do not turn off your computer. Typically, Unix terminals are left continuously running to avoid damaging the computer. Booting a Unix computer can be a lengthy process. Preferably, just leave idle or disabled computers alone. In an emergency, you might be able to find the on–off switch. However, you might then have to face an angry system administrator. Note that the monitors automatically shut off to conserve energy and prevent burning the login message onto the screen.

2.6 PROTECTING YOURSELF AND YOUR ACCOUNT

Respect general considerations and responsibilities inherent in using any networked computer. Even if you independently own and operate a computer, abide by general rules of etiquette and national laws.

2.6.1 General Computer Use and Responsibility

Each computer site, Unix or otherwise, follows its own rules. Consult with your site administrator(s) about local policies.

2.6.2 Protecting Your Account from Intruders

Beware of "crackers"—people who try to cause computer mayhem. Crackers have powerful programs that might figure out, or "crack," your password and access your account. Follow these tips to protect yourself:

- Never share your account or tell anyone your password.
- Your password should contain at least six characters, at least one of which should be a number. Unix distinguishes between upper- and lowercase letters. Unix will often accept other symbols as well.
- Your password should not contain something obvious about yourself, such as your birthday or address.
- Your password should not contain common words or expressions. For instance, FORWHOMTHEBELLTOLLS would be a bad choice.
- Never use anagrams of your username for your password. For example, username *dalessio* should not have the password *soladies*.
- Change your password frequently.

TABLE 2.3 Unix Troubleshooting

Problem	Proposed Solution
The screen is blank before logging on.	Press an inert key (**Shift,** for example) or jiggle the mouse.
Someone else is already logged on, or `who am i` reports the wrong user.	<ul><li>Double-check your assigned username.</li><li>Look around—maybe that person stepped away and did not log out.</li><li>Write down the username and log the person out. Then, log in and e-mail a reminder about the dangers of leaving an unattended computer.</li></ul>
After you log in, the computer accepts your username, but then immediately logs you out.	See a system administrator—you might have exceeded your disk quota.
After logging in, you get a message saying `Login incorrect`.	<ul><li>Do you have a valid account?</li><li>Did you enter the right username and password?</li><li>Did you choose the correct case while typing?</li></ul>
After you log in, the computer "hangs"; that is, no output is reported for a long time.	Don't be impatient; sometimes the computer takes a while to log you on.
You type a command and nothing happens.	Did you press **Return** after typing?
During your session, the computer hangs.	Too many users can slow a system. Be patient.
You type or press keys, but nothing appears on the screen.	<ul><li>Did the system hang? Wait a few moments.</li><li>Did you accidentally press `^S`? This control sequence suppresses the output. To make the output visible again, press `^Q`.</li><li>Are you using a GUI? If so, try pointing your mouse inside the terminal window in which you intend to type.</li></ul>
All your commands appear in UPPERCASE.	Press **CapsLock**. Now try typing again.
You typed the wrong command, and Unix is taking exceedingly long to perform this instruction.	<ul><li>Wait and see what happens. You might learn something.</li><li>Kill the process with `^C`.</li><li>If `^C` does not work, suspend the process with `^Z`.</li><li>Sometimes `^D` (exit) can help. But beware! `^D` might log you out.</li></ul>
The screen just went completely blank!	Press **Shift** or an arrow key. Also, try jiggling the mouse. Monitors turn the picture off to prevent burning the image onto the screen.
It's an emergency, or you're completely stuck—and worse yet, there are no consultants to be found.	<ul><li>Turn the computer off and on. Wait to see if you get logged out. Always save this option as a *last resort!*</li><li>Bug that person sitting next to you: Claim total ignorance. You never know, but one day that person might be *you* helping out another confused user.</li></ul>

To change your password, use the **passwd** command:

Step 2.7: Changing Your Password

```
unix> passwd                                    Change your password.
passwd: Changing password for dis              Unix reports what's happening.
Old password:                   Enter your old password. You will not see the output.
New password:                                  Enter the new password.
Re-enter new password:                         Reenter your new password.
unix>                           If Unix accepts your new password, the prompt reappears.
```

If Unix does not accept your new password, Unix reports an error message. Try changing the password again. Don't take it personally! Sometimes it takes a few tries. Password programs are often restrictive in order to maintain security. Also, the change is not always instantaneous. If you ever forget your password, visit your system administrator.

2.6.3   Warning: Carpal Tunnel Syndrome

Dangers accompany everything in life, the use of computers included. In fact, one sub-discipline of industrial engineering is *ergonomics*: how the human body interacts with the workplace environment. The human body is just not designed to sit still for many hours on end. Improper posture, poor typing practices, and extensive hours working can physically harm your fingers, wrists, arms, and back. Conditions such as **carpal tunnel syndrome** (CTS) often result from excessive typing with poor posture. CTS can cause numbness, tingling, and pain in your hands and wrists. Check with your system administrator for handouts and guides for proper typing procedures, stretches, and exerciese and consult the bibliography for suggested references on CTS.

PRACTICE!

> 17.   Does the word *qwertyuiop* make a good password? Why or why not?

2.7   APPLICATIONS: FUN WITH UNIX

Unix offers a bewildering number of commands. In this section, I hope that I can motivate your exploration of Unix by showing you some handy commands that I use. I will also demonstrate some of Unix's power by providing a hint on how Unix allows you to create your own commands.

Step 2.8:   What's Today?

Ever forget what day it is? Unix can help! See also **time**:
```
unix> date                                          Ask Unix to report the date.
Sat Mar 26 13:43:21 EST 2005                        Hello from March of 2005!
```

Step 2.9:   Calendar

On what day were you born? Not your birthday...the day of your birthday in the year you were born. Well, Unix can tell you. The **cal** *command will output any calendar:*
```
unix> cal 10 1923                                   Output the calendar for October 1923.
October 1923                                        For more fun, try just cal and cal 1923.
 S  M Tu  W Th  F  S                                What do those commands do?
    1  2  3  4  5  6
 7  8  9 10 11 12 13
14 15 16 17 18 19 20
21 22 23 24 25 26 27
28 29 30 31
```

Step 2.10:   Banner

Suppose you want a really big version of some word in ASCII. Try **banner word**:
```
unix> banner CRUD                                   Output a really big version of the word CRUD.
```
You will see a gigantic version of the word CRUD in your window. For more fun, look up www.figlet.org.

Step 2.11: Finger

Instead of silly output, perhaps you would rather see if you can find someone online who shares my last name. If your **finger** *command isn't disabled by your system administrator, try this:*

```
unix> finger schwartz                          Or, if you prefer, try someone else's last name.
```

If anyone has that last name, Unix will output his or her information. In fact, if you dig around, you can create a file called a finger plan that outputs a message to anyone who fingers you.

Step 2.12: Lynx

Speaking of looking things up, Unix supports a text-based Web browser. Yes! If you don't mind browsing the Web with no graphics and just pure text, **lynx** *provides a quick and dirty way to surf the web:*

```
unix> lynx                                            Surf the web without graphics!
```

Type **G** *(for "go"). You will be prompted to enter a URL. You might find the whole interface and system extremely primitive. So why would you bother with such an archaic program? If your connection is very slow,* **lynx** *provides a terrific means to grab information at a brisk pace.*

Step 2.13: History

On your own computer, perhaps you're having trouble remembering all the commands you entered. Or perhaps you would like to reenter a command that you're tired of typing. Well, Unix to the rescue again!

```
unix> history                                    Ask Unix to output recent commands.
```

Unix will show a list of commands. The depth to which Unix remembers is a variable that you can customize— but wait until you learn how to modify your configuration files.

Step 2.14: Repeat

To repeat a command, find the number that labels a command line from a history list. Then enter !*num:*

```
unix> !10                     Redo commandline 10 (assuming that history shows at least 10 commands).
```

Unix will reenter your 10th-from-last command line without your having to retype the whole thing.

Step 2.15: Customizing

Suppose you simply miss DOS and just can't remember that **ls** *stands for the list command. By entering* **alias customname command** *you can create your own commands:*

```
unix> alias dir ls            Tell Unix that for this session in the current window, dir means to do ls.
unix> dir                                     Unix will list your files as if you had executed ls.
UnixBook   Mail   Courses                                        Unix shows a listing.
unix> ls                                      Just confirming that dir really does mean ls!
UnixBook   Mail   Courses                                        Unix shows the same listing.
```

There are many, many options I have left out. But hopefully, you will take some time to look for other interesting and helpful commands.

Step 2.16: Spreadsheet

Your implementation of Unix might have an interesting text-based spreadsheet program called **sc** *(spreadsheet calculator). Yes, someone really did program an entire spreadsheet in text mode:*

```
unix> sc                                        Run a text-based spreadsheet program
```

Actually, this program might be bit challenging. Many GUI-based versions of **sc** *are available on the Internet if you prefer something more user friendly.*

2.7.1   Compound Commands

One of Unix's "cool" features is how you can customize the system by modifying and creating your own commands. In English, you can connect independent clauses together with all kinds of punctuation; in fact, I am doing so with this sentence—it pays to know some grammar (notwithstanding my abuse of it)! In Unix, the semicolon (**;**) can connect two command lines:

Step 2.17: Connect Two Command Lines

> unix> **who am i; who**   *Tell Unix to show you who you are*
> *Possibly a large amount of output is not shown.*   *and then show everyone else logged in.*

2.8 APPLICATION: PIPING IN UNIX

What if you could send the output of one argument *into* another? For example, chances are that the **who** command spits out a hoard of users, but you would prefer just knowing how many people are logged in. So we need a way first to find out everyone (**who**) and then count the number of lines. Well, the command for counting the number of lines in a file is **wc -l** (*word count*, using the *lines* option). For example, **wc -l data.txt** would tell me how many lines are inside file data.txt. Thus, one way to handle this problem is to output the result of **who** into a file. Then, in a separate command, count the lines in that file. In fact, you will learn how to do this (a process called *redirection*) later.

To avoid the extra step in creating a file, how do you send the output of one command *into* another for processing? Use the pipe (|), following the command-line syntax **command1 | command2**. Unix will then process **command1** and send the output into **command2**. Give it a try:

Step 2.18: Pipe One Command's Output into Another

> unix> **who | wc -l**   *Generate a list of users, count the number of lines,*
>   *and then report the value.*
>
> 127   *Unix will report the number of people currently logged in.*

If you have trouble seeing how the pipe works, try pretending that the command you entered was **wc -l output_from_who**. Piping and other useful applications will be discussed in further detail later on.

CHAPTER SUMMARY

- The Unix "language" is a collection of keyboard symbols used to create Unix commands that have syntax and semantics.
- Unix commands are case sensitive.
- The sequence of commands and other statements entered at the prompt is called a command line.
- You can edit a command line before entering it into the computer.
- The command-line structure is command–options–argument.
- Your account has been set with a default shell. Know that shell!
- You must watch for possible errors in case you have entered an incorrect command.
- Do not share your password…ever!
- Do not leave your computer unattended.
- Always remember to log out.
- Take breaks from typing now and then.

KEY TERMS

account	command line	semantics
ASCII	control characters	syntax
carpal tunnel syndrome	environment variable	username
case sensitive	password	

COMMAND SUMMARY

alias	customize a command
banner	output an obnoxiously sized message
cal	show calendar
date	show current date
echo	output the value of a variable
finger	output information about a user
history	show commands recently entered
lp	print hard copy
ls	list files
lynx	invoke text-based Web browser
man	find help on a Unix command
more	view contents of text file
passwd	reset Unix password
sc	invoke spreadsheet calculator
time	show current time
wc	count words in a file
who	show users currently logged on

Problems

1. If you have not done so already, obtain a Unix account.
2. Obtain site documents about policies, user accounts, and logging in. If your site provides Unix reference manuals, obtain those as well.
3. Where is consulting or Unix advice available at your computing site?
4. What are two names for the ASCII character "/"?
5. What is the difference between logging on and logging in?
6. What is the difference between logging on and logging off?
7. Log on and change your password.
8. What default shell is used by your Unix system?
9. Which version or type of Unix does your system use?
10. Does your system understand the command **whoami**? What is one way of checking? Does the command work?
11. Suppose that someone entered the command line **ECHO $SHELL** and Unix reported ECHO: Command not found. What mistake did this person likely make? How should the command line have been typed?
12. Do you think that the password **chester** would be acceptable? Why or why not?
13. Name several considerations to ponder in creating a safe password.
14. Who should know your password?
15. Consult your site's policies on responsible account usage. Name at least three guidelines.
16. What is CTS? Why should you be concerned? Does your site provide reference material on CTS?

3

File Editing

3.1 BASICS OF FILES

Engineers and scientists must manage all kinds of information. Conducting experiments, analyzing devices, designing systems, testing software, performing economic studies, and writing reports all generate lots of data. Also, you will likely learn to program your software. The programs that you will write will contain bodies of text, which resemble data. This section introduces important principles of managing these data on a computer.

3.1.1 File Management

Files are collections of data, or documents that include reports, drawings, and papers. Data, such as numbers, characters, pictures, and drawings, constitute typical information. Think of files as just places for your "stuff." Computers have eased the labor involved in storing such information by using file management programs. File management involves copying and moving files into directories that contain related information. Recall from Chapter 1 the directory tree shown in Figure 1.4 to picture how directories and files are organized. In this chapter, you will create your first files. Other portions of the text cover directories and associated file-management commands.

OBJECTIVES

After reading this chapter, you should be able to:

- Understand the basics of ASCII text.
- Name files that you create.
- Perform basic viewing and listing of files to assist with editing.
- Learn and practice basic text-file editing with `pico`.
- Learn and practice basic text-file editing with `vi`.
- Learn and practice basic text-file editing with `emacs`.
- Investigate the available GUI editors on your system.

Although elementary and high schools now commonly have their own computer labs, many students still suffer from computer phobias. Some even feel ashamed or embarrassed about their lack of skill. I have often been vehemently told by a variety of students, young and old, that "computers *hate* me!"

Let me dispel this myth: Computers do not *feel* anything, let alone hate. Although we anthropomorphize computers, they are lifeless. Computers certainly never hold any particular grudges. Crackers might indeed have scores to settle, but computers do not. Moreover, I have witnessed students trembling in fear, worried that the next key they press will cause a horrible explosion or other tragic event. Granted, banging a table in anger about a bug-ridden program does carry certain risks to your hard drive. (Yes, I am guilty!) But you have little chance of causing damage simply by typing commands. The wrong sequence of commands might mess up your account; responsible studying, however, can help prevent damage from that.

Experimentation is crucial with computers. Learn software according to this approach: Locate and start the program, learn command syntax, solve problems, and demonstrate your work. Often, your system administrator, office, or school has supplied review sheets that tell you how to activate programs. Find them! They will help! (But they won't lessen your need to practice.) Bring this book along with you to a computer. Read each section and then try the commands. Look inside the book. Then look up at your screen. Compare the two. Do you see what you expected to see? Read each portion of text during and after the command entry. Before entering a command, try to anticipate the output.

At first, you might feel frustrated and incompetent, but these feelings do not indicate any lack of intelligence. Consider such feelings a challenge: Becoming fed up with learning is a sign that you care to learn! After all, if you didn't care about learning, why would you feel anything at all? With practice, the commands will eventually sink in. Be sure to seek help if you get stuck—and have faith that one day all of these commands will seem like second nature—because they will.

So, does your account contain any files? I guarantee that even if you haven't created anything yet, your account administrators supplied you with some initial files that configure your account. To see everything you currently have in your directory tree, log on and enter **ls -aR**, which lists (**ls**) all (**a**) your files in every directory, and their directories, and so forth (**R**):[1]

Step 3.1:   List Everything

```
unix> ls -aR                    List all directories and their contents, starting from the current directory.
                                Unix might show a lot of stuff if you have been doing some work. If the listing takes awhile, press ^C to quit.
```

If you are using a GUI, look for a program called *File Manager*, or something similar, which will show you a directory's contents by clicking on it.

3.1.2   File Types

Many of the files that you will encounter and use are ASCII ***text files***, which are files composed of printable and viewable ASCII characters. ASCII includes the characters you see on your keyboard: lower- and uppercase letters, symbols, and digits. Other ASCII characters, called *nonprinting characters*, perform actions such as "new-line"

---

[1]The **R** stands for *recursion*, which you will discover if you learn how to program for two semesters or so. For now, you can think of the **-R** option as "look at everything until there are no more things to look at." In reality, the **-R** tells **ls** to follow the left branches of the directory tree until there are no more branches. Then, Unix backtracks to the right branches, working its way all the way to the right, showing files along the way from top to bottom.

(NL) and "null" (NUL).[2] Other files, such as **binary files**, are composed of byte sequences that only the computer can read. Some examples of binary files are Unix utilities, proprietary formats for application software, and archived files.

To check a particular file's type, use `file filename`. If you see any files after running `ls -a`, try to check their types. For example, you might see a file called `.login` and wonder what type it is. Try the following step:

Step 3.2:   Check File Type

```
unix> file .login                              Check the file type of .login in your Unix hierarchy.
.login:    assembler program text                          It is a special kind of text file.
```

Although you probably won't know what *assembler program text* actually is, don't worry. The idea is that Unix is clueing you into the fact that `.login` is a text file, which carries an implication that you can edit it. The `.login`, `.cshrc`, `.profile`, and other "dot-files" you might see contain commands to set up and customize your Unix environment. Don't mess with them…yet!

3.1.3   ASCII Text Files

Although using ASCII limits presentation quality, ASCII text files are universal: You can transport your work among different computers throughout the world. Windows users should experiment with *Notepad* and *Wordpad* to create text files and try to view them in Unix. If you get weird characters at the ends of the lines try `dos2unix oldfile newfile`, assuming that your system has the command. Another handy trick is to view a text file in a Web browser and then save it directly to your computer ("save as text"), which works regardless of the operating system.

Some common applications of text files are computer programs and *HTML* (hypertext markup language) for websites. Other formatting programs, such as *TeX* and *PostScript*, employ ASCII text commands to produce fonts, figures, and tables by using only text input. Other common uses of text files include electronic mail (e-mail), programming, and data files. Students interested in exploring document processing a bit further might wish to investigate *Unicode*, which is a modern system for representing over 65,000 text characters. Figure 3.1 shows a small sample of this system that includes smiley-face characters. (See also *http://www.unicode.org*.)

3.1.4   File Sizes

Each ASCII character contributes one byte to the file size—the total memory consumed by a file's contents. Larger chunks, such as kilobytes and megabytes (see Table 1.1), usually help measure file sizes. If you would like to see the sizes of all your current files, using kilo- and megabyte notation, try `ls -alh` (list all files, long format, human-readable sizes):

Step 3.3:   Obtaining File Sizes

```
unix> ls -alh                              Long list of all files, with sizes shown in readable format.
-rw-r--r-- 1 dis dis 2.5K Feb 21 14:48 x.txt   Sample long listing for a file called x.txt.
```

---

[2]A long time ago, computers would send signals to teletype machines with these nonprinting characters. So the characters would cause actions such as backspacing, returning, etc. Look up *ASCII table* on the Internet, and you'll find complete tables. If you learn to program, you will often see *escape characters*—for examples, \n and \f—that have the same behaviors.

In the preceeding listing, don't worry about all the "mumbo jumbo." I just want you to spot the 2.5K, which is the size of my file x.txt (which I doubt you have), namely, 2.5 kilobytes. As you progress through Unix, you will learn about each of the items that ls -l reports.

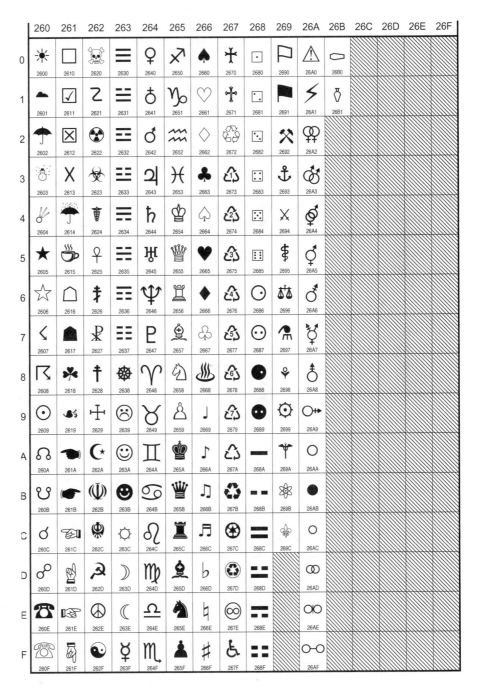

Figure 3.1 Chart of Miscellaneous Unicode Symbols. U+2600-267F. *Reproduced with Permission of Unicode, Inc.*

3.1.5 Filenames

A **filename** is a unique name assigned to a file in order to help organize and identify your work. A Unix filename can include upwards of 255 characters and is normally restricted to ASCII characters. Unix prohibits only the slash (/) and ASCII NUL characters, but you should generally select only letters, digits, the dot (.), and the underscore (_) to make filenames. Also, remember that Unix is case sensitive!

To help identify the type of a file, which is based on its contents, use a **file extension**, a small group of letters tacked onto a name, starting with a dot (.). For example, data.txt has the extension txt, signifying that data.txt is likely, although not guaranteed, to be a text file. Other command extensions you might encounter are ps (*PostScript*) and jpg (JPEG image format). Note that the file extension is included as part of the filename and is not required.

Some examples of filenames are my_file.txt, Homework1, and _1data_set.save. Beware of using spaces in filenames (e.g., bad   file name.txt), because filenames with spaces and other strange characters can be difficult to manage.

PRACTICE!

1. Calculate the size of a file, in kilobytes, containing 1024 ASCII characters.
2. Determine how many bytes are contained in the following sentence:
   Unix is our friend!
3. Suppose that you store a project in a file called project#1_b.txt. Did you choose an acceptable filename? Why or why not?

3.1.6 Text Editors

A **text editor** can create, change, and view the contents of a text file. Modern full-screen editors have antiquated older line-by-line editors, but editing a file still consists of four basic steps:

- Starting the editing program.
- Moving the cursor.
- Inserting or deleting text.
- Saving or destroying your work.

Whether you create a new file or change an older file, you still edit that file! There are numerous packages out there for editing text files. Some programs run directly in a window, whereas others are GUI based.

Which editor should you use? Every version of Unix has rather archaic programs called *line editors*, which let you edit only one line at a time. So, if you feel adventurous, try either **ed** or **ex**. Realizing the need to see a full screen, the makers of Unix have for years provided **vi** (pronounced *vee-eye*), Unix's standard editor, and that editor is included in this chapter. Given the complexity of **vi**, programs such as **pico** and **emacs** are popular, though technically nonstandard. I focus first on **pico** because of its simplicity and provide the essentials of **emacs**. Wrapping up the chapter, I introduce the basic GUI editor **nedit** and an alternative GUI-based version of emacs called **xemacs**.

3.1.7 Word Processors and Publishing

Although I need to focus on text editors (as pretty much every book on Unix has to), you do have access to powerful and highly customizable word processors, spreadsheets, drawing programs, and more in Unix. I suggest that you start with **OpenOffice** (OO, *http://openoffice.org*), which is an open-source alternative to packages such as Microsoft Office. OO can even save and open Microsoft Office documents! Ask your system administrator if you can access the program. (Solaris users will likely have *StarOffice*, the commercial equivalent.)

PRACTICE!

> 4. Check whether the text editors mentioned in Section 3.1.6 are available on your system. (*Hint*: Use **man**.)
> 5. Can you find at least one text editor on your system that I did not mention?

3.2   PICO

pico is a simple, basic text editor that is available for Unix and Microsoft Windows. You can download it for free as part of **pine**, which is an e-mail program. Unfortunately, I cannot guarantee that your system has **pico**. See if the following step works:

Step 3.4:   Run Pico

```
unix> pico                                    Run pico. If you want to exit, press ^X.
unix> man pico                      Find help. You might need to press Spacebar a few times.
```

Assuming that you were able to access **pico** (Figure 3.2), continue with this section. Otherwise, ask your instructor or system administrator to install it soon! In what follows, I try to explain every nuance there is to editing, figuring that many students reading this book are new to Unix. So, if you already have some experience, you might want to skip ahead to **vi**, **emacs**, and **nedit**.

3.2.1   Using Pico

pico requires you to use **Control**-key combinations. For example, to exit **pico**, you simply enter **^X**. Just as with Unix **Control**-key commands, you can use lower- or uppercase **X**. **pico's** most common operations are listed in its window, as shown in Figure 3.2. To view the complete list of commands, see Table 3.1, which I created by using **pico's** own listing from **^G**.

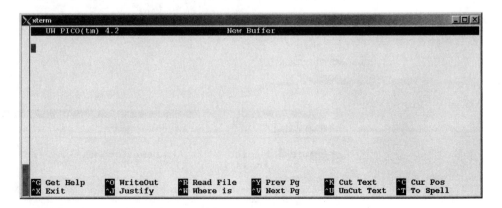

Figure 3.2   **pico**: Window

TABLE 3.1 `pico` Commands (Adapted from `pico`'s Help Listing)

General Commands		Cursor Movement	
`^G`	**Get help** (this table of command descriptions).	`^C`	Report current **cursor** position.
`^L`	Refresh the display.	`^W`	Search for (**where** is) text, neglecting case.
`^T`	Invoke the spell checker.	`^F`	Move cursor **forward** one character.
`^C`	Cancel another command; otherwise, show cursor position.	`^B`	Move cursor **backward** one character.
Cutting/Pasting		`^P`	Move cursor to **previous** line.
`^D`	**Delete** the character at the cursor position.	`^N`	Move cursor to **next** line.
`^^`	Mark position to start (de)selecting text.	`^A`	Move cursor to beginning of current line.
`^K`	Cut selected text (displayed in inverse characters).	`^E`	Move cursor to **end** of current line.
`^U`	Paste (**uncut**) previous cut text and insert at cursor.	`^V`	Move cursor forward one page of text.
`^R`	Insert a file at the current cursor.	`^Y`	Move cursor backward one page of text.
Backspace, **delete** (delete one character)		arrow keys	Move cursor in any direction.
Saving/Quitting		**Whitespace/Justification**	
`^O`	Output the current buffer to a file, saving it.	**Return** and **Enter** (start new line)	
`^X`	Exit `pico`, saving buffer.	`^I`	**Insert** tab at cursor position.
		`^J`	**Justify** text.

3.2.2   Saving Your Work

I encourage you to save your work often, especially since systems do occasionally crash.[3] `pico` does not automatically save your work as you enter text. Instead, it will place everything you type in a ***buffer***, which is computer memory that stores your work. So, everything in the `pico` window or screen from top to bottom is in the buffer. To send the contents of `pico`'s buffer to a file, you need to enter `^O` (the letter O) to write out those contents to a file. `pico` will prompt you for a filename, as shown in Figure 3.3.

Step 3.5:   Write Out Buffer

> *Enter* `^O`. *When* `pico` *prompts you for a file, type* `test.txt` *and press* **Return** *or* **Enter**. *If the filename you picked was already in use,* `pico` *will ask if you want to* OVERWRITE *that file. If you enter* **Y**, `pico` *will delete the old version of the file and create the new version, using the buffer's current contents. If you enter* **N**, *select a different filename.*

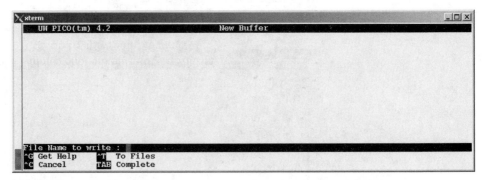

Figure 3.3 `pico`: Writing Out Buffer Contents to Text File

---

[3]Do you believe in premonitions? A group member and I once worked a few hours straight on a class report. After a while, overcome with a sense of dread, I had asked him whether he had saved the work at any point. He hadn't! I insisted that he save everything immediately. About a minute later, the entire network crashed. My recommendation is not to trust in such prescience!

If you need help with these commands, look at the bottom of **pico**'s window or screen. You will see new commands, including help on all of them. Note that the file you have created, `test.txt`, has no contents and will show a file size of zero if you check **ls -l**.

3.2.3   Exiting `pico`

To exit **pico**, enter **^X**. If you have made any changes, **pico** will ask you whether you want to save your new version of the file. If you say **N**, you will lose all your changes and quit. So be careful what you say! If you change your mind and prefer not to quit, enter **^C** to cancel your request to exit.

3.2.4   Starting `pico`

So far, I have had you start **pico** using the lone command **pico**. You can actually pick a filename right at the command line with **pico *filename***. If the filename exists, **pico** will load the associated file into the **pico** screen or window. Otherwise, **pico** will assume that what you enter while editing is intended for ***filename*** when you exit. Also, **pico** has many command-line options that you can review by entering **man pico**. For example, **pico -m** will activate the mouse.

3.2.5   Text Entry

After you start **pico**, it places your cursor at the top left corner of the screen or window. As you enter text, the cursor moves to the right, just as it does at the command line. As shown in Table 3.1, you have many options to move the cursor, either by arrow keys or by **Control** sequences. I particularly like **^A** and **^E** to jump to the head and end, respectively, of a line. Unlike old, unsophisticated text editors, **pico** lets you move freely in all directions.

Step 3.6:   Type Stuff

See if you can duplicate the screen shown in Figure 3.4. Don't worry if you make a mistake. You will learn about fixing mistakes in the next step and section.

Along the way, you should continue to save your work with **^O**, because I will use `test.txt` a few more times.

3.2.6   Cutting and Pasting Text

Sooner or later, you will type something wrong or will want to change something. You can use **Backspace** (delete one character to the left) and **Delete** (possibly delete one

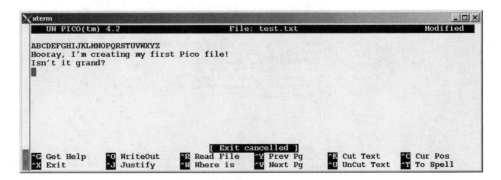

Figure 3.4   `pico`: Text Entry

character to the right). Note that **Delete** may or may not act as **Backspace**, depending on your system and configuration. So, instead of relying on **Delete**, use ^D. In cutting lines, `pico` needs a bit of explanation. To cut and paste a single line,

- Move your cursor anywhere on the line and enter ^K.
- Move the cursor to one line *below* the line where you would like to place the line you just cut. Enter ^U.

Note that until you cut another portion of text with ^K, `pico` will keep pasting the same line when you enter ^U. The area in memory where the program stores the cut text is often called the *clipboard*. Once you put something new on the clipboard through ^K, the old chunk is removed. `pico`'s clipboard stores only one cut chunk of text at a time.

Step 3.7: Cut and Paste Line of Text

Using what you typed in Step 3.6, make your text identical to the contents of Figure 3.4. Then, cut the first line and paste it five times at the bottom of the file. Refer to Figure 3.5.

If you want to cut a block of text, you have to be careful. You need to keep entering ^K without pressing any other key. `pico` will let you cut lines of text, including blank lines, but you cannot deviate from the cutting process.

Step 3.8: Cut and Paste Block of Text

Using your work from Step 3.7, cut the entire block of the bottom five lines (ABC...) without pressing any other key. Move your cursor onto the H in Hooray. Then, enter ^U, which will paste the block above, as shown in Figure 3.6.

`pico` has another bit of sophisticated editing. You can mark a position anywhere with ^^ (**Control-^** or **Control-6**, not **Control-Control!**) and then move the cursor to another position. As you move your cursor, `pico` will highlight the text that you are marking for cutting. The action strongly resembles dragging your mouse over text to highlight it. (In fact, had you activated `pico` with `pico  -m`, you could use your mouse for highlighting.) If you move the cursor in the other direction, you can "unhighlight" the marked text. Once you've highlighted the text, enter ^K to cut it. Now, `pico` will not automatically cut the entire line.

Figure 3.5 `pico`: Editing

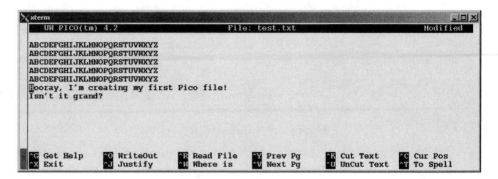

Figure 3.6 `pico`: Block Editing

Step 3.9: Marking Text

As shown in Figure 3.7, I first put my cursor on the D *in* ABCD.... *Then, I entered* ^^. *To indicate that you have marked the start of text to cut, the bottom of the* **pico** *window or screen says* Mark Set. *Next, move the cursor to the left, using the right arrow until you reach the* X. *Finally, enter* ^K *to cut everything from left to right that you highlighted.* **pico** *will start from the mark at* D *and stop one character before the cursor position. So you have now cut* DEFGHIJKLMNOPQRSTUVW, *which you can paste anywhere by using* ^U.

Remember that once you cut something else (which places it in the buffer), you cannot retrieve the text you cut previously.

3.2.7 Line Continuation and Justification

Now and then, something you type or paste into **pico** (especially long website names) causes **pico** to show a portion of the text, terminating with a dollar sign ($). You can also get a $ if you shrink a **pico** window after you type in it. The $ is a continuation symbol in **pico**, which means that **pico** is telling you that there is at least one more character to the right that cannot be seen. You have four choices to get rid of the blasted $:

- Ignore it. Perhaps you are printing on paper that is wider than your screen or window.
- Enter ^E to go the line's end, and press **Spacebar**, **Return**, or **Enter**.
- Enter ^A to go the line's front, and press **Spacebar**, **Tab**, or ^I (insert tab).
- Click somewhere on the line, and enter ^J to justify the line.

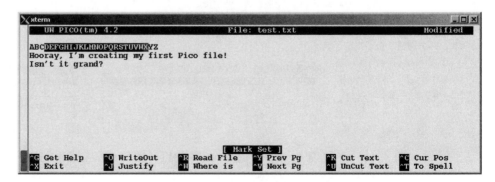

Figure 3.7 `pico`: Marking Text

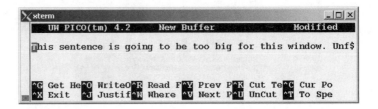

Figure 3.8 `pico`: Text Justification

When you justify a line (or lines) of text, `pico` tries to make a block of text fit within the confines of the current screen or window. So, for a line with a $, justification will break the line so that it fits one line and "spills over" (*wraps*) the remaining text to the next line. If the next line is still too long, `pico` will keep justifying the text until the last line does not exceed the maximum width.

Step 3.10: Justify Text

*As shown in Figure 3.8, I have created a line that exceeds the window length. To do something similar, write a rather lengthy line and then shrink a window. Or use **Backspace** at the front of a line to connect it to the previous line. After doing so, enter ^J to justify the whole mess.*

When you have a block of text that you would like to connect and fit within the confines of a window or screen, you can use ^J:

- First, ensure that each line has the same number of spaces (possibly none) at its beginning.
- Next, separate blocks that you do not wish to justify with blank lines.
- Finally, enter ^J anywhere in the block that you would like to justify.

Just as with lines with $, `pico` will force the block to fill as much of each line as possible, starting at the top of the block of text.

Step 3.11: Justify Block

As shown in Figure 3.9, start `pico` again and enter the text as shown. Note how each of the four lines starts in the same column. When you are finished, move the cursor onto any of the lines, anywhere in the line, and enter ^J. `pico` will justify the text on the basis of the window or screen size that you have chosen.

Note that after you justify a block of text, you can unjustify it with ^U.

Figure 3.9 `pico`: Block Justification

PRACTICE!

6.   Create a new text file called `practicePico.txt`.
7.   Inside the text file, import `test.txt`.
8.   Add your name to the top of the file.
9.   Save your work with the new filename `practicePico2.txt`.
10. Exit **pico**.
11. Use **more** to confirm the contents of the two new files that you created.

3.3   VI

In this section, I focus on Unix's standard (and classic!) text editor, which is called **vi** (*visual editor*) and is pronounced *vee-eye*. In general, I prefer **emacs**, although **vi**'s new incarnation, **vim** (*vi improved*), has a large following. Like **pico**, **vi** and **vim** consume relatively little memory compared with **emacs**. This section provides an overview of **vi**, which you will definitely need to practice, as the command structure differs greatly from that of **pico**. If you enjoy **vi**, I recommend that you investigate **vim**. (Note that you might prefer to substitute the command **vedit** for **vi**, as **vedit** provides a slightly more user-friendly version of **vi**.)

3.3.1   Creating Text Files with **vi**

To create a text file with **vi**, start the editor by entering the command **vi**. You may also choose an existing text file or create a file with a specific name, using the input **vi** *filename*. To ease your learning of **vi**, we will use **vedit** to provide an easier interface:

Step 3.12:   Start **vi**

unix> **vedit**   *Start the **vi** text editor. You can also enter **vi**.*
Your window or screen will appear as shown in Figure 3.10.

As with all other Unix commands, **vi** has many command-line options, which you can find with **man vi**. Note that the **vi** options also work for **vedit**.

3.3.2   **vi** Modes and Command Mode

A column of tildes (~) spanning the entire height of the window or screen should appear in it. The **vi** editor starts in ***command mode***, one of three **vi** modes whose connections are depicted in Figure 3.11.

Figure 3.10   **vi**: Initial Screen

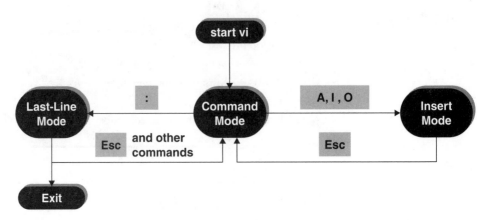

Figure 3.11 vi: Modes

While inside command mode, you can move the cursor back and forth on the current line, delete and paste text, and toggle into other modes. Table 3.2 summarizes many common commands that you can enter from within command mode. (See **man vi** for more.) To return to command mode from other modes, press **Esc** just once. If you make a mistake, get incongruous results, or become confused, return to this mode.

3.3.3   insert Mode

vi's ***insert mode*** lets you insert text into the file that you are editing. From within the command mode, you may *type* **i** to toggle into insert mode. You can now *insert* text at the cursor's current position. If you are using **vedit** instead of **vi**, the window or screen will now alert you that you are in insert mode. To finish one line and start the next, press **Return** or **Enter**. The following step has you practice inserting text:

Step 3.13: Insert Text with vi

Run **vedit** *if you have not done so yet. The cursor in Figure 3.10 shows you the current position in which to insert text. Press* **Esc** *to ensure that are you indeed in command mode. Then type* **i** *to change to insert mode if you are using* **vi**. *As shown next, you will type one line at a time. If you make a mistake, move the cursor backwards with* **Backspace** *or* **Del** *and type your correction.*

```
Name: David I. Schwartz            Type your name. When done, press Return.
User: dis                          Type your user ID. You remain in edit mode until you press Esc.
~                                  vi will indicate new areas for text entry with a ~ on each line.
~                                  vi removes the ~ when you start editing a line.
~                                  New areas are always at the bottom of your text.
```

Your window or screen should appear as shown in Figure 3.12.

Recall that **vi** is case sensitive! For instance, from within command mode, **I** inserts text at the beginning of a line and **i** inserts text to the left of the cursor. You can find other ways to insert text in Table 3.2 and **man vi**.

Figure 3.12 vi: Insert Mode

TABLE 3.2 vi: Summary of Commands

Cursor Movement		Inserting Text	
l, →	Move one character right	A	Append at end of line
h, ←	Move one character left	a	Append to right of cursor
j, ↓	Move one line down	I	Insert at beginning of line
k, ↑	Move one line up	i	Insert to left of cursor
$	Move to end of line	O	Open new line above current line
0	Move to beginning of line	o	Open new line below current line
Cutting/Pasting		**Deleting Text**	
yy, Y	Copy ("yank") line into memory	x	Delete current character
y$	Copy to end of line	d$	Delete to end of line
P	Paste line after or below cursor	d0	Delete to beginning of line
p	Paste line before or above cursor	dd	Delete current line
Undoing		**Searching**	
u	Undo previous command	/text	Search forward for text
U	Undo editing changes to line	?text	Search backward for text
Saving		**Quitting**	
:w	Save work to current file	:q!	Quit; ignore any changes
:w file	Save work to file	:q	Quit (assumes no changes)
:wq file	Save work to file and quit	:wq	Save changes and quit

3.3.4 Last-Line Mode

To save your work, you must switch to ***last-line mode***, which lets you save and quit, set
vi options, search for text, and name or rename files. To enter last-line mode, type a
colon (:) from within command mode. Then, enter **wq** *filename* to save your text as
filename inside your account.

Step 3.14: Saving Your Work in VI

*Restore the work you were doing in Step 3.13 if you have closed it. You are now going to save that work in a file
called* userinfo.txt. *To get to last-line mode to enter the save-and-quit command, you first need to enter
command mode with* **Esc**. *Next, type*: *(which puts you in last-line mode), followed by* **wq userinfo.txt**.
Your screen or window will appear as shown in Figure 3.13. When you press **Return**, *vi will write the current
buffer to* userinfo.txt *and quit.*

Figure 3.13 **vi**: Saving and Quitting

To help remember **wq**, note that the **w** command instructs Unix to *write* all your text into a file and **q** tells Unix to *quit*.

3.3.5 Handy Tip: Keeping Track of Modes

New **vi** users usually get frustrated concerning which mode they are in. Use **vedit** until you become more comfortable. Here are some tricks to help you:

- You know that you are in insert mode when the words INSERT MODE are near the bottom right corner of your screen or window.
- If you do not see INSERT MODE and your cursor is somewhere in the body of your text, you are in command mode.
- If your cursor is at the bottom of the screen after you have entered a **:**, **?**, **!**, or **/**, then you are in last-line mode.

Give it time…you will eventually get used to **vi**!

3.3.6 Summary of **vi** Editing

In general, follow this pattern when editing with **vi**:

- **vi** starts from command mode, in which you can move the cursor around and delete text. Change your mode when you finish moving and deleting.
- Next, toggle to insert mode. Use **a**, **A**, **i**, **I**, **o**, or **O** to insert text on one line. Press **Return** for a new line, or press **Esc** to return to command mode. Repeat this cycle until you finish editing.
- Finally, press **:** to initiate last-line mode. Save your work and exit with **wq**.

3.3.7 Customizing **vi**

You will eventually discover that you might need to configure various options. For example, if you discover that **vi** isn't wrapping excessively long lines of text, access last-line mode and enter **set wrapmargin=1**. You can also have **vi** automatically load commands. Inside your home directory, create a text file called .exrc. (**vi**'s roots become apparent!) For example, use the following:

```
set wrapmargin=1
set showmode
```

Do not include extra lines; **vi** will treat each line in your .exrc as a command entered in last-line mode. To see all options that have been (and could be) set, enter **set all** in last-line mode. You can apply and modify these options in your .exrc file. I recommend digging around the Internet also, as many useful examples abound.

PRACTICE!

12. Using **vedit**, create a text file with the contents of test.txt as shown in Figure 3.6.
13. Cut two lines that begin with ABC....
14. Paste those two lines at the bottom of the file.
15. Change the pico to vi in the body of the text.
16. Delete letters D through S (inclusive) in the lines with ABC.....
17. At the bottom of the file, describe your favorite text editor that you have worked with so far.
18. Inside your file, use **vi** to search for the string ABC.
19. Save your work to a file called test-vi.txt, and quit.
20. Check the contents of test-vi.txt with **more**.

3.4   EMACS

emacs belongs to Unix's standard distribution, but it is very popular and very likely installed on your system. Although I'm a bigger fan of **emacs** than of other editors, I have deliberately placed a stronger emphasis on **pico**, assuming that my readers are still new to command-line environments. This section focuses on getting you started with **emacs** and on using some of its commands. The program is quite sweeping, allowing you to check e-mail and more. There are numerous resources on the Internet that cover **emacs** in great detail.[4]

3.4.1   Running Emacs

As with other text editors, you can start emacs with or without arguments:

* **emacs *options***: start emacs with no particular text file.
* **emacs *options filename***: edit (or create) a new text file.

In both versions, the options are indeed optional. You can learn about these command-line options with **man emacs**. Assuming that you enter **emacs** and your system hasn't customized the command, you should see a screen or window akin to Figure 3.14.

If your system complains about not being able to open an **emacs** window, try **emacs -nw**, which means "run *emacs* with no window."

3.4.2   Emacs Command Key Sequences

As summarized in **emacs**'s introductory message, you need to learn special notation:

* *Control commands* (**C-*char***): Press and *hold* **Control** and then press ***char***'s key. So, for **C-h**, you would press and hold **Control** and, while holding it, press the **H** key (with or without **Shift**). Then let go of both keys. Do not press **Enter** or **Return**.
* *Meta commands* (**M-*char***): The **M** refers to **Meta**, which you would hold down while pressing the **X** key (with or without **Shift**). If your keyboard lacks **Meta**, either *hold* **Alt** or *press and release* **Esc**. For example, for **M-x**, I press **Esc** (and let go) and then press the **X** key.

---

[4]See *http://www.gnu.org/software/emacs* and *http://www.emacs.org*.

```
X xterm                                                               _ □ x
Buffers Files Tools Edit Search Mule Help
Welcome to GNU Emacs

Get help            C-h  (Hold down CTRL and press h)
Undo changes        C-x u       Exit Emacs              C-x C-c
Get a tutorial      C-h t       Use Info to read docs   C-h i
Activate menubar    F10  or  ESC `  or  M-`
(`C-' means use the CTRL key.  `M-' means use the Meta (or Alt) key.
If you have no Meta key, you may instead type ESC followed by the character.)

GNU Emacs 20.4.1 (sparc-sun-solaris2.6, X toolkit)
 of Fri Jul 23 1999 on ringding
Copyright (C) 1999 Free Software Foundation, Inc.

GNU Emacs comes with ABSOLUTELY NO WARRANTY; type C-h C-w for full details.
Emacs is Free Software--Free as in Freedom--so you can redistribute copies
of Emacs and modify it; type C-h C-c to see the conditions.
Type C-h C-d for information on getting the latest version.




----:---F1 *scratch*         (Lisp Interaction)--L1--All-------------------
For information about the GNU Project and its goals, type C-h C-p.
```

Figure 3.14 Running `emacs`

- Case sensitivity (**Shift**, **S-***key*): Most of **emacs** commands are not case sensitive. For example, **C-h** and **C-H** both access **emacs** help. But I have seen a few commands that do require **Shift**. In such cases, you use the notation **S-**, as in **S-Insert**, which means holding down **Shift**, pressing **Insert**, and then releasing both keys.

Sometimes **emacs** will require sequences, such as **C-x C-c**, which means that you press **C-x** and then **C-c** immediately afterwards. You will see the key sequences at the bottom of the **emacs** screen or window (an area called the **emacs minibuffer**) as you enter them.

3.4.3   `emacs` Frame

emacs will either completely fill a screen or spawn a window, depending on how you run it. (Your system administrators may have configured it.) Either way, I can still provide an overview of what you see on your screen, which is called the **emacs frame**, as shown in Figure 3.15.

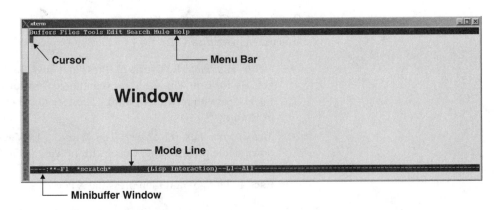

Figure 3.15 `emacs`: Frame Contents

The **emacs** frame has the following features:

- *Window*: In **emacs**, the main area where you will enter text for editing is the window. I would have preferred the term *panel*, but no such luck: The reason for *window* is that you can create multiple windows to edit multiple files within the same frame.
- *Minibuffer window* or *echo area*: **emacs** will echo your commands in the minibuffer window. In fact, you can enter commands directly into the minibuffer by entering **M-x**.
- *Menu bar*: Depending on the type of the file that you edit, **emacs** supplies menu selections for common commands. The menu bar is more intuitive if you use a windows-based version of **emacs**.
- *Cursor*: When using **emacs** in a window, you must move and click your mouse to indicate the selected window. **emacs** will place text wherever your cursor appears.
- *Mode line*: **emacs** supplies different commands for different types of files and modes, which can include standard editing, programming, and even e-mail and other tasks.

emacs even lets you know that, for example, you are editing in "frame 1," by reporting F1 in the mode line. You will see the minibuffer and mode line "in action" as you begin to edit text files throughout this section.

3.4.4   Getting Help

Besides the help offered through **emacs**'s websites and **man**, **emacs** tells you how to get help directly from within **emacs** itself. For example, to run the tutorial, enter **C-h t**.

3.4.5   Cancelling a Command

If you ever make a mistake, do not enter **C-c** Instead, **emacs**'s basic *quit* function is **C-g**. In fact, I like to press **C-g C-g** so that I can see Quit appear in the minibuffer.

3.4.6   Basic Editing

You can start entering text immediately into **emacs** right after you run the program. Usually, I recommend that you first create a filename, especially to rid yourself of that buffer explanation at the file's top. But I want to take you through some initial editing steps to get a feel for **emacs**.

Step 3.15:   Entering Text

Enter text at the cursor's position after you run **emacs**. *See figure below:*

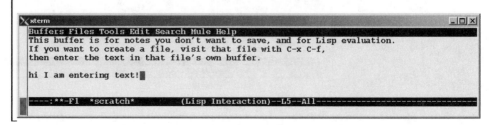

Step 3.16: Moving the Cursor

You have a few choices. To move the cursor to the top of the window, either enter **M-<** *(or* **M-S-,***) or use the arrow keys. If you use* **M-<**, *your minibuffer will report* Mark set, *which you can ignore for now. See figure below:*

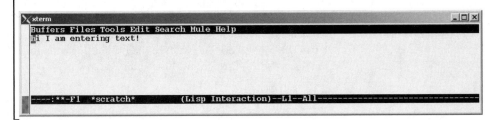

Step 3.17: Deleting Text

To delete text, use **C-k**, *which kills (deletes) one line. Use it four times. If you want to be fancier, move the cursor to the* h *in* hi..., *and use* **C-w**. *This command deletes a region starting at the mark (see previous step) and ending just before the current cursor position. You can also set the mark with* **C-Spacebar**. *See figure below:*

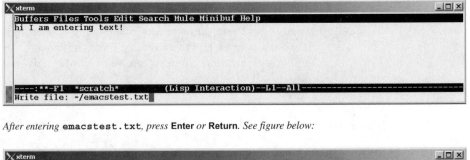

Step 3.18: Writing a Text File

Again, you have a few options. Normally, you would save your work with **C-x s**, *but in this case you can write out your text to a specific filename (use* emacstest.txt*) with* **C-x w**. *See figure below:*

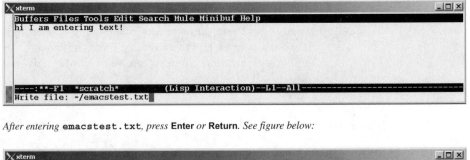

After entering **emacstest.txt**, *press* **Enter** *or* **Return**. *See figure below:*

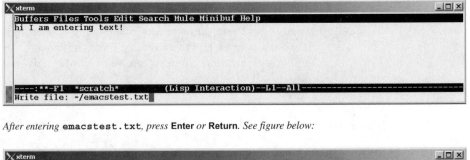

Note how **emacs** recognizes the txt file extension and changes the major mode to Text.

3.4.7   Saving, Quitting, and Exiting Emacs

As with other text editors, **emacs** uses a *buffer* to store your text. As shown in Step 3.18, you can use **C-x C-w** to select a specific file to which **emacs** will dump its buffer. To save changes to a file without quitting, use **C-x C-s**. (**C-x s** will prompt you to save.) If you would like to quit **emacs**, use **C-x C-c**. If you have made changes to the current buffer, **emacs** will prompt you as to whether you would like to save before quitting. You may also get prompted to terminate other buffers.

3.4.8   Autosaving

Unlike **vi** and **pico**, **emacs** will frequently *autosave* your work. So, if you are editing a specific file, **emacs** will occasionally save your work that is in the buffer to a file. (There's an internal variable that you can set to determine the frequency.) **emacs** stores the updated file that has the same name, starting with a #. In the following steps, I demonstrate how you can recover an autosaved file:

Step 3.19:   Autosaving

Alter emacstest.txt *and then wait a few seconds. The minibuffer will report that autosaving is taking place. See figure below:*

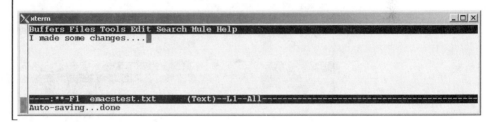

Step 3.20:   Quit without Saving

Let's say you forget to save or simply choose to quit. After **C-x C-c**, *press* **q** *to quit. See figure below:*

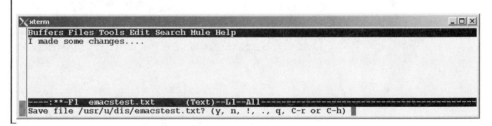

Step 3.21:   Recover a File

After you quit **emacs**, *restart it with* **emacs emacstest.txt**. **emacs** *will alert you that you have an autosaved file which differs from the file you saved manually. See figure below:*

To recover the file, enter **M-x**, *which moves your cursor to the minibuffer. Then enter* `recover-file`. *(Be sure to press* **Enter** *or* **Return**). `emacs` *will now prompt you for a file. Enter* `emacstest.txt`. *See figure below:*

`emacs` *now gives you a choice between the autosaved file (which begins with #) or your previous manually saved version. If you enter* **yes**, `emacs` *will load the autosaved file into the buffer. See figure below:*

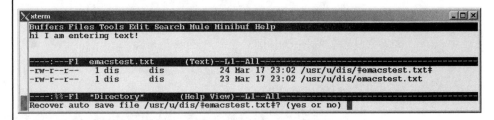

You should now see the altered version, which you could formally save with **C-x C-s**:

3.4.9 Deleting and Cutting

`emacs` provides great flexibility for changing your text. Unfortunately, I can only review the basics, but that should be enough to get you started. Here are some common delete commands:

- *Characters*: To delete one character forward, use **C-d**. To delete one character backward, use **Delete**.[5]
- *Words*: Use **M-d** to delete the next word (the word to the right of the cursor). **M-Delete** has already deleted the previous word.
- *Lines*: **C-k** deletes all text to the right of the cursor.
- *Region*: Use **C-w**, but be careful how you select your text. A region is an area of text that starts at a mark, which you can set with **C-Spacebar**. By moving the cursor to a new place and entering **C-w**, you can delete the region between the two places. I need to be a bit more specific about how the region is defined, and I will do so next.

As shown in Figure 3.16, you can mark a region anywhere:

---

[5]Depending on your computer, **Backspace** might trigger **C-h**, because ^H is an ASCII nonprinting character (ASCII value 8). But **C-h** gets help in `emacs`, which causes a conflict for users who expect **Backspace**!

```
        1 2 3 4 5                    1 2 3 4 5  Region includes
Mark  A [B] C D E F    ────────▶     A          mark
      G H I J ■
            Cursor

Cursor [1] 2 3 4 5
       A B C D E F     ────────▶     H I J      Region excludes
       G [H] I J                                mark
              Mark
```

Figure 3.16 `emacs`: Setting and Cutting Regions

- If you move the cursor right or left, the region includes the rest of the current line to the right or left, respectively.
- If you move the cursor up or down, the region includes all lines above or below the current line, respectively.

One way to think of a region is that the mark and final cursor position form a diagonal inside an *approximately* rectangular portion of text.

In a GUI, you can also use your mouse to select text for deletion and then use **C-w**. Note that **emacs** provides other ways to mark text besides **C-Spacebar**. Now let's have you give it a try.

Step 3.22: Mark and cut region

Inside emacstest.txt, *set up a block of text as follows: Move the cursor to the* d *and enter* **C-Spacebar**, *which marks the* d *as the first character of the region.*

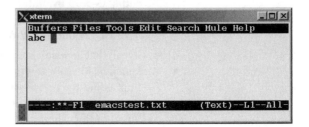

Next, move the cursor to the end of the text. I want to delete the entire region after abc. *Note that* **emacs** *does not show you the mark!*

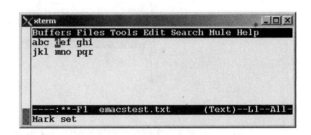

To toggle the cursor between the mark and the current position, use **C-x C-x**. *Once the cursor is back to the space after the* r, *enter* **C-w**. **emacs** *will delete all text between the mark and the current cursor.*

If you want to cut a *rectangular* block, mark a corner, mark a region, and enter **C-x r k** (rectangle cut). **emacs** will cut out only the rectangle from the mark up to (but not including) the cursor. In this case, you use the diagonal between the mark and the cursor.

3.4.10 Pasting

To paste a portion of text that you have cut, move the cursor to the point where you want the first character of the text pasted. Then execute **C-y**, which stands for *yank* (as in yanking text from a clipboard). For practice, you will restore emacstest.txt to its original state (see Step 3.22):

Step 3.23: Paste region

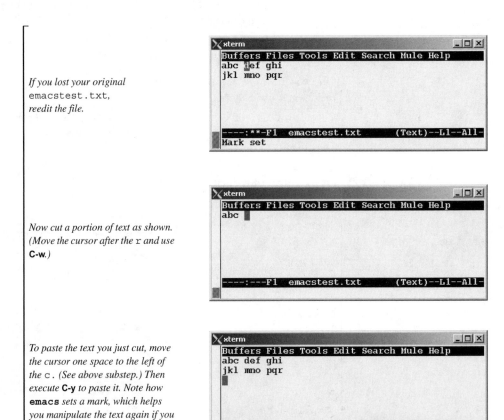

If you lost your original emacstest.txt, *reedit the file.*

Now cut a portion of text as shown. (Move the cursor after the r *and use* **C-w**.*)*

To paste the text you just cut, move the cursor one space to the left of the c. *(See above substep.) Then execute* **C-y** *to paste it. Note how* **emacs** *sets a mark, which helps you manipulate the text again if you change your mind.*

If you want to undo your most recent edit, you do not have to cut the text: just use **C-x u**, **C-/**, which means "undo." Actually, **emacs** remembers all your edits! You can keep executing **C-x u** over and over again, working back to the beginning of your session.

3.4.11 Multiple Windows

Recall that an **emacs** window is a separate panel within the **emacs** frame, which is contained inside your screen or GUI window. Yes, I realize I used the word "window" twice. I am going to be referring to **emacs**'s version of window in this section. Why bother? Because you can split your frame into multiple windows and assign each window to a different buffer. Then, since a window may have its own buffer, you can associate a window with its own file or program. So, **emacs** mimics a GUI! In the next step, you will work on two separate files in the same **emacs** frame.

Step 3.24: **emacs** Windows

Edit a new text file called a.txt *with* **emacs a.txt**. *Once inside, split the window vertically with* **C-x 2**. *See figure below:*

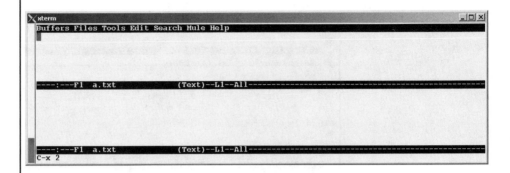

To move the cursor to another window (you can say "toggle between windows"), use **C-x o** *(not zero!). Indeed, using* **C-x o**, *you can toggle* all *windows inside the same frame. See figure below:*

You are seeing one buffer (and file), a.txt. *Both windows "see" the same buffer!* **emacs** *even alerts you about the* a.txt *buffer in both mode lines. So, if you start typing in one window, the text automatically appears in the other window. In a little bit, you will actually assign a window to a different file. But for now, type* **hello!** *in one window to see how the other window will (nearly) simultaneously show the same text. See figure below:*

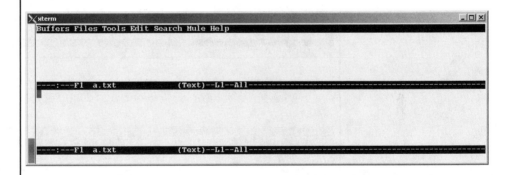

You can also split a window horizontally. Using **C-x 3**, *split the bottom window into two subwindows and toggle the cursor (***C-x o***) to the bottom right window. See figure below:*

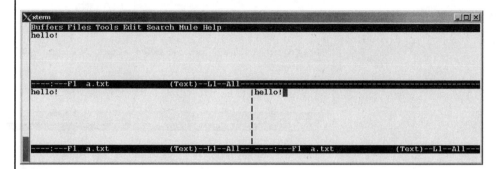

Now you will assign the bottom right window to a new text file, b.txt. *Make sure that your cursor is in that window, and then use* **C-x b** *(change buffer), followed by* **b.txt** *inside the minibuffer. Then press* **Enter** *or* **Return**. *See figure below:*

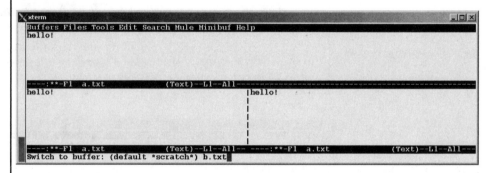

Look at the mode line at the bottom of the frame. The bottom right window now stores the buffer for b.txt. *You can edit different text in the buffers. See figure below:*

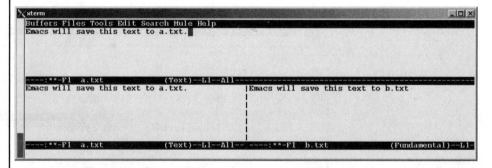

Save your work and exit from **emacs**. *Then, check your work using* **more**, *which views a file's contents in the command window:*

```
unix> more a.txt                              View the contents of a.txt.
emacs will save this text to a.txt.    You have one a.txt, though you had three windows.
unix> more b.txt                              View the contents of b.txt.
emacs will save this text to b.txt.         b.txt was separate from a.txt.
```

Note that the pull-down menu Buffers can assist with buffer switching. If you would like to *remove* a particular window from a frame, use **C-x 0** (zero this time!).

```
Xterm                                                              _|□|x|
 Buffers Files Tools Edit Search Mule Minibuf Help




 ----:---F1  funstuff          (Fundamental)--L1--All----------------
 In this buffer, type RET to select the completion near point.

 Possible completions are:
 2C-associate-buffer                  2C-command
 2C-split                             2C-two-columns
 Buffer-menu-1-window                 Buffer-menu-2-window
 Buffer-menu-backup-unmark            Buffer-menu-bury
 Buffer-menu-delete                   Buffer-menu-delete-backwards
 Buffer-menu-execute                  Buffer-menu-mark
 ----:---F1  *Completions*     (Completion List)--L1--Top-----------
 M-x
```

Figure 3.17 emacs Functions

3.4.12 Running Special Programs

You wouldn't believe how much **emacs** can do. In this section, I give you only a small glimpse of what's possible. As shown in Figure 3.17, you can access all **emacs** functions by executing **M-x**. **emacs** will then move your cursor to the minibuffer and wait for you to type something. Instead, press only **Spacebar**, which activates **emacs**'s completion routine: **emacs** will search for *all* of its functions. You will see a huge list, which you can skim through by changing your window with **C-x o**. (All navigation commands still work.) Note that some functions are identical to **C** and **M** keystrokes; a function can be *bound* to a keystroke, as several functions already are.

Step 3.25: Sample Emacs Program

Restart **emacs** *with any file (say,* funstuff*) and execute* **M-x yow**. *What happens next is that after you enter* **M-x**, **emacs** *will move your cursor to the minibuffer. Then you type* **yow** *and press* **Enter** *or* **Return**. *This program produces unpredictable results. So you might see something quite different from what you expect. Note that my screen capture is not faked! It really said this:*

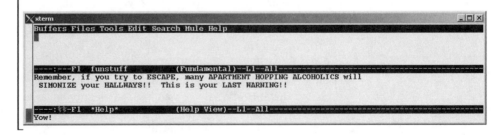

For more fun, restart **emacs** and try **M-x doctor** and **M-x hanoi**. But **emacs** is not all fun and games: Try **M-x shell**, which allows you to run a command prompt from within **emacs**. You can even access and send e-mail. So, you could feasibly use **emacs** as a pseudo operating system!

3.4.13 Customizing Emacs

Explaining **emacs** in its entirety would take another whole book. In fact, such books exist. I offer you a tidbit of the ways in which you can customize your sessions. For instance, if you are like me, you must have pressed **Backspace** too many times by now. Unfortunately for many of us, **emacs** may think that **Backspace** means **C-h**, which triggers helps.[6] So, you might have been triggering help every time you pressed **Backspace**. To rid yourself of this nuisance, you can "permanently" change the behavior of **Backspace** by creating a file called .emacs in your account. This text file contains instructions that **emacs** will follow every time you run the program. If you suffer from **Backspace** pain (pun intended) and are using Version 21 or higher, try the following:

Step 3.26:   Customize Emacs

unix> `cd`	*I am changing directories to make that sure you are in your home account.*
unix> `emacs .emacs`	*Yes, it looks weird. Just edit a file called* .emacs.
`;;; Ensure that BACKSPACE deletes backwards`	*Comment on your change.*
	emacs *will ignore this line.*
`(normal-erase-is-backspace-mode 1)`	*Instruct* **emacs** *to change* **Backspace**'s *behavior.*
	Save and exit from your work.
unix> `emacs b.txt`	*Edit a new text file.*
`Type me, then try to Backspace me!`	*If you do not trigger help, your customizing worked!*

One downside to this modification is that you cannot use **C-h C-h** for help. Instead, use **M-x help**. You may have discovered that your system administrator already gave you a .emacs file, perhaps containing the preceding setting. Once you have edited your .emacs file, **emacs** will continue to exhibit your customizations. You can override your changes by reediting .emacs or setting options in the minibuffer during a session. For more fun, search around on the Internet. You will find entire sites devoted to **emacs** customization files.

PRACTICE!

21. Try each of the following settings inside your .emacs file, one at a time. For each, describe its effect when you edit a file. Feel free to keep these settings!

    `(normal-erase-is-backspace-mode 1)`

    `(fset 'yes-or-no-p 'y-or-n-p)`

    `(setq column-number-mode t)`

22. `(global-set-key "\C-cg" 'goto-line)`

3.4.14 Command Summary

Table 3.3 lists a number of **emacs** commands. Note that I did not include the wide variety of functions, special keys, and mouse operations in **emacs**. In fact, I left out hundreds of commands! You can find a more comprehensive reference list in Unix. On my system, I would enter the following command:

gs /usr/local/gnu/emacs-21.2/share/emacs/21.2/etc/refcard/ps.

On your system, you first need to figure out **emacs**'s location. So, you might want to wait until you feel more comfortable with directory navigation. To print a copy for yourself, use **lp** or **lpr**. In fact, the resulting printout will explain **M-y**, which I couldn't cram into Table 3.3. If you want a *complete* list of commands, use **emacs**'s help to display all bindings with **C-h b** (or **F1-b**). Try **M-x Spacebar** as well.

---

[6]Why? **^h** represents the ASCII nonprinting character for—you guessed it!—deleting backwards!

TABLE 3.3   emacs Command Summary

Movement		Cutting and Pasting		File Commands	
C-f, →	Forward character	**C-d**	Delete current character	**C-x C-f**	Find file
C-b, ←	Backward character	**Del**	Delete previous character	**C-x C-v**	Read new file
M-f	Forward word	**M-d**	Delete next word	**C-x i**	Insert file
M-b	Backward word	**M-Del**	Delete previous word	**C-x C-w**	Write buffer to new file
C-n, ↓	Next line	**C-k**	Delete to end of line	**C-x C-s**	Save file
C-p, ↑	Previous line	**M-0 C-k**	Delete to head of line	**C-x C-c**	Quit emacs
C-e	End of line	**C-w**	Kill region	**Marking**	
C-a	Head of line	**C-y**	Paste yanked text	**C-Spacebar**	Set mark
M-v	Down page	**M-y**	Too long to explain	**C-@**	Set mark
C-v	Up page	**Search and Replace**		**C-x C-x**	Exchange point and mark
M->	Bottom file	**C-s**	Search forward	**M-h**	Mark paragraph
M-<	Top file	**C-r**	Search backward	**C-x C-p**	Mark page
C-x o	Move to other buffer	**M-%**	Search and replace	**C-x h**	Mark buffer

Control		Spelling	
C-g	Quit	**M-$**	Spell word
C-/, C-_	Undo	**M-x ispell-buffer**	Spell entire buffer

Buffers		Formatting		Windows	
C-x b	Select other buffer	**Tab**	Indent line	**C-x 2**	Split vertically
C-x C-b	List all buffers	**C-M-**	Indent region	**C-x 3**	Split horizontally
C-x k	Kill buffer	**C-s**	Center line	**C-x 0**	Delete window

PRACTICE!

23. Using **emacs**, edit a file that contains your name and address.
24. Replace each letter a with y, using **emacs**'s replace command.
25. Delete all text except for the first column of letters.

3.5   GUI EDITORS

In the "old days" before today's GUIs, full-screen editors such as **vi** and **emacs** were considered blessings. However, they do require quite a bit of memorization because of all the command sequences they use. Given that nowadays practically all of the computers you will interact with have GUIs, I will briefly demonstrate two common examples on Unix. Note that your systems may have different software.

3.5.1   NEdit

Running **nedit** will give you a window, as shown in Figure 3.18. As explained in **man nedit**, the program is "streamlined," which means that it is intended for basic text editing. For Microsoft Windows users, think "Notepad for Unix." Although there are numerous commands for programming, all you really need to do is use the mouse to point, click, and select. Standard editing keys, such as **Tab**, **Backspace**, **Return**, and others, have definitions typical of their counterpart keys in word processors.

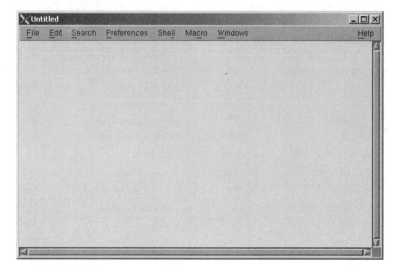

Figure 3.18 NEdit

3.5.2 XEmacs

emacs can run in a GUI environment, but all you really end up doing is opening a Unix window that contains the **emacs** frame. For an environment that capitalizes more on GUI operations and capabilities, try **xemacs**. The start-up window, shown in Figure 3.19, should seem vaguely familiar. As with **nedit**, you may now use the mouse extensively by selecting menus and toolbar icons. However, the GUI provides an easier interface for **emacs**'s functions, command bindings, and variables. In fact, several of the menu options remind you about the keyboard shortcuts. You can also goof off quite a bit: Check out the **Games** menu under **Apps**.

PRACTICE!

26. Use **nedit** to write a short essay on the advantages and disadvantages of using keyboard shortcuts for text editing.
27. Use **xemacs** to play a game of *Tetris*.

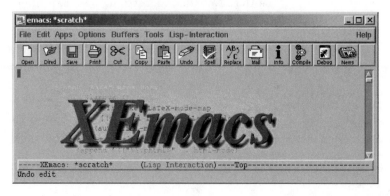

Figure 3.19 XEmacs

3.6   APPLICATION: PROGRAMMING IN JAVA

Why bother so much with text editing? As discussed at the beginning of this chapter, programming relies heavily on text editing. For example, you can create a simple program and run it on Unix. If you have never programmed before, the following steps will give you a brief taste of the experience.

Step 3.27: Create the file

```
unix> emacs Hello.java                              Create a text file called Hello.java.
public class Hello {                                       Java is case sensitive.
    public static void main(String[] args) {       Be sure to match my punctuation.
        System.out.println("Hello, world!");           Your program will greet you!
    }                                                        Don't forget this brace.
}                                                           Don't forget this brace.
```

When you are done editing, save and exit. Some languages, including Java, require you to *compile* your text. The compilation process converts the text to another language, which is called *bytecode* in Java. You may think of compiled code as patterns of bits that the computer understands, but that most likely do not correspond to ASCII bit patterns.

Step 3.28: Compile Code

```
unix> javac Hello.java                          Compile your program into bytecode.
unix>                                   If your code has a mistake, the compiler might warn you.
```

If the compiler complains, go back and fix your mistakes. If your work compiled, **javac** puts the bytecode in a *class* file, called Hello.class. To try seeing this compiled code, enter **more Hello.class**. You will see some text mixed with some other "garbage," because **more** views text files. Trying to view nontext formats will cause trouble. Now you should test your program to see if it actually works!

Step 3.29: Run Program

```
unix> java Hello                        Use only the name Hello, without the extension.
unix> Hello, world!                         Your program is designed to greet the user.
```

Obviously, programming involves much more depth than I have shown. But I want you to see how text can be used for extremely practical purposes. Moreover, someone had to program the commands you are using in Unix, which meant that they needed a text editor.

CHAPTER SUMMARY

- Files store information on a computer.
- Text files store collections of characters, which are usually just keyboard characters.
- ASCII text is a universal format, understood by essentially all computers.
- You can modify **ls** (and most other Unix commands) with options.
- Text editing has important applications (programming, webpages, data, and more).
- Text editors usually store the text that you type in a buffer, which is part of computer memory. Saving your work dumps the buffer into a text file in your account.

- **pico** is a simple text editor that shows you all commands at the bottom of the screen.
- **pico** commands are control sequences with single characters.
- **vi** is a more complex text editor that relies on different modes: *command*, *insert*, and *last-line*. In command mode, you can cut and paste, move the cursor, and access other modes. In insert mode, you enter your text. In last-line mode, you can perform text operations, such as *search* and *replace*, and save or quit.
- **emacs** is an incredibly powerful text editor that can run other programs, such as e-mail, news, Unix shells, and more.
- **emacs** commands tend to be **Control** and **Meta** (**Esc**) key sequences. You can find listings via **emacs** help system (**C-h b**, **F1**, **M-x help**).
- **emacs** has many functions that you can discover with **M-x Spacebar**.
- The screen or window in which you run **emacs** is called a *frame*. The frame has an **emacs** window (for text entry), a menu bar (in case you don't know key sequences), mode line (to keep track of what you're doing), and a minibuffer (which shows your key sequences).
- To cut and paste text in **emacs**, you need to mark regions; move your cursor left, right, up, or down from the mark; and use a cut or kill command followed by a yank command.
- You can split an **emacs** frame into multiple windows, each of which can hold different buffers. You can associate each of these buffers with different files.
- Unix supports many GUI text editors, including **nedit** and **xemacs**.

KEY TERMS

binary file	file	text editor
buffer	file extension	text file
command mode	filename	
emacs	insert mode	
emacsframe	last-line mode	
emacs minibuffer	OpenOffice	

COMMAND SUMMARY

dos2unix	convert text file in DOS format to Unix format
ed	invoke primitive text editor
emacs	invoke GNU **emacs** text editor
ex	invoke line editor; still rather primitive
file	check file type
gs	view PostScript file
java	run Java program
javac	compile Java program into bytecode
lp	print file
lpr	print file
ls	list files
more	view text file
nedit	invoke basic GUI text editor
pico	invoke simple, but handy and great, full-screen text editor
vedit	invoke more instructive version of **vi**
vi	invoke **vi** text editor
vim	invoke improved version of **vi**
xemacs	invoke GUI alternative to **emacs**

Problems

1. What is a computer file?

2. Name at least three uses for files.

3. How many standard ASCII characters are available for use in constructing text files?

4. How many ASCII characters are used in the following line:

   Interval Addition: [1,2] + [3,4] = [4,6]

5. What are three uses for a text editor?

6. How many bytes are in a file composed of three blank lines? Assume that this file was created by inserting three blank lines with **vi**.

7. Is the **vi** last-line-mode command **:qw** the same as **:wq**? Which command sequence is permissible?

8. Are the filenames HELLO.txt and hello.txt identical? Why or why not?

9. Is the command line **vi vi** valid if you are working inside your account?

10. If you start **vi** without a filename, how do you save your work to a file called **save_this.txt** from within **vi**?

11. Is the command **less** available on your system? If so, what does **less** do?

12. Try the commands **tail** and **head** on a large text file. What do these commands do?

13. Project 1: Create a text file called hw1.txt. Type in all of the problems and their solutions for this chapter.

14. Project 2: Create a text file called emacscommands.txt. Describe, in an organized and clear fashion, 10 useful key sequences that I did not cover in this book.

15. Project 3: Write a one- to three-page, double-spaced essay about why are you studying Unix. Somewhere in the essay, describe how and why you are interested in science or engineering. Do not be afraid to be candid. Edit your work entirely with a text editor. Be sure to manually check your grammar, spelling, and overall style. Also, try **spell *filename***. Enter your name at the top of the file. Print and submit your file when it is finished.

4

File Operations

4.1 INTRODUCTION

In this chapter, I will demonstrate a variety of commands that help you work with files, most of which will be text files. If you use GUIs, you already have done many of the operations herein. Even Microsoft Windows users who haven't accessed a DOS window might be surprised. Just enter **HELP** at the DOS prompt to see a wealth of commands. Although some of these commands might seem archaic, the idea is that Unix provides a *tool set*, commands from which you can create programs called shell scripts. Moreover, sometimes it is simply faster to type a short command.

Step 4.1: Find Unix commands

*Unfortunately, you usually cannot just enter **help** at the prompt. Instead, to get an idea of how many Unix commands there are, you need to snoop around a bit. In this step you will investigate parts of the Unix file system:*

```
unix> ls /usr/bin | more       Show a listing of a directory
                               that usually holds many commands.
```
*Lengthy listing of files....Use **Spacebar** to page through the results.*

In the preceding step, I use some Unix code that might seem very new. For now, I simply want to give you a feel for how vast Unix truly is, although I realize it might give you a headache. Fear not! This chapter focuses on an important subset of commands that help to answer the following sorts of questions, especially regarding text files:

- What files do I have? Can I see inside a file? Can I find text in a particular file?
- Can I look at groups of files? Can I find certain files?

OBJECTIVES

After reading this chapter, you should be able to:

- List groups of files in a directory.
- Use `cat`, `more`, `less`, `head`, and `tail` to view text files.
- Count the characters, words, and lines, spell-check, and sort the contents of a file.
- Compare files in different fashions.
- Understand how to write a basic regular expression.
- Search for text in a file or a group of files in the same directory with a regular expression.
- Print a file without wasting paper, show a printing queue, and stop a print job.
- View and modify file permissions.

There is a very simple secret to performing well on homework and tests: *Go to class!*

- *Go to class*: Consider the following questions: Where will the assignment be posted? What material does the homework cover? What material will you be tested on? Now, what's the answer in each case? *Go to class*. On the due date of an assignment, often a student asks, "When is the homework due?" Usually, I look at my watch and retort, "In about five minutes." *Go to class!*

- *Learn before you learn*: Part of classroom boredom arises from complete bafflement. Most of us cannot pay attention for lengthy periods of time, and when we are unprepared, the chances for absorption are slim at best. However, skimming the textbook ahead of time helps. After all, learning is often a function of repetition. (*Go to class!*) For this text, even *attempting* commands beforehand will ease laboratory instruction.

- *Listen*: Most students prefer taking notes in class; writing anything seems preferable to falling asleep. There's nothing really wrong with taking notes; the problem is doing so indiscriminately. Did you know that some students, and not necessarily the naturally gifted, can pass difficult classes without ever taking a single note? Their trick is listening. What your professor says, and how he or she says it, is often the indicator of what the professor judges most important to know. Guess what usually shows up on tests?

- *Take notes*: Combine listening with note-taking. Let your professor's voice guide your writing. Also, combine what your professor discusses in class with any written notes he or she might distribute.

- *Ask questions*: What portions of the text seemed most confusing during your skimming? Has the professor reached that portion of the text? If so, has the material been clarified? No? Raise your hand! You can ask an insightful question because you previously reviewed the material. But even if your question won't be insightful, or if you're not sure, ask anyway. Chances are that more than half the class is wondering the same thing.

- *Now, go to class!*

- How do I organize all my files into directories? Wait a minute....How do I make directories?
- How much space am I consuming? Can I archive or shrink my work?
- How do I protect my files? How can I share them?
- How do I make printouts?

I help you to answer these questions in the sections that follow. Comparing and searching directories will be discussed in Chapter 5, as these topics require an explanation of the Unix file system.

4.2 BASIC LISTING REVISITED

In this section, I review and remind everyone about listing and I start explaining directories in a bit more detail because I need students to start working with files. To help, I also introduce the notion of a *filename metacharacter* (*).

4.2.1 Introduction to HOME Directory

When you log into Unix, you log into your account, which reserves your personal space. Your account actually exists as part of the Unix file system as a directory in which to store your own files and other directories. As shown in Figure 4.1, many users are listed

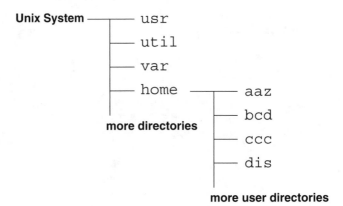

Figure 4.1   Example of Unix File System and User Accounts

somewhere in the directory hierarchy. If you enter **cd ~/.. ; ls**, you will see a list of users on your system.[1]

Thankfully, remembering a potentially vast collection of "stuff" and where it resides is unnecessary. When you log in, Unix starts inside **HOME**, the "top" directory for your account. **HOME** is a variable, not a command, that is set by your Unix system.

Step 4.2:   Where is your **HOME**?

```
unix> echo $HOME                          Tell Unix to say where your HOME is.
/home/dis                           My HOME happens to be in a directory called /home.
```

Your **HOME** might be quite different. But as long as you have an account, you have a **HOME**, which your system administrator set.

4.2.2   Listing Revisited

To see what is in **HOME**'s contents, use the listing command **ls**, which lists files and directories in formation:

Step 4.3:   List Files

```
unix> ls                                  List the files in your current directory.
a.txt b.txt c.txt          If you finished Chapter 3, you should have lots of text files.
```

Actually, I'm being a bit cagey with you: **ls** just happens to list your account. Why? When you log in, Unix sets your command line to **HOME**, which makes it a default directory. So, commands which look for files will assume that you mean **HOME** unless you specify a different location. To see a variety of files, try the following modifications of **ls**:

Step 4.4:   Different kinds of listings

```
unix> ls -a                               List all files in the current directory.
.emacs .exrc a.txt            Unix shows your files, including hidden files.
unix> ls -l                               List unhidden files in long format.
-rw------- 1 dis dis 35874 Apr 28 2004 gdiac.jpg     Long list of several files.
```

---

[1]If you are the type that actually reads these seemingly extraneous footnotes, I've got a surprise for you. Try **ls ~/../*** instead. Unfortunately, not everyone knows about file permissions, which you will learn about in this chapter. If you want a head start hiding all your work, enter **chmod go-rwx ~**.

```
unix> ls -al                                    Long list of all files, including hidden files
-rwx------ 1 dis dis 10180 Feb 27 21:40 .aliases*              Lots of files now!
unix> ls -alR | more                            Recursively list all files in long format.
You will see everything you own.                        Use Spacebar to page or ^C to quit.
```

In the preceding examples, the **-a** option tell Unix to include hidden files, which are files whose names begin with a dot (**.**). For more information, see **man ls**.

4.2.3 Introduction to File-Matching Metacharacters

Now and then you will want to operate on multiple files. One extremely handy way of indicating groups of files is with *****, which is a file-matching metacharacter that shells know and support. A ***metacharacter*** is a character that means something other than its literal value or appearance. When you use ***** in a filename, Unix will try to match all file-names for that portion of text. For example, ***.txt** tells Unix that you mean all files that end with **.txt**. If you say **.***, you are telling Unix that you mean all the hidden files.

Step 4.5: File-matching metacharacter (*)

```
unix> ls *.txt                                      List all files ending with .txt.
a.txt  b.txt  info.txt                              You might have different files.
```

Occasionally, you may see the term ***globbing***, which refers to the process of matching filenames. Section 5.10.1 covers this topic in greater detail.

PRACTICE!

1. What is the command to list files along with their types?
2. How do you list files in multiple columns sorted across the screen?
3. How do you list all files whose names start with the letter A?

4.3 VIEWING TEXT FILES

Get used to checking your work. If you accidentally pasted a love letter in your home-work file, I'm sure your grader would be amused, but your work will certainly become legendary.[2] Rather than using a text editor to check your work, you can use a variety of other tools: **cat**, **more**, **less**, **head**, and **tail**. See also **page**.

4.3.1 **cat**

In this instance, I'll avoid the variety of jokes on **cat**'s[3] behalf. Although named after its primary purpose (con<u>cat</u>enating, or appending, files), **cat** provides a quick and dirty way to view a file. In fact, **cat** can number each line:

Step 4.6: Use **cat**

```
unix> pico info.txt                             Edit a text file to use for testing.
Name: David I. Schwartz                             You can type something else
Username: dis                                               if your prefer.
Favorite Color: blue                                    Maybe you prefer mauve?
unix> cat -n info.txt                           Show info.txt and number the lines.
   1  Name: David I. Schwartz
   2  Username: dis
   3  Favorite Color: blue
```

---

[2]Actually, I used to write stories and messages just to see if my teaching assistant was paying attention.
[3]I did find a **dogs** command on my system, but it doesn't work and has no documentation.

Later on, you will understand what I mean when I say, "To append files with **cat**, use the redirection operator **>**, as in **a.txt b.txt > c.txt**." This operator creates a file, c.txt, that contains the contents of b.txt pasted *after* the contents of a.txt.

In general, the file you intend to create should not already exist.

4.3.2   **more** or **less**

Although I have no proof, I suspect that the creator of **more** understood that people viewing long files realized that they needed a tool to provide one page a time, thus allowing the user to prompt for *more*. So, you can use **more   *filename*** to view a file, especially one that exceeds a screen or window size. The command **more** is called a *pager*, because you can "page" through portions of a long file at your own pace.

- Use **Spacebar** for a complete page, which corresponds to the current size of the screen or window.

- Use **Enter** to step through a file one line at a time.

- Use **^L** to clear the screen if the viewing becomes garbled (usually when you try to resize a window containing a viewing in progress).

- Use **q** or **^C** to quit.

In the next example, I take a look at my system's dictionary. Unix will report No such file or directory if the requested file does not exist.

Step 4.7:   View a file with **more**

At the prompt, enter **more /usr/ dict/words**. *If your system has the same configuration as mine, you will see something like the image in Step 4.7. The* 0% *indicates that I have seen only a little of the file so far! Press* ^C *to quit.*

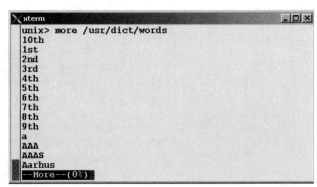

An improved version of **more**, called **less** (named in ironic reaction to **more**), has better performance and more functionality. Step 4.8 gives an example.

Although **more** has similar functionality, you might be happier with **less**. I will pass along some advice I was given long ago: "**less** is more than **more**, and **more** is less than **less**." For more information about the wonders of **less**, see **man less**.

PRACTICE!

4.   What does **more -ec *** do?

5.   How do you scroll backwards in **less**?

Step 4.8:   View a file with `less`

At the prompt, enter `less /usr/dict/words`. *Assuming that your system has the file, you will see a view similar to that which you saw with* `more`. *Enter* `/cat`, *which tells* `less` *that you want to search for the word* cat *inside the current file.*

`less` *will highlight each occurrence of* cat *on the current screen or window, starting from the top and working from left to right. To search for more occurrences, type* **n** *for "next", as I have done a few times.*

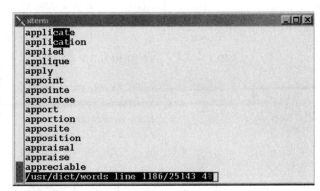

4.3.3   `head` or `tail`

Yes, I enjoy silly section headings. In fact, in the first draft of this book I wanted the section on computer responsibility to be titled "To Pee or Not To Pee," but my editor was displeased. Such is life. Anyway, **head** and **tail** provide handy viewing shortcuts:

- **head**: view lines at the beginning of a file.
- **tail**: view lines at the end of a file.

I really hope that you do have access to a big file, like the dictionary I've been using, because it will help demonstrate these two commands:

```
unix> head -3 /usr/dict/words        View the first 5 lines of the dictionary file.
10th
1st
2nd
unix> tail -2 /usr/dict/words        View the last 10 lines of the dictionary file.
Zurich
zygote
```

PRACTICE!

6. How many lines does **head** show if you do not modify its behavior?
7. How many lines does **tail** show if you do not modify its behavior?

4.4   ANALYZING THE CONTENTS OF A FILE

When I say "analyze," I am referring to ways you might want to inspect a particular file: its name, type and contents, spellings, counts (bytes, characters, words, lines), and other things I'm going to wish I remembered for this book. In this section, I demonstrate commands that help you do these things:

Step 4.9:   File type revisited

```
unix> file info.txt                              Check type of text file.
info.txt:   ascii text                           Yep, it's ASCII.
```

Step 4.10:   View information about a single file

```
unix> ls -lh /usr/dict/words           You can use ls to describe a single file.
-r--r--r-- 1 root bin 202K Apr 6 2002 /usr/dict/words   Long listing, human size.
```

Step 4.11:   Change time stamp

```
unix> ls -l info.txt                             Check your info.txt file.
-rw-r--r-- 1 dis dis 59 Mar 26 18:56 info.txt    Long listing, earlier time.
unix> touch info.txt                             Change time stamp to right now!
unix> ls -l info.txt                             Check the file again.
-rw-r--r-- 1 dis dis 59 Mar 26 20:48 info.txt    Please don't use touch to cheat.
```

Step 4.12:   Count things inside a text file

```
unix> wc info.txt                                Count items inside info.txt.
unix>   3   9   59 info.txt              Shows count of lines, words, and characters.
```

Step 4.13:   Check spelling

```
unix> spell info.txt                             Check spelling inside info.txt.
Username                                         spell reports upsetting words.
dis                              Don't forget about spell-checkers in text editors.
```

For interactive spell-checking (what you have used in text editors), use **ispell**. As I've been reminding you, you can use **man** to discover more about **ispell** and the other commands listed.

PRACTICE!

8.   What does **touch *file*** do if ***file*** does not exist?
9.   How many words are your system's dictionary?
10. Use **ispell** to check info.txt.

4.5   REORGANIZING A FILE

If you ever work with databases, you might find Unix very helpful, especially in creating your own custom programs. In this section, I cover two common operations: sorting and removing repeated lines.

4.5.1   Sorting

If you have ever used a spreadsheet, you have likely sorted data numerically or alpha-betically. Yes, Unix can do those operations, too—with **sort**. Unfortunately, the **man** page on **sort** is quite complicated. For now, all you need to know are the basics—namely, sorting in ascending or descending order.

Step 4.14: Make data file to sort

```
unix> pico data.txt                                    Create simple data file.
b                                                 Use letters in scrambled order.
d                                               Save your work and quit when done.
a                                               We will use this file a few more times,
c                                                             so please hang onto it.
```

Step 4.15: Sort in ascending order

```
unix> sort data.txt                                   Sort data in ascending order.
a                                                  sort outputs in increasing order.
b
c
d
```

Step 4.16: Sort in descending order

```
unix> sort -r data.txt                               Sort data in descending order.
d                                                  The -r option stands for reverse.
c                                                  sort outputs in increasing order.
b
a
```

Note that data.txt does not change. In fact, how *do* you save the output of **sort**? There are two ways, one of which requires that mysterious redirection operator (Chapter 8): **sort data.txt > *filename***. Alternatively, you can use **sort**'s **-o** (*output file*) option:

Step 4.17: Sort and save

```
unix> sort -r -o sorteddown.txt data.txt                    Sort data and save.
unix> more sorteddown.txt                                      View sorted data.
d
c
b
a
```

In the preceding command, sorteddown.txt is a value for the **-o** option. The data.txt value is for **sort**, the file you wanted sorted into sorteddown.txt. The curious students out there may now be wondering, "Can we sort data back into the *same* file?" Well, yes, you can! Just replace sorteddown.txt with data.txt in the command line, above.

4.5.2 Removing Repeated Lines

What happens if your file contains repeated information? If you do something called sorting by multiple keys, **sort** needs to keep track of which elements are associated with the repeated data. If you would rather rid a file of repeated lines, use **uniq**:

Step 4.18: Remove repeated lines

```
unix> more repeated.txt                          Create a text file with this content.
a
a
b
b
b
c
unix> uniq repeated.txt                           Remove repeated lines.
a
b
c
unix> uniq repeated.txt cleaned.txt         Remove repeated lines and save output.
```

4.5.3 Splitting a File

You can also use Unix to split large files into smaller chunks. When you enter **split -n filename prefix**, Unix will find the first **n** lines of **filename**, put them in a file called **prefixaa**, then find the next **n** lines, put them in **prefixab**, and so forth.

Step 4.19: Split a file

```
unix> pico data.txt                          Create a data file with seven lines (not shown).
unix> split -2 data.txt stuff                  Split the data into files with two lines each.
unix> ls stuff*                                      List only files starting with stuff.
stuffaa   stuffab   stuffac   stuffad    If you view each file, you will see parts of data.txt.
```

I use the asterisk (*****) in the preceding code to seek a match with all files in the current directory that start with **stuff**. I will explain this operation in more detail later. Note that **stuffad** has only one line inside of it, as the data had an odd number of lines. Once you have learned about **cat**, you can append some of these files together, essentially reorganizing your original data. For example, try **cat stuffab stuffac > newdata.txt**. See **man split** and **man csplit** for more information.

PRACTICE!

11. What should you do if you want to sort files with dates?
12. Use **uniq** to report how many times a line repeats in a file.

4.6 COMPARING FILES

We are going to need two files with which to work for this discussion:

Step 4.20: Create some data files

```
unix> pico data1.txt
jay
pat
sam
joe
unix> pico data2.txt
pat
kit
sam
joe
```

Unix can help you compare files (especially text files) with the use of several commands. Because of the richness and complexity of these commands, I will discuss only basic operations. I strongly suggest that you consult **man** when you feel ready to accept the greater challenge.

4.6.1 **comm**

The **comm** command is very handy when your files' widths are relatively small. **comm** *file1 file2* will report three columns: unique lines in *file1*, unique lines in *file2*, and duplicate lines (lines common to both files):

Step 4.21: Compare files side by side

Compare data1.txt *(column 1) and* data2.txt *(column 2) with* **comm data1.txt data2.txt**.

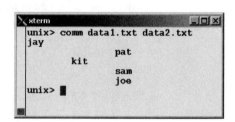

comm has nifty command-line options to suppress different columns.

4.6.2 **diff**

You might find **diff** perplexing and cryptic at first, but hang in there. As a first pass, simply try the syntax that you would normally expect, **diff *file1 file2***:

Step 4.22: Using **diff**

```
unix> diff data1.txt data2.txt          Check for differences between two files.
1d0                                                              Bizarre.
< jay                                              Seems to indicate file1.
2a2                                                         Also bizarre.
> kit                                              Seems to indicate file2.
```

I hope that you are curious about what the output means. Believe it or not, Unix does have meanings for all these symbols. When you use number–letter–number, as in 1d0 and 2a2, Unix is telling you three things:

- The first character, a number, indicates a line in the *first* file.

- The middle character (letter a, c, or d) indicates an **ed** command. (Remember that? It's a *line editor.*) a means "append," c means "change" (or "replace lines"), and d means "delete."
- The third character, a number, indicates a line in the *second* file.

The information that follows each three-character code is the offending line:

- Think of < as ←, pointing to the first file, which has the different line.
- Think of > as →, pointing to the second file, which has the different line.

I can now interpret **diff**'s output in the preceding example:

- 1d0 means that the difference that follows (jay in data1.txt) can be resolved by deleting line 1 of the first file and doing nothing with the second file.
- 2a2 is a little easier to explain backwards (as suggested by **man diff**). Think of d as the opposite of a. By deleting kit (the second line of the second file), you can make the lines in both files match. The assumption is that you follow 1d0 and delete jay as well.

Note that sometimes **diff** will report three hyphens (---) to distinguish the contents of files.

If you would like to be a bit fancier, **emacs**'s feature of multiple windows with different buffers can be extremely handy. As shown in Figure 4.2, I start **emacs** and split the main window into three windows (**C-x 2** and then **C-x 3**; remember that **C-x o** moves the cursor between buffers). In the top two buffers, I loaded the data files (**C-x b**, **Enter**, **C-x C-v**). In the bottom window, I loaded a Unix shell (**M-x shell**), which now acts as Unix.

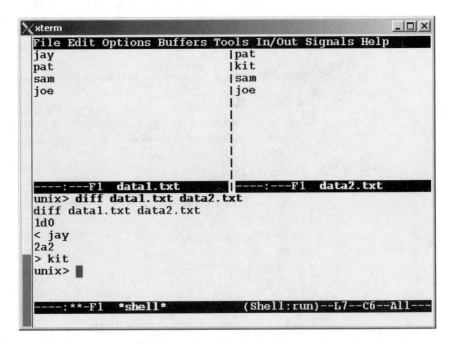

Figure 4.2 Using **emacs** Windows to Assist with **diff**

PRACTICE!

13. How does **sdiff** compare with the **emacs** example I have presented?
14. Run **diff data2.txt data1.txt** and explain the analysis.

4.7 SEARCHING FOR TEXT IN FILES

To search for text, you could feasibly use **more** or **less**, combined with the **/** search command for each file. Unix, however, can rescue you from this mindless tedium! In this section, I provide a basic overview of the 'rep family of commands: **grep**, **egrep**, and **fgrep**. Like other sections, this one only primes you for later study should you need more Unix, so I will concentrate on the basic behaviors.

4.7.1 Characters, Strings, Words

Given that Unix is a text-based environment, many commands either require or do text processing. Learning some terminology will help me reduce how much I need to gloss over certain aspects of the language. Starting with the basics, we think of text in terms of *characters*. (See **man ascii** for the full set.) Ignoring the more than 65,000 Unicode characters, we will concentrate on keyboard characters. You can group characters into a **string**, which many languages signify with a variety of quoting styles: "a", 'blarmy', "abc xyz", '123*', `qwerty`. Note that a string can include any character, including spaces and other symbols. Do not confuse strings with **words**, which are collections of characters separated by whitespace or punctuation. For example, "Kneel before Zod!" is a string with 17 characters (spaces count) and three words.

4.7.2 Patterns

Lest I overwhelm you with details and make my editor mad by adding 50 more pages, I am providing just a taste of patterns and regular expressions. When looking for text in a file, you might already know what you want, such as when you look for the word *Lubricant*. In this case, you are looking for a *fixed pattern*—a specific collection of characters. But perhaps you want to find all words that have *L* and *u* as their first and second characters? In that case, you are looking for a *general pattern* (or just **pattern**)—a specified organization of characters that fit a template. So there might be many strings in a file that start with *Lu*.

4.7.3 Regular Expressions

A **regular expression** (also called **regex** in Unix) is a mechanism that allows one to describe a set of strings by another string that follows predefined rules. This special string is usually called the regular expression. For example, I could ask you to write every single letter from "a" to "z." In response, you could write "a," "b," and so forth. Or, you could simply write **[a-z]**. The **[]** indicate that you are to select one character from inside the **[]**. The **a-z** means "every character from 'a' to 'z'". The **[]** characters are metacharacters. So, my example **[a-z]** does not mean *strings with square brackets*. Following is an explanation of some of Unix's basic **regex** metacharacters:

- **.** matches any single character except *newline*. For example, **.at** matches *aat, bat, cat, ...*

- **[]** matches one character between the brackets. For example, **[abc]** matches *a*, *b*, or *c*.

- **-** indicates a range. For example, **a-z** means all characters from "*a*" to "*z*," inclusive.

- ***** matches zero or more instances of the character preceding the asterisk. For example, **ba*** matches *b*, *ba*, *baa*, ... because the **a** precedes the *****.

- **** treats the next character literally. For example, ***** matches * and does not mean the metacharacter *****.

- **^** matches the start of a line. So, **^cat** matches with every line that starts with *cat*. For example, catastrophe.

- **$** matches the end of a line. So, **cat$** matches every line that ends with *cat*. For example, aristocat.

For a complete list, refer to **man -s5 regex**. The Internet has many resources that dive into further detail. Besides a whole host of theoretical implications in computer science, there are several practical applications of these commands—and you guessed it: Many Unix commands use **regex**, as you will see in the sections that follow.

Note that regular-expression metacharacters are *not* equivalent to filename metacharacters! (See Section 4.2.3.) I like the advice in *Bulletproof Unix*[4], which I quote here: "If it's a *filename*, I use a file-matching metacharacter, but if I am looking *inside* the file, I use regular expressions."

4.7.4 Basic **grep**

The most agreed-upon explanation for **grep**'s name that I found is *global regular expression print*. Well, now you can see why I made you slug through a whole section on regular expressions. The concept behind **grep** is that you want to find the lines inside a text file that contain words that match a pattern of characters. For basic searches with known strings, use **grep *string files***:

Step 4.23: Basic search for strings

```
unix> grep pat data1.txt data2.txt          Search these two files for the string pat.
data1.txt:pat                               data1.txt has the string pat somewhere inside.
data2.txt:pat                               data2.txt has the string pat somewhere inside.

unix> grep -n pat data1.txt data2.txt       Show line numbers this time.
data1.txt:2:pat                             data1.txt has the string pat on line 1.
data2.txt:1:pat                             data2.txt has the string pat on line 2.
```

If you want to search a lot of files, you need to use a potentially confusing concept. Shells have something called *filename metacharacters*. For example, if you enter **more -ec *.txt**, the *shell* interprets the filename as *any name ending in* .txt in the current directory. (This command will display all .txt files in the current directory, letting you page through them one at a time.) More filename metacharacters will be introduced when you learn about directories. Now you can search an entire directory for files that contain a pattern:

---

[4]A variety of comprehensive resources are available in the Bibliography for those looking to delve further into Unix.

Step 4.24: Basic search for strings

```
unix> grep pat *.txt                                Search all files ending in .txt for Name:.
See output of Step 4.23.
```

In this example, I surrounded my fixed pattern with quotes because I want to be safe: You might not know all of the shell's metacharacters. In fact, when you use a **regex**, you should always use quotes, especially since the shell's ***** means something completely different than a **regex**'s *****!

4.7.5   regexes and grep

Now that you (hopefully) feel comfortable with **grep**, you can use a **regex**. The syntax follows the same form: **grep *regex files***. As explained in the previous section, surround your **regex** with single quotes to avoid confusion with the shell's metacharacters. For example, I can search my system directory for all words that start with cat.

Step 4.25: Search for text with **regex**

```
unix> grep -n '^cat' /usr/dict/words         Search dictionary for words that start with cat.
3852:cat                                First instance of line starting with cat is line 3852.
3853:catabolic                                              More cat words follow.
3854:cataclysm
Words fly past....                  To go slower, use grep '^cat' /usr/dict/words | less.
unix> grep '^z[u,a]' /usr/dict/words        Search all words that start with zu and za.
zag
zagging
zap
zazen
zucchini
unix> grep -n 'aaa*' /usr/dict/words              Search for all words with two or
                                                            more a's in a row.
2112:bazaar
3592:Canaan
10298:Haag
10299:Haas
12358:Isaac
12359:Isaacson
19624:Salaam
24248:Waals
```

If you need to search only for a string and not a pattern (i.e., a fixed pattern—a string that you need to match in its entirety), you should use **fgrep**, which does not employ regular expressions.

4.7.6   egrep

As people began to realize the usefulness of regular expressions, they created an extended set that includes additional metacharacters. Some of that extended set is as follows:

- **+** matches one or more of it's preceding character. For example, **abc2+** will match with *abc2*, *abc22*, *abc222*, ... because the **2** precedes the **+**.

- **?** matches to zero or one of the characters that precedes it. For example, **abc?** matches with *ab* and *abc*.
- **|** signifies an alternative or disjunction. For example, **a | b** means *a* or *b*.

For extended regular expressions, use **egrep**:

Step 4.26: Use egrep

```
unix> egrep 'uu+|ww+' /usr/dict/words          Search for all lines with at least 2 u's or 2 w's.
continuum
hollowware
residuum
screwworm                                       Yes, my system really has this word!
vacuum
unix> egrep '(z|v)' info.txt                    Search for lines that have z or v in info.txt.
Name: David I. Schwartz
Favorite Color: blue
```

PRACTICE!

15. How would you search for the string **dis** inside all files in your current directory?
16. How would you search a file called **stuff.txt** for lines with numbers?

4.8 PRINTING FILES

Sooner or later, you will have to submit something for grading or review. Typically, engineers and scientists must print their work in the form of **hard copy**—file contents that are printed on paper. Sometimes hard copy is called a *printout*.

4.8.1 Printing on Default Printer

A common print command is **lp**, which stands for *line printer*. The trick I use for remembering this command is *laser printing*, which started back when my alma mater had endless amounts of free printing. Some versions of Unix use the BSD print command, **lpr**. For basic printing, **lp** has the syntax **lp *filename***, which sends ***filename*** to a default printer on your system. **lp** works by **spooling** a file, a process that does the following:

- First, **lp** informs Unix which file to print.
- Next, Unix instructs the printer on how to format the printout, which means how the file looks on paper.

Try to print **info.txt** on your default system printer, which is called *jaded* for me:

Step 4.27: Print Files

```
unix> lp info.txt                              Print a file called info.txt.
request id is jaded-2 (1 file)                 Unix reports your request.
```

Unix's response to **lp** needs some explanation. **request id** has the form *printer–job number*. I am printing on a printer called *jaded* and my job is the second print *job*, or printing action. To learn your default system's printer name ahead of time, try entering **echo $PRINTER** or **echo $LPDEST**. These variables tell **lp** where to print if you do not specify a printer.

Step 4.28: Default Printer

```
unix> echo $PRINTER                                    What is my default printer?
jaded                                          Your shell will report a different variable.
```

4.8.2   Printing on Different Printers

To learn about other printers, use your system's **printers** command (if it has one):

Step 4.29: Find other printers

```
unix> printers                       Report list of printers. Not available on all systems.
# Printer     Type            location     owner/user
#====================================================================
# astrolabe   lexmark T614N   4119 Up      Office Duplex
Lengthy list continues....
```

Otherwise, I guarantee that your system administrators have posted a list somewhere. Once you know another printer's name, specify the *destination* with **lp -d** *printer* *filename*. The BSD syntax is **lpr -P** printer filename.

Step 4.30: Print to destination

```
If you want these two commands to work, you'll need to create a.txt and b.txt if you haven't already. I do
not show the output:

unix> lp -d astrolabe a.txt                             Print a.txt on astrolabe.
unix> lpr -P astrolabe b.txt                            Print b.txt on astrolabe.
```

4.8.3   Monitor Printing

If you print to a public printer, you may have to wait for your printout, especially if 10 people ahead of you are printing their life stories. In general, I find that my printouts are vitally more important than everyone else's, so I share your (potential) indignation. You can monitor the status of your print job with **lpstat** (*status*, associated with **lp**) or **lpq** (*queue*, associated with **lpr**):

Step 4.31: Printing status

```
unix> lpstat                                What is the status of pending print jobs?
jaded-1793 dis 163 Nov 22 18:30                        The print job is still pending.
unix> lpq                                                 Wait a while and check again.
jaded@blather 0 jobs                            lpq and lpstat have different output formats.
```

Unix usually reports the request ID, username, file size in bytes, and date and time of the request. Pending print jobs might be waiting for other files to print or might actually be currently printing. If **lpstat** reports nothing at all, your request might have been processed faster than you could enter **lpstat**. **lpq** is handy in this respect.

4.8.4   Canceling a Print Job

Be wary of what you print! Many sites are quite public, and a scathing message probably should remain private. To cancel a print job, use **cancel *requestID***, as in **cancel jaded-1796**. Unix will endeavor to remove the print job from the spool, assuming that the file has not already been printed:

4.8.5   Canceling Printing

unix> **lp info.txt**	*Print a file.*
request id is jaded-1796 (1 file)	*Unix reports job information.*
Quickly enter the following command!	*Hopefully, your printer is slow today.*
unix> **cancel jaded-1796**	*Cancel a specific job.*
request "jaded-1796" cancelled	*Unix successfully cancelled.*

For **lpq**, the equivalent command is **lprm -P *printer requestid***. To remove everything you have printed (sometimes the easiest thing to do), use **cancel -u *username***. You can remove only your *own* jobs, which you might find unfortunate now and then.

PRACTICE!

17. Create a new text file called new.txt, using **lpr** and **lp**.
18. Determine your default system printer.
19. Print new.txt on your default printer. Is another printer available? If so, print new.txt with that printer as well.
20. How do you determine when the print job is finished?

4.9   TEXT PROCESSING AND FORMATTING

Unix does not restrict you to text files. In fact, you may want to format your files so that they look "pretty," meaning that they are formatted, just like this book. Given the prevalence of GUI publishers (e.g., Adobe FrameMaker, which I am using), many people do not think about command-line programs. However, you can use programs that convert ASCII text to the document you want to see. For example, Hypertext Markup Language (HTML) understands that the text **<bold>stuff</bold>** means that you want a Web browser to show the word "stuff" as **stuff**. This section only gives you a glimpse of Unix's capabilities.

4.9.1   PostScript

PostScript (PS) is a text-based language that can describe graphical images and text—pretty much whatever you want to put in a document. You should be able to print a PS document anywhere, although it seems that I see this format only on Unix these days. You can even generate a PS document from a text file with **genscript**. Next, I send the output (which is the PS translation of the input file, info.txt) to another file with a special Unix operator >:

Step 4.32:   Generate PostScript from text

unix> **genscript info.txt > info.ps**	*Generate PS file version of* info.txt.
unix> **more info.ps**	*You might be surprised about the output length.*

```
%!PS-Adobe-3.0                                    This line indicates a PS file printer.
The remaining contents describe programs that use PS to display the document.
```

To view the PS version of `info.ps`, you need a GUI. Use **ghostview** or **gs**, which will open a window containing the graphical view of your input file:

Step 4.33:   View PostScript document

```
unix> gs info.ps                                            View the PS file info.ps.
gs will report all kinds of information, which I don't show here. Below, I show the last line:
>>showpage, press <return> to continue<<    Press Enter to page through the PS document.
GS> quit                                                    Enter quit or ^C to quit.
```

A great aspect of PS is that once you have a PS file, you can print it on any Unix printer. In fact, you can use print-to-file options in Unix GUIs to create PS files, allowing you to archive your work as files. You can then print the files without having to reload the program:

Step 4.34:   Print PostScript document

```
unix> lp -d jaded info.ps                         Print a PS document on a printer.
```

Note, however, that a PostScript file generally cannot be unmade. So, if I print a FrameMaker document to PS and then delete the document, I cannot load PS back into FrameMaker to restore the file's original format. But you can do some conversions at the Unix command line. Check out the following commands:

- **pdf2ps**: convert PDF (see next section) file to PS format.
- **ps2pdf**: convert PS to PDF.
- **ps2ascii**: convert PS to plain ASCII by stripping out all formatting and images.

If you feel especially courageous, you can actually *program* in PS, creating files by hand.

4.9.2   PDF

Although I ought to relegate **PDF** (Portable Document Format) to another section, I suspect that you are curious about **ps2pdf** and **pdf2ps**. PDF is a file format with tremendous, near-universal support, but you need a special GUI viewer to see the files. On your system, try **acroread** or **xpdf**.

Step 4.35:   Viewing and Printing PDF Files

```
unix> acroread something.pdf                                 Open a PDF file.
```

If you do not have a PDF file, just enter **acroread**. I have loaded a PDF file, as shown in Figure 4.3. To print, you can either select **Printer Command** and use Unix's **lp** or **lpr** (with options!) or select **File** to create a new PS file. Besides **acroread** and **xpdf**, your system might have other commands. Note also that your system's Web browser likely has PDF support.

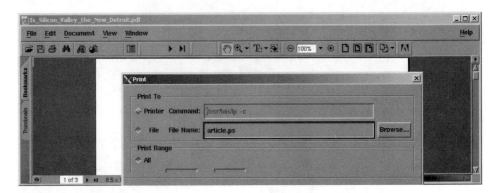

Figure 4.3 Print PDF File to PS

4.9.3 Everything Else

Given the depth of text formatting and the scope of Unix, all I can do is point you toward available resources and commands that might help you later on:

- *Markup languages*: There are many reference works on creating HTML, XML, MML, SGML, and other markup languages. The idea is that you describe text documents with processing commands. Chapter 6 has a brief example of HTML to show you how to create a webpage. You can see an HTML file by accessing a webpage and saving the page as *source*.

- *TeX and LaTex*: If you write mathematical and scientific documents later in your career, you will discover that many journals and professional societies require LaTex, a text-based typesetting system that can produce documents equivalent to those produced by GUI publishers. Investigate *www.latex-project.org* for more information. Some helpful Unix commands are **latex**, **tex**, and **dvips**.

- *Unix text processing*: Some books devote entire chapters to this topic. I have shown you some commands in this chapter, but ignored **troff**, **nroff**, **eqn**, **neqn**, **awk**, **nawk**, and numerous others.

If you want a taste of text formatting outside of Unix, create a document in Microsoft Word and save it as *RTF* (Rich Text Format). Using Notepad or another text editor, open the .rtf file, and you will see how Word can understand formatting in ASCII!

4.10 PROTECTING YOUR FILES

As with all things in life, you bear responsibility for your actions. Because you are likely working on a networked computer, you must not engage in malicious activity, and you should protect your own work. This section helps you get started in deciding who can and cannot see your files. To begin with, enter this command: **chmod go-wrx ~**. This section and its companion in the next chapter will clarify **chmod** and the **~**.

4.10.1 Ownership and Permission

Consider each user as an ***owner***. You own the files that you create and store in your account. Thus, Unix automatically provides you with permission to access, view, or modify your own files and directories. Outside of your account, Unix does not necessarily grant you the same permissions. Only system administrators have complete access to the entire system. Don't worry! They will not pry into your account unless that is absolutely necessary.

4.10.2 Long Listing

How do you find out ownership and permission of directory contents? Try listing directory contents in long format with **ls -l**:

Step 4.36: Long listing

```
unix> ls -l                                            Long list of the current directory.
-rw-r--r--  1   dis    dis      16 Mar 27 14:17 data1.txt
-rw-r--r--  1   dis    dis      16 Mar 27 14:17 data2.txt
-rw-r--r--  1   dis    dis      59 Mar 26 21:50 info.txt
   ①        ②    ③     ④       ⑤    ⑥     ⑦        ⑧        See next for descriptions.
```

From left to right, the long list shows eight fields:

① File type and permissions (discussed in next section).

② Links (skip this for now; see Section 5.9).

③ Owner.

④ Group.

⑤ Size in bytes.

⑥ Last modification date.

⑦ Last modification time.

⑧ Filename.

In this example, the fields for info.txt describe a 59-byte file that was last modified on March 26 at 7:50 P.M. The directory is owned by user dis, who belongs to dis, a **group**. (In my case, my home account doesn't belong to a group.) A group is a collection of users with common identification. You can enter **groups** to display the groups to which you belong.

4.10.3 Permissions

All items in the directory have **file permissions** that determine who can read, write, and execute the files. For instance, you, the owner, have permission to copy and delete your own files. Directories have permissions too (discussed later in Section 5.10.5.)

The first 10 characters in the long listing indicate first the file type and then nine permissions. Look at Step 4.36, item ①. The file info.txt has the type and permission fields -rw-r--r--. Think of these 10 fields as *slots*, as shown in Figure 4.4. Each slot must be filled. Starting from the left, the first slot is the *type*. A dash (-) indicates a file. (You will see more types, such as d for directory, in the other slots.) The next nine slots show *permissions*. These slots divide further into three sets of three slots:

- The first three slots show permissions of the owner, or *user*.
- The second three slots show permissions for the user's *group*.
- The final three slots show permissions for the world, or *other*.

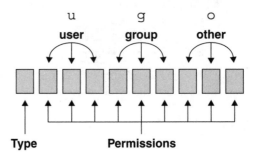

Figure 4.4 Type and Permission Fields

Unix abbreviates user, group, and other fields as u, g, and o, respectively. Each of the three slots in the *user*, *group*, and *other* fields corresponds to a level of accessibility and is filled with the appropriate letter or a dash. In each group of three slots, the first slot shows *read* permission, the second shows *write* permission, and the third shows *execute* permission. The dash indicates *no permission* for the given field.

One of four characters can fill each permission slot:

- A dash (-) indicates no permission given.
- r grants read permissions, such as copying a file and listing a directory.
- w allows writing permissions, such as adding to, creating, and deleting files.
- x provides execute permission.

Table 4.1 summarizes the permission values. I have included directories for completeness.

According to these rules, -rwxr--r--, for example, indicates a *file* (slot 1) with all *user* permissions (next three slots), but only *read* permission for *group* and *other* (slots 5 and 8). So, the user can read, write, and execute this file, but anyone else may only read it. Totally restricting permissions on a file yields ----------, while allowing total access for everyone would yield -rwxrwxrwx, which might be asking for trouble. Figure 4.5 gives some examples.

As you discover more Unix, you might start snooping around in public directories, especially when you are looking for a command. Does your system prevent you from deleting itself? For example, investigate the permissions of **ls**.

Step 4.37: Investigate permissions of system command

```
unix> ls -l /usr/bin/ls                                    List information about ls.
-r-xr-xr-x 1 root bin 19084 Apr 6 2002 /usr/bin/ls    You can run and look, but not edit.
```

TABLE 4.1 File Permissions

	Symbol Meaning	File Permissions Granted	Directory Permissions Granted
-	none	none	none
r	read	view contents	list contents
w	write	edit, delete	modify, add, or remove files
x	execute	execute a program	enter, or access, a directory

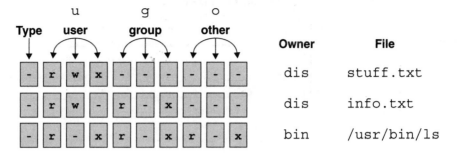

Figure 4.5   Sample File Permissions

The command **ls** is indeed a program that you can run. Unix stores all programs as files. In fact, you had a small bit of programming in Section 3.6. You can check the type with **file /usr/bin/ls**. Because the system has group and world execute permission, you can (thankfully) use **ls**. Since **ls** lacks w permission, you cannot edit it to mean something malicious, such as "copy credit card number to my account."

PRACTICE!

21.   Explain the file permissions in Step 4.37.
22.   Why does the **ls** in Step 4.37 lack user w permission?

4.10.4 Changing Permissions

The command **chmod**, *change mode*, sets file permissions. Using **chmod**, the owner of a file or directory can add or remove read, write, and execute permissions to or from the user, group, or other fields. The basis syntax for **chmod** is as follows:

- Add permission: **chmod *users* + *permissions files***.
- Remove permission: **chmod *users* - *permissions files***.

To save time, Unix allows you to apply multiple additions or removals in the same command, according to these rules:

- Choose any combination of ***users*** from **u**, **g**, or **o**, such as **ug** or **go**. To change permissions for all three, you may use **a** (*all*) in place of **ugo**.
- Use the plus (**+**) to add permissions to slots and minus (**-**) to subtract permissions from slots.
- Use combinations of **r**, **w**, and **x** to choose the ***permissions*** that you wish to change. For example, **o+rx** would allow the world to read and execute a file or access a directory.
- Identify files. For now, concentrate on files in your **HOME** directory. Next, you will modify directory permissions.

Suppose that user **jre** enters **chmod go-rx ~**. This command line removes group and world access permissions on her **HOME**, which is now safe from prying eyes. Once you block **HOME**, no one (other than system administrators) has permission to go there. Next, I show you how to modify permissions:

Step 4.38: Setting file permissions

```
unix> chmod go-r info.txt                    Remove group and world read permission on info.txt.
unix> ls -l info.txt                                                         Check the file.
-rw-------  1  dis    dis      59 Mar 26 21:50 info.txt
unix> chmod a+r *                    Add read permission to "main" files in the current directory.
unix> ls -l                                                              List everything
-rw-r--r-- Remaining output not shown.    Look at all the file permissions. The 2nd slots should all be r.
unix> chmod go-rwx .*                   Remove group and world permissions from hidden files.
unix> chmod go-rwx *                       Remove group and world permissions from "main" files.
unix> ls -al * ; ls -al .*                                            Long list everything.
-rw------- for each file             All group and world permission should be removed from everything.
```

As you will learn later, there are commands (see **umask**) to help you automatically set default permissions for every time you create a file. **chmod** also has numerical codes to represent permissions, which you will see when you investigate **umask**.

4.10.5 Encrypting and Decrypting a File

If you like spy movies, you will especially like this section. Besides setting access permissions, you can scramble a file's contents such that only you and anyone you trust with a special password can view that file. The process of *encrypting* a file means translating it into a form that cannot be read without decryption. For example, a simple encryption involves taking every letter of some body of text and adding 1 to its value. So, A = 2, B = 3, ...; e.g., the word *Drum* becomes *ESVN*. *Decrypting* ESVN involves knowing—or guessing—the encryption scheme and applying it backwards. So, you can easily decrypt *ESVN* by subtracting 1 from each letter. Unix provides **crypt**, which can encrypt and decrypt a file. I suggest the following syntax:

- Encrypt a file: **crypt < *file* > *file*.enc**.
- Decrypt a file: **crypt < *file*.enc > *file*.dec**.

In Chapter 8, I explain the angle brackets in greater detail, for now the operator **<** sends a file into the command, and the operator **>** sends the output of the command into a file. In both versions, Unix will prompt you to enter a password. Think of something *unrelated* to your actual password, because you may want to share the new password with someone. Next, try a simple password (**12345**) to encrypt a text file:

Step 4.39: Encrypt a file

```
unix> pico secret.txt                                        Create an important data file.
Trans fat is evil.                                           Write something crucial.
unix> crypt < secret.txt > secret.enc                               Encrypt your data.
Enter key:                     Enter 12345 at the prompt. Unix will not display this password.
```

If you do not believe in **crypt**, try **more secretdata.enc**. Unix will prompt you to view a binary file! Now, decrypt your file:

Step 4.40: Decrypt a file

```
unix> crypt < secret.enc > secret.dec                              Decrypt your data.
Enter key:                     Enter 12345 at the prompt. Unix will not display this password.
unix> more secret.dec                                          View the decrypted file.
Trans fat is evil.                                            Unix shows your message.
```

If you would like to implement another form of encryption, check out *PGP* (Pretty Good Privacy) with **pgp -h** and on the Internet.

PRACTICE!

23. Enter **chmod u-rwx info.txt**. Now try to view the file. Explain what happens.
24. You can restore your permission on info.txt. Why?
25. Restore the permission on info.txt only for yourself.
26. Should you grant yourself execute permission on info.txt? Explain your answer in terms of the **file** command.

4.11   APPLICATION: FUN (AND USEFUL) WAYS TO PRINT

For this chapter's application, I will show you ways of saving paper by formatting your output. The following commands are prevalent, but may not be on your system. If not, you should alert your system administrator, because they are very useful.

4.11.1   mpage

If you absolutely must print something, consider printing *multiple* pages to one sheet of paper with **mpage**, which is typically included in Linux distributions. This command provides a relatively straightforward set of options that allows you to print one, two, four, or eight pages on one side of a sheet of paper. You can also send the output directly to a printer or save it as a PS file. In fact, you can even print other PS documents! Here are some examples of the use of **mpage**:

Step 4.41:   Print multiple pages

```
unix> mpage -2 data1.txt > f1.ps          Split data1.txt into 2 panels.
unix> mpage -8 *.txt > data.ps            Print all txt files, using 8 panels per side.
unix> mpage -2 a.txt b.ps > c.ps          Put a.txt and b.ps into 2 panels.
unix> mpage -1 stuff.txt > stuff.ps       Print stuff.txt in landscape format.
```

Note that **mpage** will report the number of pages it produces each time. Several more options are interesting as well. I strongly recommend that you do not send the output of **mpage** directly to a printer until you become comfortable with doing so. If you inadvertently print a PS file as text, you will waste a shocking amount of paper.

4.11.2   enscript

To be honest, my own system lacks **mpage**! So, I use **enscript**, which I feel is a bit more cryptic. Just wait until you see the bewildering set of options—plus you cannot include PS files as part of the input, as you can with **mpage**. I usually save my command lines in a separate file. For example, I am obsessive about movies and like to keep a list of films I want to see in a file called movies.txt. If I ever go to a rental store, I completely forget the films I want to see. So, I bring the list! Given how busy I am, the list is getting rather long, so I use **enscript** to process my movie list.

Step 4.42: Make handy list of movies

```
unix> pico movies.txt                                    Edit a list of movies.
Dude, Where's My Car?
Zardoz
Cube, The
Fantastic Planet
and many more.
unix> sort -o temp.txt movies.txt        Alphabetize the list and store in a temporary file.
unix> uniq temp.txt sortedmovies.txt            Remove duplicate names and store.
Why uniq? Sometimes I forget that I already added a movie. uniq will not output adjacent, duplicate lines.
unix> less sortedmovies.txt                                Check the final list.
```

Do you see too many items beginning with The or A? If so, you should reedit the file (e.g., Ten Commandments, The). Once your list satisfies you, print it!

Step 4.43: Print movie list

```
unix> enscript -r -B --columns=4 -f Helvetica10 -p movies.ps sortedmovies.txt
unix> gs movies.ps                                          View your list.
GS> quit                                                      Quit gs.
unix> lp movies.ps                          If the list is OK, print to hard copy.
```

The **enscript** command prints a PS file (**-p movies.ps**) in landscape (**-r**), with no header (**-B**), four columns (**--columns=4**) in a plain font (**-f Helvetica10**). Maybe I will see you at the rental store, list in hand!

CHAPTER SUMMARY

- You can perform a variety of operations on text files.
- Frequently used operations consist of analyzing a file's contents, comparing files, and searching for text.
- When you log on, you start in your **HOME** directory.
- A filename metacharacter is a special type of character that the shell interprets. The * is an example that matches to any group of characters in a filename.
- Use a pager, such as **less**, for viewing long text files.
- **Less** is more than **more**, and **more** is less than **less**.
- Many commands, such as **sort**, require you to specify an output file for an operation.
- When comparing two files (as in **diff file1 file2**), keep track of which file is which in order to understand the organization of the output. (You might find **sdiff** handy.)
- Regular expressions represent a pattern of strings.
- When searching for strings in files, **grep** and **egrep** use regular expressions to find the lines that contain the specified search patterns.
- There are two sets of commands for printing and related tasks: the primary commands **lp**, **lpstat**, and **cancel**; and the BSD commands **lpr**, **lpq**, and **lprm**.
- If you do not specify a printer, Unix will use the default printer (**$PRINTER**).
- You can print a PostScript document directly on a Unix printer.

- You must remember to protect your account. Enter **chmod go-rwx ~** to be safe.
- To view file permissions, use **ls -l** or **ls -al**.
- File permissions have 10 fields: 1 for *type*, 3 for *user*, 3 for *group*, and 3 for *world*. Each group of three fields has *read*, *write*, and *execute* permission.
- You can encrypt and decrypt a file with **crypt** and **pgp**.
- You should remove *group* and *world* permissions until you are familiar enough with Unix to open up certain directories to others.

KEY TERMS

encryption	owner	regular expression
decryption	pager	spooling
globbing	pattern	string
group	PDF	word
hard copy	permission	
metacharacter	PostScript (PS)	

COMMAND SUMMARY

acroread	View PDF file.
cancel	Cancel a print job.
cat	View a file; concatenate a file.
chmod	Change a file's access permissions.
comm	Compare two files and show results in three columns.
crypt	Encrypt or decrypt a file.
diff	Compare two files and show differences through codes.
echo	View a variable.
egrep	Search for lines containing text with extended regular expressions.
enscript	Special form of printing.
fgrep	Search inside files for strings with no regular expressions.
file	Try to determine the file type.
genscript	Create PS from text.
grep	Search for lines containing text with basic regular expressions.
groups	Report system groups to which you belong.
gs	View PS file.
head	View the top of the file.
ispell	Spell-check a text file interactively.
less	View a text file.
lp	Print a file.
lpq	Show the printing queue.
lpr	Print a file.
lprm	Remove a print job.
lpstat	Show the printing queue and status.
ls	List files.
man	Find information.
more	View a text file.
mpage	Special form of printing.
pgp	Pretty Good Privacy program.
printers	Show list of printers.

sdiff	Side-by-side version of **diff**.
sort	Sort text in ascending or descending order or according to key.
spell	Spell-check text inside a file, but not interactively.
split	Divide a file into groups of lines and store in other files.
tail	View the bottom of a file.
touch	Change the time stamp of a file.
uniq	Check for duplicate lines.
wc	Count characters, words, and lines.

Problems

1. Name five operations you can perform on a file.
2. Do pagers work on nontext files? Give an example of a command line. What happens if you execute the command?
3. Describe the default behaviors of **head** and **tail**.
4. Explain why **less** is more than **more**.
5. Write a command line to view a text file's contents with line numbers.
6. Write a command line to show only the number of lines inside a file.
7. Write a command line that will output the number of hidden files in a current directory. (*Hint*: You might need to use the **-A** option with **ls**. How many hidden files do you have in your **HOME** directory?)
8. Write a command line that will output the total number of unhidden files in a current directory.
9. How many words are in your system dictionary? Show the command line.
10. Write a command line to compare two data files (d1.txt, d2.txt) with **comm**, whereby the output shows only the duplicated files. For extra credit (assuming that your instructor gives it), output the result to d3.txt.
11. Refer to Section 4.6.2. Add a fifth line (kim) to the bottom of **data1.txt**. Run **diff data1.txt data2.txt** and explain the analysis.
12. Write a command line that demonstrates **diff3** comparing three data files.
13. Write a regular expression that matches all blank lines.
14. Write a regular expression that matches integers.
15. Write a regular expression that matches any word beginning with a capital letter and ending with a number.
16. Can **emacs** use regular expressions? Give an example of a function or key binding that searches with regular expressions.
17. Write a command line that will find and number all lines in test.txt that contain vowels, not counting y. For extra credit, see if you can account for y. (*Hint*: Look up rules for when y is a vowel.)
18. Write a command line that will find all lines in a text file that contain nonalphabetic characters (i.e., everything except **A-Z** and **a-z**).
19. Distinguish between **grep** and **fgrep**. In particular, when should you use **fgrep** instead of **grep**?
20. Write a command line that will look for all instances of the word *lubricant* in all unhidden text files in a current directory.

21. Write a command line that will mail you after a print job finishes.

22. Write a command line that will print 666 copies of a file. Explain why printing that many copies is a bad idea.

23. If a user enters **cancel**, should the system administrators worry? Why or why not?

24. Print a large text file as four columns in landscape format. The PS file should number each panel and have an outline.

25. Convert your `info.txt` file into PDF format.

26. Write a command which sets the permission on your account such that no one can view, change, or execute any of your files.

27. Write a command line (or a group of command lines) that adds complete user permission, removes group read permission, and adds world execute permission to a file called `blubber.txt`.

28. Write a command line that adds group and world read and execute permission to `info.txt`.

5

Directories and File Management

5.1   DIRECTORIES

Whereas files store your "stuff," directories store your files. Look at Figure 5.1. To help organize a large collection of papers, you can store them inside folders or filing-cabinet drawers. Computer files can be stored in an analogous fashion with the use of ***directories***. A directory is actually a special kind of file that contains information about which files are "inside" of it. New Unix users should not need to worry about this technicality at this stage. Instead, you will focus on the basic notion of directories as places to put files of "stuff."

SECTIONS

OBJECTIVES

After reading this chapter, you should be able to:

- Understand the parent–child relationship of directories and their contents.
- Distinguish between relative and absolute pathnames.
- Run file management commands on files and directories.
- Use shortcuts for the current working directory (.), the parent (..), the root (/), and your home directory (~).
- Construct a directory tree to organize your Unix account.
- Protect your account with restrictive permissions.
- Navigate a directory tree.
- Duplicate and rename files and directories.
- Delete files and directories without removing your entire account.
- Create hard and symbolic links between files.
- Compress and archive your work to save space on your account.
- Search and find files and directories in a directory tree.

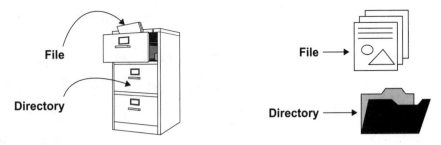

Figure 5.1 Filing-Cabinet and Folder Analogies to Computer Files and Directories

5.1.1 Directory Tree

Picture a tree, with its main trunk and large branches splitting off into smaller branches and twigs. Eventually, the extremities terminate in leaves. As illustrated in Figure 5.2, a directory tree adapts a tree model by forming an organized hierarchy of files and directories; simply turn the book upside down to see a rough approximation of a tree.

Figure 5.3 shows a portion of a sample directory tree. In Unix, the uppermost directory (the start of the *trunk*) is called **root** and is represented by a lone forward slash (/). The root directory contains *everything* in your system. Directories act as a tree's **branches**. Each time a directory is placed into another directory, the tree splits outward and downward. Files and empty directories terminate the branches and are called **leaves** because they do not contain other files.

5.1.2 Parent–Child Relationship

A directory that contains files or other directories is called a *parent*, while a file or directory contained inside another directory is called a *child*. The child of one directory, of course, may be a parent as well, yielding, in its turn, its own file and directory children.

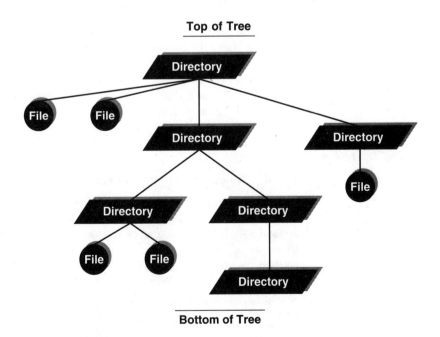

Figure 5.2 Directory Tree

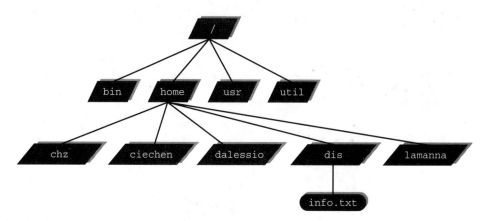

Figure 5.3 Sample Directory Hierarchy

In Figure 5.3 (/), dis is the child of the parent home. The directory home, in turn, is the child of *root*. Because the tree terminates with *root*, *root* is the ancestor—the parent of all other parents. A common example of this structure is your genealogy. Your parents each had parents who each had parents, all the way back to whoever you believe are your most distant ancestors. At each level, if the children of any set of parents did not procreate (you know, make more children!), then those nonchildbearing children were *leaves*. Otherwise, people who had their children continued the genealogy tree down to you. Kind of makes you feel responsible, doesn't it?

5.1.3   Why Directories?

If you place all your files in your **HOME** directory,[1] I guarantee that the clutter will eventually overwhelm you. Not to slam Microsoft Windows, but how often have you seen a completely flooded desktop?[2] Just as you would (or should) do at home, you place items in specified places. Or imagine moving to a new home. When you organize your stuff, you should label the containers. Computer science even has a name for this labeling of collections of stuff: *abstraction*. For example, in programming, abstraction helps software engineers hide low-level details with high-level names and structures. So, a box labeled "pots" clearly indicates that you should put that box in the kitchen in your new home assuming that you actually filled it correctly. Computer directories have the same role. With a clear and descriptive name, you can readily determine the files that a directory contains! So, how do you name a directory?

5.1.4   Rules for Naming Directories

Rules for naming directories are the same as rules for naming files. You can create a directory with the command **mkdir name**. As you will learn in Section 5.2.4, you can append a slash (/) at the end of a name if it is the last directory in a *path*. For example, to create a directory **test** inside your *current directory*, you can enter either **mkdir Test** or **mkdir Test/**. You may also wish to use *titlecase* names (names,

---

[1]Note that in Unix *everything is a file*. You will discover that a directory is simply a special kind of file. But for now, I think that you should continue to distinguish between the two concepts.

[2]Here is a question for Microsoft Windows users: What is your equivalent of **HOME**? After you read a few more sections of this book and learn what I mean by **cd /home/dis**, look for the Windows equivalent at the DOS prompt (DOS knows **cd**!).

such as *Titlecase*, whose first letter is capitalized), because **ls** lists uppercase letters before lowercase letters. I do *not* recommend spaces in directory names! (Later on you will learn how to deal with spaces just in case you encounter someone else silly enough to do so.) The concepts of path and current directory are discussed in the next sections.

PRACTICE!

1. Determine which of the following names Unix will interpret as valid directory names: A, a, a.a, a/, #@#, /, //.
2. In the preceding exercise, is any directory name useful?

5.2   PATHNAME

This section introduces the notion of a *pathname*, which is a name that locates a file or directory in a file system. Knowing how to write a pathname will enable you to write Unix commands for files in other directories, not just your **HOME** directory.

5.2.1   File Location (Graphical View)

To show a file's location in the file-system hierarchy, many GUIs (including those of Unix) support file managers. For example, if your system supports **dtfile** (*desktop file manager*) try the following:

Step 5.1:   View Unix file-system hierarchy

```
unix> dtfile &                                          Run Unix GUI file manager.
```
The & allows you to keep working at the prompt without killing the File Manager window.

In Figure 5.4, I show my current **HOME**. Each folder contains several folders and so forth. To see a particular folder's contents, double click on it with the mouse. If you prefer to see a treelike structure, select **View→Set View Options...** and activate **By tree**. I show a tree view in Figure 5.5. Otherwise, you can execute **dtfile -tree on** at the prompt next time.

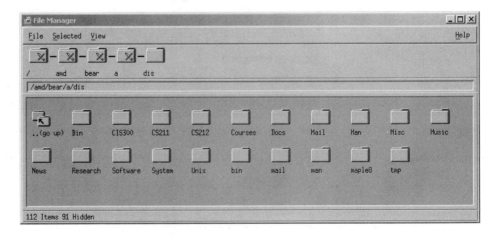

Figure 5.4   DT File Manager (Normal View)

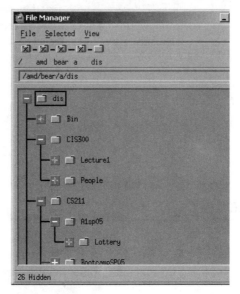

Figure 5.5 DT File Manager (Tree View)

5.2.2 File Location (Text and 2-D View)

Many Unix systems have a pine e-mail program installed. The **pine** package includes the **pico** text editor and **pilot**, which is a file and directory browser. With **pilot**, you can navigate a directory tree, view files, and even run Unix commands. Like **pico**, **pilot** shows all commands at the bottom of the screen, together with their **Control**-key sequences, as illustrated in Figure 5.6.

Step 5.2:   Browse tree with **pilot**

```
unix> pilot                                      Run pilot (not part of the formal Unix package).
```

5.2.3 File Location (Text and 1-D View)

Each file in the Unix file system has a specific "address" that you can specify by following the path from the root to the current file (or directory). For example, you can find

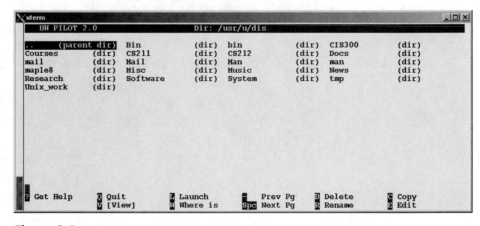

Figure 5.6 pilot

`info.txt` in Figure 5.3 in this sequence: *root* (/), `home`, `dis`, `info.txt`. Now, looking at Figures 5.4 and 5.5, we see a field that shows `/amd/bear/a/dis`, which is the actual name of my **HOME**.[3] The forward slashes[4] not only separate the directory names, but indicate which directory contains another. For example, `/home/dis` means that *root* (the leftmost /) contains `home`, which in turn contains `dis` (my **HOME** directory). This one-dimensional line of text composed of directory names and filenames is called a ***pathname***. The pathname works from left to right, representing the graphical view that works from top to bottom. (Simply rotate the book a quarter circle clockwise.)

PRACTICE!

3. Why is a pathname considered 1-D?

4. In the context of pathnames, explain why two files in the same directory cannot share a name.

5.2.4 Pathname Rules

A pathname does not need to start at the root. For example, `Data/test.txt` means that directory `Data` stores `test.txt`. But I do not know where `Data` resides. However, Unix will know, depending on a location called the *current working directory* that I will discuss later. For now, I want you to concentrate on simply writing pathnames. Here is a summary of the rules:

- To specify the location of a file in Unix, you must use a pathname, which has the form $dir^1/dir^2/.../name$. The final item in the pathname may be a directory or a file.

- Each name in the path must follow Unix's filename convention.

- If the last name is a directory, you may terminate the whole pathname with a /.

- You can start a pathname with /, which represents the topmost directory called *root*.

Note that I will occasionally say *path* instead of *pathname* for the sake of brevity.

The sections that follow explain in more detail the choice of whether to start a pathname with *root*. Although not covered in this book, you might wish to explore **dirname** and **basename**, which may help you analyze pathnames.

5.2.5 Absolute Pathnames

What is the path to my office? My "current working residence" is Ithaca, New York. More specifically, I live in the city of Ithaca, located in the state of New York, located in the United States of America. Expanding even further, the United States is located in North America, which in turn is located in the Northern Hemisphere, located on the planet Earth. Indeed, someone looking for my office has quite a path to follow. The root directory is like the universe: the highest level from which to specify directions.

An ***absolute pathname*** incorporates the *complete* trail to follow to a directory or file, starting from *root* and ending with the item of interest. When looking at the

---

[3]I can still write `/home/dis` and not lie, because that directory happens to point to the same place. You need to learn about *links* before I can attempt to explain the mechanism.

[4]Windows and DOS users might find this notion familiar, because DOS uses the backslash (\) for the same purpose. See also the **TREE** command in DOS.

pathname as text, you work from left to right, starting with **/**. In fact, a sole forward slash in the command line signifies *root*. Here are some absolute pathnames:

Step 5.3:   Practice with absolute pathnames

```
unix> ls /home/dis                          List the contents of your HOME.
Output not shown.                 /home/dis is the absolute pathname of your HOME.
unix> ls -l /home/dis/info.txt                    Long list info.txt.
Output not shown.                  Unix finds info.txt from the absolute path.
unix> ls /                       List all files and directories contained by root.
bin dev etc local usr util                ... and more. You should see a long list.
```

In fact, you will discover that you can express the syntax of **ls** as **ls *pathname***.

PRACTICE!

> 5. I have been using the pathname /home/dis/info.txt. Why is this pathname absolute? Describe the location of info.txt.
>
> 6. Try to figure out how to list the contents of your home directory with an absolute pathname. (*Hint*: Do you remember what **echo $HOME** does?)
>
> 7. Describe what **ls /home** does. For more fun, have Unix count the results of that listing.

5.2.6   Relative Pathnames

Anyone who lives in Ithaca does not need directions to Ithaca. Residents would require only directions *relative* to places within Ithaca. In Unix, complete directions in the form of absolute pathnames are typically unnecessary. After all, if you are working from within your **HOME** account (still pending a formal explanation!), you shouldn't need to keep writing **/home/*user***! Unix provides a mechanism called a ***relative pathname*** to save time. A relative pathname starts at a particular directory, usually the directory from which you working, rather than at *root*.

Using Figure 5.3, pretend that directory home is a room into which you can walk. From inside the room, you see doors to other rooms: chz, ciechen, dalessio, dis, and lamanna. From your current perspective, these places (the directories) have relative locations (relative pathnames). For example, you could say, "the path from my current location to dis's directory is simply dis." Likewise, the relative pathname of info.txt within home is simply dis/info.txt. Actually, this relative location is the current working directory that I have been mentioning. You will see more of it in the context of writing command lines. So far, you have already been using relative pathnames:

Step 5.4:   Practice with relative pathnames

```
unix> more info.txt                         View info.txt inside HOME.
Output not shown.                You could have entered more /home/dis/info.txt!
unix> mkdir Stuff                   Create a subdirectory called Stuff inside HOME.
                                           Stuff has the path /home/dis/Stuff.
unix> ls Stuff/*.txt                 List all .txt inside Stuff, which is in HOME.
No output because you don't have anything in Stuff. And I have to teach you about mkdir!
```

The notion of relative pathnames is strongly related to another notion, called the *current working directory*. The next section ties these concepts together and introduces very important pathname shortcuts.

PRACTICE!

> 8. What is the absolute pathname of the directory `chz`? (Use Figure 5.3.)
>
> 9. What is the relative pathname of `info.txt` if you are inside `dis`? (Use Figure 5.3.)

5.3   IMPORTANT DIRECTORY SHORTCUTS

Fortunately, there are only a few directory names that you need to memorize without question. Their names are short, too: `/`, `~`, `.`, and `..`. I realize that these names seem cryptic, so I will explain them one at a time in this section.

5.3.1   Root (/)

You have already seen *root* (`/`), which is the topmost directory in Unix. As a reminder, you represent *root* as the first `/` in a pathname. In Step 5.5, you experimented with `ls /`, which shows only the contents of the file system just below `/`. Would you like to see everything that has read permission on your file system? Use `ls -R path`, which exhaustively (actually, it's *recursively*) lists the complete contents of the rightmost item in the path:

Step 5.5:   Experiment with root (/)

```
unix> ls -R /                          Exhaustively list all files and directories contained by root.
You should see a gigantic list. Enter ^C to quit. Or try ls -R / | less to page through everything.
```

5.3.2   Current Working Directory

Forget about Unix for a moment. Now suppose that you need to find mouthwash, which you lost somewhere in your residence. You should go look for the item in different rooms. You will walk into a room, dig around, and either cheer in victory or cry out in dismay, returning to your starting point. That starting point then becomes the main location, perhaps a hallway with doors to those other rooms. Now suppose that the missing item is in the bathroom, under the sink. Then the path from your starting point to the item is *bathroom/sink/cabinet/mouthwash*. Note that I did not specify the complete path, which would look something like this:

>   universe/milkyway/solarsystem/earth/country/address/house/bathroom/sink/cabinet/mouthwash.

Instead, if you keep track of the hallway as your starting point, the shorter path suffices. In fact, maybe your home is already a universe of stuff!

Dealing with a directory tree is no different. Unix keeps track of a ***current working directory*** (CWD), which is the current location in the file-system hierarchy. The CWD affects the command line. For example, if you enter `more info.txt`, Unix assumes that `info.txt` is located inside the CWD. If `info.txt` is absent, Unix will complain. To help you keep track of the CWD, use **pwd** (*print working directory*):

Step 5.6:   Display the current working directory

```
unix> pwd                                     Display current working directory.
/home/dis                        You should be at HOME unless you have learned cd.
```

Note how **pwd** reports the absolute pathname of your CWD. To assist with remembering **pwd**, try vocalizing it as "path to working directory." To help visualize your CWD, you can use **dtfile** (or any file manager) by selecting a particular directory in the tree.

In **dtfile**, you can double click with the left mouse button on any directory. So, when I double click on CIS300 (one of my directories in Figure 5.4),[5] **dtfile** shows the contents of CIS300, as illustrated in Figure 5.7. The view effectively treats CIS300 as a top-level directory with its own contents. I can now investigate any of those contents with mouse actions.

At the command line, to indicate your CWD, you have two choices:

- Provide no pathname in a command line (e.g., **ls**).
- Use a single dot (**.**) as the path (e.g., **ls .**).

The lone period (**.**) literally means your CWD's absolute pathname. So, you can use it as part of another path whenever you need to say "the working directory." For now, I will have you write some redundant command lines so that you get used to the **.**:

Step 5.7:   Listing with current directory (**.**)

unix> **ls**	**ls** *assumes you mean the CWD, because you didn't specify a path.*
Output for your working directory, which is likely still **HOME**.	*In fact, why not check with* **pwd**?
unix> **ls .**	*List your CWD.*
Output for your working directory.	*The* **.** *in this case is redundant.*
unix> **ls -l /home/dis/info.txt**	*Long list* info.txt, *assuming it is in* **HOME**.
Output using absolute pathname for comparison.	*Notice how much typing the absolute path needs.*
unix> **ls -l ./info.txt**	*Long list* info.txt, *which is inside your CWD.*

Unix will output the listing for info.txt, *assuming that your CWD truly contains the file!*

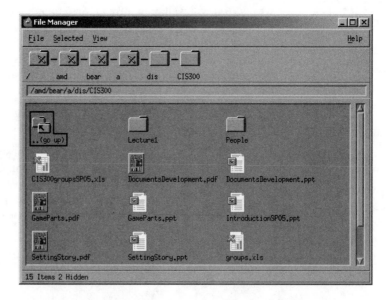

Figure 5.7   Graphical View of CWD

---

[5]Check out *http://www.cis.cornell.edu/courses/cis300*, which is my course titled "Introduction to Computer Game Design." The course number might change in the next few years, so you might need to start with *http://www.cis.cornell.edu*.

Note how **ls**, **ls .**, and **ls -l ./info.txt** all used relative pathnames! For comparison, I shows the absolute path version **ls -l /home/dis/info.txt**, which does not depend on the CWD. The **.** is not superfluous! In the preceding example, I used the relative path **./info.txt**, which nicely abbreviates the absolute version of /home/dis/info.txt. For the most part, you will use the single dot when you prefer a shortcut.

PRACTICE!

10. Log off and then log on. What is your current working directory?
11. Create a file called mystuff.txt inside your **HOME** directory. What is the relative path to mystufff.txt? Describe the path in terms of **..**
12. Suppose you had a directory called Junk inside your **HOME**. Write two command lines to list the contents of Junk, assuming that your CWD is **HOME**.
13. Depending on your shell and settings, **echo $cwd** might work. If so, what would this command do? (Try it!)

5.3.3   Home Directory

Unix stores your files in your Unix account. **HOME** contains the system memory allotted to each user. As discussed earlier, when you log in, Unix places you inside your **HOME** directory. Each user's **HOME** is a directory labeled with their unique username. Most Unix systems place users' **HOME** directories inside a /home directory. Using the folder analogy in Figure 5.8, I show my **HOME** account directory, dis, stored inside /home. (See Figures 5.5 and 5.6 for alternative views.)

Never confuse **HOME** with home if you use **/home/username**! Your shell sets the default value **HOME**, which tells Unix where your account resides. The home directory, by contrast, contains all other **HOME**s. Note that some systems store user accounts in directories with entirely different names, as you can see in Figures 5.5 and 5.6. I can now be more descriptive in what happens when you ask Unix to display your **HOME**:

Step 5.8:   Determine your **HOME**

```
unix> echo $HOME                                    Display your HOME.
/home/dis                            Unix displays the absolute pathname of your HOME.
```

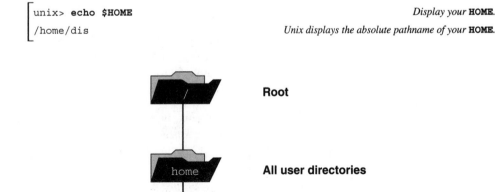

Root

home   All user directories

dis   dis's **HOME directory**

Figure 5.8   Folder View of **HOME** Directory

Because **HOME** is so vital to store your work, most Unix shells provide a convenient shortcut for the absolute pathname of **HOME**: the tilde (**~**) can be used to represent **HOME** in a pathname. (The Bourne shell **sh** does not.) So, instead of saying `/home/dis/info.txt`, you could say `~/info.txt`.

Step 5.9:   Practice with ~

```
unix> more ~/info.txt                                    View info.txt inside HOME.
Output not shown.                    The ~ is redundant here, but does illustrate how it represents HOME.
```

When you work with more directories, the ~ will save you from having to change your CWD. For example, if your CWD is `Stuff/Data1` and you want to list the contents of `Stuff/Data2`, you can enter **ls ~/Stuff/Data2**. You will see ever more applications of ~ when you learn how to copy, rename, and delete files.

Sometimes students ask how does Unix know which user's **HOME** to use for ~. For each person who logs in, Unix interprets a lone ~ to mean that person's account. For example, **ls ~** means "list my **HOME** directory."

Step 5.10:   Using ~ for **HOME**

```
unix> ls ~                                                       List HOME directory.
Output not shown.                       ls ~ is identical to ls and ls . when the CWD is HOME.
```

Note that wherever you can say ~ and the absolute pathname for **HOME**, you can say **$HOME**, which finds the value of **HOME**. So, **ls $HOME** is equivalent to **ls ~**.

When you place the tilde in front of a username, **~user**, Unix interprets the path as "the **HOME** of **user**."[6] So, if I enter **ls ~jre**, I am trying to list the contents of `jre`'s **HOME**.

Step 5.11:   Accessing another user's account with **~user**

```
unix> ls /home                                          Let's see who else has an account.
Long list. I found jre.              Again, your system's accounts might be located somewhere else.
unix> ls ~jre                                            List the contents of jre's HOME.
If jre neglected to set access permission, I can see everything.          See chmod for permissions.
```

You should now understand what the command line **chmod go-rwx ~** does: You are instructing Unix to remove group and world **rwx** permissions on your **HOME** account! But user's can still see that you have an account.

PRACTICE!

14. Complete the following statement:
    My **HOME** directory has the absolute pathname _____ .
15. Describe the parent–child relationship of your **HOME** directory with respect to your system's *root*.
16. Describe what **ls $HOME** does. What can you infer about **$HOME**?
17. Check the permissions on your account.
18. Set the permissions such that no one has access to your **HOME** except for you.

---

[6]Depending on how much you use the Internet, you may have encountered the ~ in association with people's home pages. You would see ~someone as part of the Web address (URL).

5.3.4   Parent Directory (..)

In Figure 5.7, one of CIS300's contents is an icon labelled `..` (`go up`). This notation indicates that you can double left-click on the icon to bring you to dis, which is CIS300's parent directory. (Recall that a parent directory contains other directories.) But what in the world is the double dot? The double dot (`..`) has a special meaning in Unix, which is—you guessed it!—*the parent directory*. Unix allows you to use `..` in a command line whenever you need to say "the parent of the CWD." For example, when I say **ls ..**, Unix will list the contents of the parent directory. If the CWD is your **HOME**, then Unix will provide a list of **/home**.

Step 5.12:   List parent directory (..)

```
unix> pwd                                              What's your CWD?
/home/dis                          Just ensuring you are at HOME. If not, enter cd ~.
unix> ls ..                                    List contents of parent directory.
chz   ciechen   dis and others
```

You can use `..` anywhere in a pathname as long as the parent directory exists. For example, you can use a sequence of `..`s to look up the directory tree:

Step 5.13:   .. in pathname

```
unix> ls ../..                              List the parent of the parent of the CWD.
bin etc local usr and others    ../.. resolves to root, assuming that the CWD is /home/user.
```

You can even see the `..` when you list any directory's hidden files:

Step 5.14:   Listing of ..

```
unix> ls -al                                         Long list all files in the CWD.
drwx------  48  dis   dis   8192 Mar 31 12:02 .         Long listing of CWD.
drwxr-xr-x 175 root root 4096 Mar 28 04:35 ..     Long listing of parent of CWD.
Many other files.
```

Note how the parent of **HOME** has drwxr-xr-x permissions, which means that groups and the world (which includes *you*) can list /home. Unix also alerts you to the fact that . and .. are directories by the first letter, d! When listing all your files, you can exclude . and .. with **ls -A**, because the CWD and its parent are always present in a directory.

PRACTICE!

19. What is the parent directory of **HOME**?
20. Suppose your CWD is **HOME**. Describe the command line **ls ../jre** and what might happen if you run it.

5.4   DIRECTORY NAVIGATION

So far, you have learned how to list directories and form pathnames, but unless you have discovered **cd** (which I have hinted at), your CWD has stayed at **HOME**. You haven't really gone anywhere in Unix (at least at the command line)!

5.4.1   Motivation

First, why should you want to change your CWD? When you start building your own directory hierarchy in **HOME**, you will eventually build a deep tree, especially if you are well organized. However, once you start doing file operations, the pathnames can get rather lengthy, even if you use relative paths. For example, suppose your CWD contains directory stuff.

```
unix> more Stuff/Homework1/Answers/data3.txt
unix> more Stuff/Homework1/Answers/data4.txt
unix> gs Stuff/Homework1/Assignment/hw1.ps
```

Instead, would you rather enter the following?

```
unix> cd Stuff/Homework1
unix> more Answers/data3.txt
```
and so forth....

The next several sections will explain how **cd** changes your CWD.

5.4.2   Changing Directories

Why memorize the entire tree when you can *change directories* with **cd**? The command **cd** followed by a directory will take you to that directory. You can express the directory as a relative or absolute pathname, depending on your CWD. **cd** changes the CWD to the directory to which you are going. In the following step I use an absolute pathname to change my CWD directly:

Step 5.15:   Change directory (absolute pathname)

`unix> cd /usr/bin`	*Change CWD to* /usr/bin.
`unix> pwd`	*Check your CWD.*
`/usr/bin`	*The CWD is correct.*
`unix> ls`	*List the CWD, which is now* /usr/bin.
List of many Unix command files.	*In earlier examples, I used the term "current directory" for* **ls**.

For more practice, work your way back to **HOME**, starting from *root*. Recall that *root's* name is just /, so you can change your CWD to *root* with **cd /**. By "stepping" one directory at a time, you can practice with relative pathnames:

Step 5.16:   Change directory (relative pathname)

`unix> cd /`	*Change CWD to root.*
`unix> pwd`	*Check your CWD.*
`/`	*Root.*
`unix> cd home`	*Change CWD to root's child* home.
`unix> pwd`	*Check CWD*
`/home`	*Child of root.*
`unix> cd dis`	*Change CWD to your account*
`unix> pwd`	*Check CWD.*
`/home/dis`	*Child of* home.

Of course, you could have saved effort with **cd/home/dis**. Also, remember that once you change your CWD, your relative pathname now starts at the current directory!

Step 5.17:   CWD and relative pathname

```
unix> cd /home/                            Go to /home.
unix> ls                          List contents of CWD, which is now /home!
List of user accounts
unix> ls dis                     List one of the directories inside the CWD.
```

In the preceding example, I rely on the fact that Unix remembers my CWD. Actually, your system administrator might have set your **cd** to show your CWD automatically. In my setup files, **cd** is customized as **cd !*;echo $cwd**. So, when I enter **cd *path***, the shell runs **cd *path*** (*path* replaces !*) and then **echo $cwd**. The **cwd** variable is maintained by the shell. To see if your **cd** has modified behavior, enter **alias cd**.

PRACTICE!

21. Set your CWD to *root*.
22. Show the command line for viewing info.txt inside your **HOME**.
23. Set the CWD to /home.
24. View the contents of info.txt inside your **HOME**.

5.4.3   Related Commands

Depending on your shell, you might have even more commands to change directories. For example, on my system, **man cd** provides information about **cd**, **chdir**, **pushd**, **popd**, and **dirs**. C-shell (**csh**) users have access to **pushd**, **popd**, and **chdir**. Depending on your shell, you might have access to commands that I have not discussed, and I recommend that you investigate them.

5.4.4   Changing Directories by Using Shortcuts

The handy shortcuts for **HOME**, *root*, the current directory (.), and a parent directory (..) apply whenever you specify a pathname. So, the shortcuts work with **cd**, too! However, I need to alert you about some issues and tricks:

- **cd** (without a pathname) sets your CWD to **HOME**.
- **cd ~*username*** changes your CWD to ***username***'s **HOME** directory. For example, whereas **cd ~/Stuff** lists the contents of my Stuff directory (which is in my **HOME**), **cd ~jre/Stuff** lists the contents of jre's Stuff. Putting a / between the ~ and ***username*** makes Unix refer to *your* account.

The following examples demonstrate the various shortcuts from Section 5.3.

Step 5.18:   Change directory to root

```
unix> cd /                                 Set CWD to root.
unix> pwd                              Show the CWD to confirm.
/                                          Confirmed!
```

Step 5.19:   Change directory to HOME

```
unix> cd                         Set CWD to HOME (a shortcut to a shortcut!).
unix> cd ~              Set CWD to HOME. Home is where you hang your hat.
unix> cd ~dis                    Set CWD to my HOME. (Use your account.)
unix> cd $Home                             Set CWD to Home.
As yet another reminder, the absolute pathname equivalent is usually cd /home/dis.
```

Step 5.20: Change directory to current directory

```
unix> pwd                                    What's my CWD?
/home/dis                                    I'm at HOME. Home, sweet home!
unix> cd .                                   Set CWD to CWD. Yes, it's redundant.
unix> pwd                                    Confirm CWD.
/home/dis                                    I'm at HOME. Home is a person's castle.
cd . is redundant because, wherever you are, your CWD is always at the current directory.
```

Step 5.21: Change directory to parent of current directory

```
unix> pwd                                    Confirm CWD.
/home/dis                                    I'm still at HOME. Home is where the heart is.
unix> cd ..                                  Set CWD to parent of CWD. (Or go up one directory.)
unix> pwd                                    Confirm CWD. East or west, home is best.
/home                                        My parent of HOME, /home.
```

If you would like to return to your previous CWD, your shell might provide a convenient shortcut. By entering **cd -** (hyphen), Unix might set your CWD to the CWD you had before you had the new CWD. Well, instead of "new CWD," I could say "current CWD," but that seems redundantly redundant. Instead, try the following:

Step 5.22: Change to previous directory

```
unix> cd /usr/bin                            Pick a directory and set your CWD to it.
unix> cd ~                                    Set your CWD to HOME again . There's no place like home.
unix> pwd                                     Check your CWD (what I call the "new CWD").
/home/dis                                     The CWD is HOME, as expected.
unix> cd -                                    Attempt to change to previous CWD.
unix> pwd                                      Confirm your new CWD.
/usr/bin                                      Your CWD is now what was the previous CWD.
```

In these examples, if a directory lacks **x** (access) permission, you cannot use **cd** to get into it (i.e., to set your CWD as that directory). For example, other users hopefully have entered **chmod go-rwx ~**, which removed group and world access permission (drwx------) to everything in your **HOME**. I will discuss more about directory permissions in Section 5.10.5.

PRACTICE!

25. What is the meaning of the command line **cd ~**?
26. What is the meaning of the command line **cd ~/**?
27. What is the meaning of the command line **cd ~dis**?
28. What is the meaning of the command line **cd ~/dis**? (*Hint*: This is a trick question!)
29. What is the meaning of the command line **cd ./../.**?

5.5 SUBDIRECTORIES

As you gather homework, projects, mail, personal files, and perhaps even more, in **HOME**, I guarantee that it will become cluttered. Unless you like clutter and never repeating a filename, I strongly suggest that you create your directories. Even if you prefer a slovenly online existence, others do not, and sooner or later you will want, and need, to navigate your directories.

5.5.1   Definition and Rules

A ***subdirectory*** is a directory contained inside another directory. More formally, a subdirectory is a child of a parent directory. For example, in Figure 5.3, directory `home` is the parent of subdirectory `dis`, which has numerous subdirectories of its own (Figure 5.4). As previously discussed, naming directories follows the same convention as naming files. Choose names wisely! After two years of naming my directories and files A, B, C, and so on, I had to delete the entire lot out of utter confusion. Also, I suggest that you use titlecase (Section 5.1.4), because titlecase names list before lowercase names. The notion of a pathname is crucial as well, as you identify subdirectories on a path by separating names with forward slashes (Section 5.2.4).

5.5.2   Creating Subdirectories

You can start organizing your **HOME** with subdirectories. I have used two analogies for **HOME**:

- Your residence with doors leading to rooms that hold things.
- A filing cabinet with drawers and folders that hold things.

Either way, your **HOME** has space for you to put files (and other directories) in subdirectories. To create a subdirectory, use **mkdir pathname**. The path assumes that you have write permission. If you use a pathname that includes **HOME**, then you should be OK, assuming that you haven't removed user permission! One of the best ways to learn about managing files in directories is to create a hierarchy. So, you will be creating the structure shown in Figure 5.9. The usual procedure for creating a subdirectory involves first changing your CWD to a parent directory and then adding new subdirectories.

Step 5.23:   Create a subdirectory

```
unix> cd
unix> mkdir Unix_work
unix> ls
Unix_work info.txt other files
```
Ensure that your CWD is **HOME**.
Create subdirectory in CWD.
List the CWD's files.
You might have several in **HOME** *by now.*

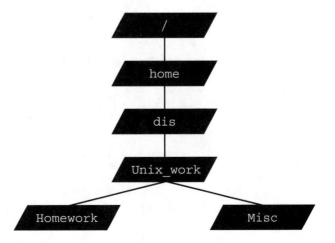

Figure 5.9   Proposed Directory Tree for Your **HOME**

As indicated in Figure 5.9, you can make subdirectories within other subdirectories. For instance, your `Unix_work` directory (a subdirectory of your **HOME** directory) might contain separate directories for Unix practice, homework, projects, and other things. For now, you will add two subdirectories inside `Unix_work`:

- `Homework`, to store homework solutions.
- `Misc`, to store other work in Unix.

You can create these directories (or any others that you prefer) by using either relative or absolute pathnames. You should label each directory according to the particular contents organized within that directory. Next, you will use both kinds of pathnames to practice with:

Step 5.24: Create subdirectory (relative path)

```
unix> cd Unix_work                          Go inside Unix_work.
unix> pwd                                    Confirm your CWD.
/home/dis/Unix_work                          I am inside Unix_work.
unix> mkdir Homework                Create a subdirectory inside Unix_work.
unix> ls                                     What do you see?
Homework                   You see both directories that you created.
```

Step 5.25: Create subdirectory (absolute path)

```
unix> mkdir /home/dis/Unix_work/Misc         Go inside Unix_work.
unix> pwd                                    Confirm your CWD.
/home/dis/Unix_work                          I am inside Unix_work.
unix> ls                                     What do you see?
Homework  Misc             You see both directories that you created.
```

If you prefer, you could have shortened Step 5.25 with **mkdir ~/Unix_work/Misc** or **mkdir $HOME/Unix_work/Misc**. If you would like to create multiple directories at the command line, you can enter **mkdir dir1 dir2**.... If you would like Unix to help you distinguish file types when listing, use **ls -F**, which shows directories with trailing slashes.

PRACTICE!

30. Why does **ls -F** show trailing slashes at the end of a directory name?
31. Without absolute pathnames, create a directory called `Temp` inside `Unix_work/Homework`.
32. Using absolute pathnames (possibly together with some relative pathnames), create a directory called `Crap` inside `Unix_work/Misc`. (It's not often I get to say "crap" in a book, so please get this one right!)
33. Using just one command line, create three directories D1, D2, and D3 inside `Unix_work`.

5.5.3 Removing Directories

To *remove* an empty directory, use **rmdir pathname**. If the directory *has* contents, Unix will complain, at which point you need to use the **rm** command. But I recommend that you avoid **rm** until a few sections from now, because it could be dangerous to your files. (Unix lacks an "undelete" command!) Suppose that you created a directory called `Test` inside `Unix_work`, but you decide that you no longer need `Test`. You can delete it!

Step 5.26: Removing empty subdirectory

```
unix> mkdir ~/Unix_work/Test                    Create a subdirectory.
unix> ls ~/Unix_work                            Check if Test is present.
Homework  Misc  Test                            You may have other contents, too.
unix> rmdir ~/Unix_work/Test                            Delete Test.
unix> ls ~/Unix_work                            Check if Test is present.
Homework  Misc                                          Test is gone!
```

Note that you cannot delete your CWD. Why? Because you cannot be within a directory that you are attempting to delete. Give it a try—Unix will complain. You will see how to delete directories with contents in Section 5.7.2.

PRACTICE!

34. Create a subdirectory called `Temp2` inside `~/Unix_work`.
35. Change your working directory to the new subdirectory `Test2`.
36. Try using relative pathnames to delete `Temp2`.

5.6 BASIC FILE COPYING AND RENAMING

As you grow older, you will gradually need more and more space for the forms, receipts, and other paperwork that clutter your life. To deal with the lifelong onslaught of paperwork, you will occasionally need to rearrange the papers and files. Unix requires similar care with the electronic files that will eventually clutter your account. Thankfully, Unix provides copy (**cp**) and move (**mv**) commands to help you stay organized. This section concentrates on copying and renaming files within the same CWD. Later sections exploit Unix's directory tree for more robust organizing.

5.6.1 Copying Files

Suppose that you need to add text to `info.txt`, but you want to keep a copy of the original file, which we call a ***backup***. In general, I recommend that you always back up your work! The syntax for **cp** is **cp *source target***, where both ***source*** and ***target*** are pathnames. For now, I will restrict our examples to the CWD, so you really could just say ***originalfile*** for ***source*** and ***copyfile***:

- ***source*** is the original file you wish to copy. ***source*** must exist in the CWD!
- ***target*** becomes a copy of the original file. ***target*** *must not* be named ***source*** and *should not* share another filename in the CWD. (**cp** can override target names, so be careful.) (See **noclobber** in Chapter 8.)

Try copying the contents of `info.txt` into a new file, `new_info.txt`, with **cp**:

Step 5.27: Basic File Copy

```
unix> cp info.txt new_info.txt          Create copy of info.txt called new_info.txt.
unix> diff info.txt new_info.txt                   Prove that the files are identical.
diff produces no output, which indicates that the two files are the same. You could also check with less.
```

On many systems, **cp** might prompt you for a `yes`/`no` response. This query indicates that your system administrator set up your account with an alias for **cp** that looks something like **alias cp 'cp -i'**. Recall from Chapter 2 that *aliases* customize and rename commands with various options. Some commands, like **cp**, include an interactive option, **-i**, to confirm or cancel instructions. If your system does not prompt you, I strongly recommend that you enter **cp -i** until you learn how to create your own aliases.

PRACTICE!

37. Edit new_info.txt and make some changes to it .
38. Does **diff** now report differences between **info.txt** new_info.txt?
39. What happens when you enter **cp info.txt info.txt**? Why?
40. What happens when you enter **cp new_info.txt info.txt**? Does Unix keep the original version of info.txt?

5.6.2   Renaming Files

Filenames are fleeting. What seems perfect today may become utterly useless tomorrow. In a pinch, p1 works well as a program name. But two years in the future, you will likely forget what p1 actually does! Rather than creating new files and directories, you can simply *rename* them with the **mv**, or *move*, command.

The **mv** command works like **cp**, except that **mv** alters the original file's *pathname*. So, you can move a file to a new location, changing what its name will be at the new destination. For example, **mv info.txt Unix_work/Homework1/mydata.txt** not only changes the name of the file to mydata.txt, but puts it in Unix_work/Homework1. For now, I want you to get used to the simplest form, **mv oldname newname**, which changes a filename in the CWD. If file **newname** already exists, **mv** will replace that file, so you need to be careful. Once more, using the interactive option, **-i**, will protect your files by forcing **mv** to prompt you with yes/no questions. Try changing the name of new_info.txt to myinfo.txt:

Step 5.28: Rename a file

```
unix> mv new_info.txt myinfo.txt          Rename new_info.txt to myinfo.txt.
unix> ls                                   Check if renamed file exists.
info.txt  myinfo.txt and others                              Confirmed!
unix> less myinfo.txt                      Check contents of myinfo.txt.
```

5.6.3   Copy and Rename Directories

cp and **mv** also work on directories, but have different rules in some cases. To copy directories, you need to use a **-r** option, which I will discuss later. To rename directories, you can use the same syntax of **mv** as **mv oldname newname**. For example, if you enter **mv Unix_work BunnyRabbit**, your Unix_work directory will now be called BunnyRabbit.

PRACTICE!

41. Create a file called crud.txt in Unix_work. Rename the file to waste.txt.

5.7   DELETION

Frankly, many of these text files are annoying. How do you solve the problem? The **deletion** of files and directories removes their contents and names from the directory tree. To rid your account of unneeded files, use the remove command, **rm**—but with great care! **rm** has the basic syntax **rm pathname**.

5.7.1   Deleting Files

Before you accidentally delete your entire account, I need you to check your system's configuration of **rm**.

Step 5.29:   Check **rm**

```
unix> cd                                          Set your CWD to HOME.
unix> pico junk.txt                               Create a meaningless text file.
Hi!                                               Meaningless text.
unix> rm junk.txt                                 Attempt to delete junk.txt.
rm: remove junk.txt (yes/no)? yes                 My system prompts me, and I enter yes.
unix> less junk.txt                               Try to view contents of junk.txt.
junk: No such file or directory                   You deleted junk.txt.
```

If your system did not output and ask rm: remove junk.txt (yes/no)?, then you have the regular (and dangerous!) version of **rm**. Why? Unix has no "undelete." Your system administrator does make regular backups, but they may not occur as frequently as you need. So, I strongly recommend that you enter only **rm -i** until you learn how to customize **rm** as **alias rm 'rm -i'**, which triggers the interactive prompt. To be safe, I will now say **rm -i**. If you do have **-i** behavior, you only need to enter only **rm**. Now that you know how to use **rm**, practice ridding yourself of a few needless files:

Step 5.30:   Practice using **rm**

```
unix> cd                                          Set CWD to HOME.
unix> cp info.txt a1.txt                          Create a file so we have something to delete.
unix> cp info.txt a2.txt                          Create another file to delete.
unix> rm -i a1.txt                                Try to delete a1.txt.
rm: remove a1.txt (yes/no)? yes                   My system prompts me, and I enter yes.
unix> rm -i ~/a2.txt                              Try to delete a2.txt using absolute pathname.
rm: remove a2.txt (yes/no)? yes                   My system prompts me, and I enter yes.
```

5.7.2   Deleting Directories

To delete empty directories, you can use **rmdir**. To delete nonempty directories, with perhaps many levels in the tree, you need to use **rm -r**. The **-r** option forces a *recursive delete*, which means deleting everything in the pathname you specify, including all the subdirectories (and their contents and so forth). However, be extremely careful when using **rm -r**. If your default **rm** lacks the interactive option, use **rm -ir**.

So, all you need to do is enter **rm -ir *dir***, where ***dir*** indicates the top-level directory to delete. **rm -ir** will prompt you to remove each item inside every other item inside the pathname. Eventually, you will delete ***dir***. Note that you cannot delete any directory if your CWD is anywhere inside ***dir***'s contents. To demonstrate this process, I strongly suggest you practice with the following step, which builds a tree and then deletes it, as shown in Figure 5.10:

Step 5.31:   Set up directory tree

```
unix> cd                                          Start at HOME.
unix> mkdir MyTree                                Create a subdirectory MyTree.
unix> cd MyTree                                   Set CWD to ~/MyTree.
```

```
unix> mkdir A B C                            Create 3 subdirectories in HOME.
unix> cd A                                                   Go to A.
unix> mkdir A B C                   Create 3 subdirectories in ~/MyTree/A.
```
Although I reuse the same names, Unix does not care. Why? directory ~/MyTree/A *is different than directory* /MyTree/A/A, *and so forth. Do you see why having unique pathnames helps you track files and directories?*
```
unix> cd B                                    Go to ~/MyTree/A/A/B.
unix> mkdir D                                 Make yet another subdirectory.
unix> pico D/ imagoner.txt      Create a text file in ~/MyTree/A/A/B/D.
bye!                                                 Type something silly.
unix> cd                                         Set your CWD to HOME.
```
           If you are courageous, you can also enter cd ../../.., *which takes you to* MyTree.
```
unix> dtfile -tree on &                   Display the tree shown in Figure 5.10.
```

Step 5.32: Recursively remove directory tree

```
unix> cd                                         Confirm CWD as HOME.
/home/dis                                        You could work in MyTree, too.
unix> rm -r MyTree                    Recursively delete everything in MyTree.
rm: examine files in directory MyTree/ (yes/no)? y        Answer yes.
```
Unix will prompt you for all those directories and one file. Keep answering y *until prompted to remove* MyTree.
```
rm: remove MyTree/: (yes/no)? n              Do not delete MyTree.
unix> ls MyTree                       See if you deleted everything in MyTree.
```
Unix should show no contents.   *You deleted all of* MyTree's *contents.*

If you get irritated with so many prompts, you could skip the **-i** option. Or if your **rm** has **-i** configured, you may risk using a backslash: **\rm -r *dir***. The backslash disables all command aliases, so use it with extreme caution.

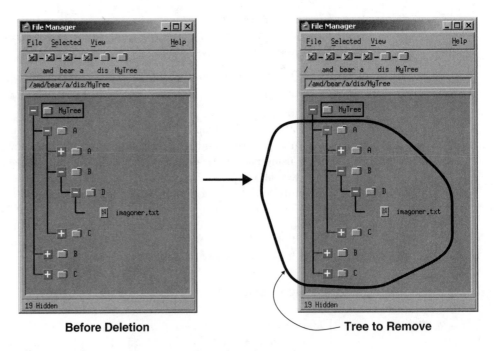

Before Deletion   **Tree to Remove**

Figure 5.10 Nested Directories (for Deletion)

PRACTICE!

42. How do you delete a file whose name starts with a hyphen?

43. Create a new subdirectory in **HOME** called `Temp`.

44. Rename `Temp` as `Birdie`.

45. Delete `Birdie`. Bye-bye, `Birdie`!

46. Figuring that you might have simply skimmed Steps 5.31 and 5.32, take the time to do them!

5.7.3   Extremely Dangerous Deletion Commands

Sooner or later, most Unix users get sloppy or confused and screw up **rm**. Rather than leaving you to guess what you can do wrong, I believe it is safer to show you what to avoid and why. There are numerous ways you can mangle your account, which I describe in Figure 5.11. To keep safe, archive your work in a separate place and take extreme care with **rm**.

DANGER DANGER DANGER DANGER DANGER DANGER DANGER DANGER DANGER DANGER
DO NOT ENTER THESE COMMANDS!

`rm -r *`	If **rm** has no **-i** option, you will delete everything at the CWD, which is often **HOME**.
`rm -r .*`	This time, you will delete all of your hidden files at the CWD.
`rm -r . *`	If you put a space between the **.** and the *****, you are telling Unix first to delete **.**, which is the CWD. Unix will not reach the *****. I made this mistake once (using the ****) and deleted half my dissertation!
`\rm -rf dir`	The **** disables an alias (usually **-i**), and the **-f** forces a deletion. The result of this command line can be devastating. In a matter of seconds, you could wipe out your entire account.

DO NOT ENTER THESE COMMANDS!
DANGER DANGER DANGER DANGER DANGER DANGER DANGER DANGER DANGER DANGER

Figure 5.11   Dangerous Commands To Avoid!

5.8   REORGANIZING FILES

Are you superstitious? An old adage states that the more critical your work, the more likely it is that your system will crash. See footnote 3 on page 32. It is a true story! If you are not blessed with prescience about system crashes, I strongly advise that you frequently save and back up your work. You can make backups with the copy command, **cp**, but all those copies will eventually clutter your account. In this section, I present some techniques for reorganizing your files into different, clutter-free directories.

5.8.1   Proposed Directory Tree

When I first showed you copying and renaming, you did not worry about pathnames because I had you operate in the CWD. Reorganizing files into subdirectories other than the CWD, however, requires you to specify pathnames. So, instead of **mv oldfile**

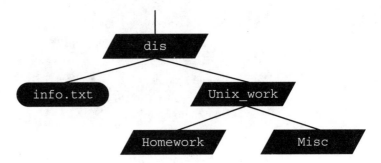

Figure 5.12 Current Directory Tree

newfile, you will now use **mv** *oldpath newpath* and likewise for **cp**. The sections that follow demonstrate how to use **mv** and **cp** with relative and absolute pathnames. To show you the process of organizing your account, I will have you reconfigure your present directory tree (Figure 5.12; see also Section 5.5.2) into a target directory tree (Figure 5.13).

PRACTICE!

47. For the examples that follow, you need the tree shown in Figure 5.12. (Note: dis is my **HOME**.) Create them if you have not done so already.

5.8.2 Copying Files into Another Directory

Your first task is copying info.txt from **HOME** to Unix_work/Misc. Using **cp** *source target* means that *source* is info.txt (along a path) and *target* is Misc (along a path). Which pathnames should you use? Well, you can express either or both pathnames as relative or absolute. Moreover, you need to decide from which CWD you will work. You could use **cd** to visit each directory, but why waste the time? (See Step 5.31.) Rather, I suggest setting the CWD to **HOME** and working from there:

Step 5.33: Copying by using relative pathnames

```
unix> cd                              Set CWD to HOME.
unix> cp info.txt Unix_Work/Misc      Copy ~/info.txt to ~/Unix_Work/Misc.
```

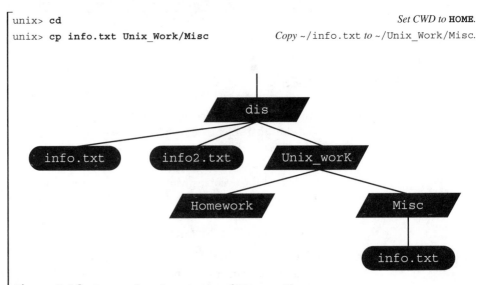

Figure 5.13 Intermediate Organization of Directory Tree

```
unix> ls Unix_Work/Misc                           Check your work inside Misc.
info.txt                            All is well. Note that the original file still exists.
```

Note that I could have entered **cp info.txt Unix_work/Misc/info.txt** or even chosen a different filename. When the copied file has the same name, you do not need to specify it again. What about absolute pathnames? Let's create info2.txt, which needs to be in **HOME**. You will work from Misc to demonstrate the handiness of absolute pathnames:

Step 5.34: Copying by using relative and absolute pathnames

```
unix> cd Unix_work/Misc                          Set CWD to ~/Unix_Work/Misc.
unix> pico info.txt              Change the contents of ~/Unix_Work/Misc/info.txt.
The contents of this info.txt do not matter.                   Make some changes.
unix> cp info.txt ~/info2.txt          Copy info.txt to info2.txt in HOME.
unix> ls ~                                             List contents of HOME.
Unix_work info.txt info2.txt and others    By now, you should have lots of files.
```

In this step, I take advantage of ~ with **~/info2.txt** to copy info2.txt in **HOME**. But you could stick with just relative pathnames! For example, from within Misc, you could have entered **cp info.txt ../../info2.txt**. In either case, your tree should now look like Figure 5.13.

PRACTICE!

> 48.   Create a text file called nvp.txt inside ~/Unix_work/Homework.
> 49.   Copy nvp.txt file to **HOME**, inside Unix_work/Homework (with a different name), inside Unix_work, and inside Unix_work/Misc.

5.8.3   Copying Directories

Copying entire directories requires the **-r** (recursive) option again. When you say **cp -r oldpath newpath**, you instruct Unix to copy everything in **oldpath** and make a new directory called **newpath**. Because the last name in a pathname is the name of interest (the file or directory upon which to operate), the last name on **oldpath** becomes the name of the copied directory (which is the last name on **newpath**). So, if you wish to put the copied directory anywhere other than the CWD, you must ensure that directories on **newpath** exist. Go back and read those sentences again. Welcome back! So, if you enter **cp -r A/B C/D**, Unix must check whether these directories exist. In particular, does the CWD contain A (which contains B) and C? If so, Unix will copy B into C and call the copied directory D. If D already exists, then B is copied into D. A brief example should help clarify these rules:

Step 5.35: Copying entire directories

```
unix> cd                                               Set CWD to HOME.
unix> mkdir CopyDir                                  Make new subdirectory.
unix> cd CopyDir                                     Set CWD to CopyDir.
unix> mkdir A C                          Make 2 subdirectories inside CopyDir.
unix> mkdir A/B                                 Make subdirectory B of A.
unix> pico A/B/stuff.txt                            Put file inside A/B.
unix> cp -r A/B C                       Copy entire B directory inside of C.
unix> more B/C/stuff.txt                       View contents of copied work.
```

If you find that you want to copy an entire directory (or anything else) to the CWD, remember that `.` stands for CWD and can be used in a path. So, if I want to copy a directory to my CWD, I can run **`cp oldpath .`**.

PRACTICE!

> 50. Display a directory tree for the example in Step 5.35.
> 51. Set your CWD to **HOME** and copy all of `~/CopyDir/A/C` there.

5.8.4 Moving Files into Another Directory

In this section, you will practice moving instead of copying. The notion of a pathname is still the same: **`mv oldpath newpath`**. However, moving does not leave the original copy: **mv** changes one pathname into another. As a result, **mv** moves files and even entire directories without having to explicitly use **-r** as you did with **cp** (Section 5.8.3). To demonstrate the process of moving files, you will reorganize your account to look like Figure 5.14.

Step 5.36: Move files into new directory

```
unix> cd                                Start from HOME.
unix> rm info.txt                       Delete needless info.txt from HOME.
unix> mkdir Unix_work/JUNK              Set up new directory.
unix> mv info2.txt Unix_work/JUNK      Move ~/info2.txt into Unix_work/JUNK.
```

As with **cp**, if you do not wish to change the filename of what you're moving, you do not need to specify the new filename as the pathname's last entry.

PRACTICE!

> 52. Move `info2.txt` back to **HOME**. (See Step 5.36.)
> 53. Now, repeat Step 5.36 with absolute pathnames.
> 54. Move `info2.txt` to `Homework`, using `Misc` as your CWD.
> 55. Move `info2.txt` back to `JUNK`.

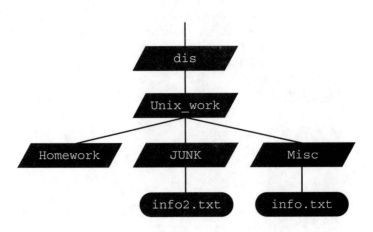

Figure 5.14 Directory Tree after Moving Files

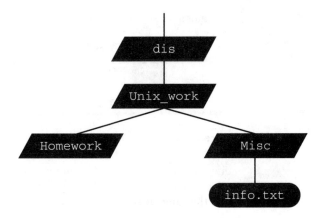

Figure 5.15 Final Organization of Directory Tree

5.8.5 Cleaning House

Now, you will practice "cleaning house" on your account by removing an unnecessary directory, namely, JUNK. When you are finished, your new tree will look like Figure 5.15. To remove everything inside JUNK (including that directory), use the recursive remove command with prompting, namely **rm -ir**:

Step 5.37: Cleaning House

```
unix> cd ~/Unix_work                          Set CWD to parent of JUNK.
unix> rm -ir JUNK                             Recursively remove all contents of JUNK.
rm: examine files in directory JUNK/ (yes/no)? y
rm: remove JUNK/info2.txt (yes/no)? y
rm: remove JUNK/: (yes/no)? y
unix> ls
Homework Misc
```

PRACTICE!

56. Create a subdirectory called DELETE_ME inside ~/Unix_work/Misc.
57. Change your CWD to DELETE_ME.
58. In ~/Unix_work/Misc copy info.txt to info_copy.txt.
59. Move info_copy.txt to DELETE_ME directory. (*Hint*: What's the relative pathname of the CWD?)
60. Now, delete DELETE_ME.

5.9 LINKS

Sooner or later you will go digging around for a Unix command and discover what seems odd notation. For example, if I produce a long list of **df** ("disk free"; Section 5.11) in /usr/bin on my system, I get the following:

```
unix> ls -l /usr/bin/df
lrwxrwxrwx 1 root root 10 Jul 23 2004 df -> ../sbin/df*
```

Two things should stand out: the file type (l) and the name (df -> ../sbin/df*). These items indicate that **/usr/bin/df** is a *link* to another file. A Unix link is a

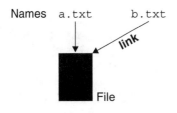
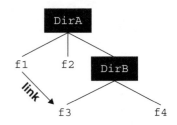

Figure 5.16 Depictions of Links

name that points to a file. So, on my system, when I run **df**, I really run **/sbin/df**. Figure 5.16 depicts two examples: b.txt is a link to a.txt, and f1 is a link to f3. So, with links, you can access a file with multiple names. Sure, that sounds great, but why? Sometimes a pathname is too long, so you can assign a link which gives you a shortcut. The following sections explain links further.

5.9.1   I-Nodes

I have avoided discussion of Unix's internal structure because it is better to teach students to use Unix for their work. But understanding the internal mechanism of any tool can greatly help you understand how to use that tool (and build a better version, too!). In Unix, one notion is the *i-node*, or index node. When you create a file, Unix carves out space in memory and assigns an i-node to that file. The i-node is a chunk of memory that stores a variety of information about a file (its permissions, owner, *i-node number*, etc.). Unix connects the filename to the i-node number, which is unique. The filename is a link to the file via the i-node number. You can see i-node numbers with **ls -i**:

Step 5.38: I-node numbers

```
unix> cd ~/Unix_work                        Work in a logical place.
unix> pico data1.txt                             Create a file.
unix> ls -i data1.txt               Show data1.txt's i-node number.
76021787 data1.txt               Your number will likely be different.
unix> pico data2.txt                           Edit another file.
unix> ls -i data.txt               Show data2.txt's i-node number.
76021789 data2.txt           Each file has a unique i-node number.
```

I-node numbers help explain certain features of Unix:

- Directories are a special kind of file. Why? Because directory names are links to their own i-node numbers. For example, try **ls -di ~/Unix_work** (list directory name and i-node number). I get the output 76021762 Unix_work, which means that Unix_work has an i-node number.

- Unix has no undelete because **rm** removes a link to an i-node. As demonstrated in the next section, you can have multiple links to the same i-node, but if you remove all the links, Unix reclaims the memory.

So, other than by copying and editing, how do you create links to files?

5.9.2   Hard Links

As discussed at the beginning of this section, a link allows you to associate multiple names with the same file (which means that each name has the same i-node number). One form of link is the ***hard link***, which you form which **ln** *source target*. A hard link will associate a filename with another filename, but you cannot make the association across file systems. So, if `file` exists in `/somewhere`, you cannot link a name that resides in `/somewhereelse` to `file`. Nor can you link a directory to another directory: **`ln dir1 dir2`** will not work. For practice with files, try to associate `b.txt` with `a.txt`, as follows (see Figure 5.16):

Step 5.39: Hard link

```
unix> pico a.txt                                          Edit a.txt.
I am a.txt!                                          Write some text.
unix> ln a.txt b.txt               Create link b.txt that points to a.txt.
```

Now you will confirm that `b.txt` links to `a.txt`:

Step 5.40: Confirm hard links

```
unix> ls -i a.txt b.txt                            Show i-node numbers.
76021787 a.txt  76021787 b.txt     They're identical because b.txt points to a.txt.
unix> more b.txt                                          View b.txt.
I am a.txt                            You see a.txt because of the link.
unix> pico b.txt                   Editing b.txt means editing a.txt.
I was here.                       Change b.txt, which changes a.txt.
unix> more a.txt                                          View a.txt.
I was here.
```

When you edit `b.txt`, you are really editing `a.txt`, because `b.txt` is simply another name for `a.txt`. The name `b.txt` just points to `a.txt` and does not form a different file.

5.9.3   Symbolic Links

If you would like to link across file systems (and link directories), create a ***symbolic link*** (or *soft link*) with **`ln -s source target`**. This kind of link can create a shortcut to a file or directory "far away." For example, create the link `f1→f3` in the second structure in Figure 5.16:

Step 5.41: Create directory tree

```
unix> mkdir DirA                                  Create new subdirectory.
unix> cd DirA                                       Set CWD to DirA.
unix> mkdir DirB                                    Create DirA/DirB.
unix> pico DirB/f3                             Create f3 inside DirA/DirB.
Hello, I am f3.                                     Write some text.
unix> ln -s DirB/f3 f1                        Link DirA/f1 to DirA/DirB/f3.
unix> more f1                                     Check symbolic link f1.
Hello, I am f3.                                   f1 points to DirB/f3.
```

You can use **`ls`** to indicate symbolic links:

Step 5.42: Show links when listing

```
unix> ls -F                                  List file types of CWD (DirA).
DirB/  f1@                   Symbols: directory ( / ), symbolic link (@).
unix> ls -l f1                                   Long list a symbolic link.
lrwxrwxrwx 1 dis dis 7 Apr 2 01:52 f1 -> DirB/f3    Unix indicates the link.
```

As a reminder, when you generate a long list of a symbolic link, Unix shows the first field as 1 and the last field as the link pointing to the source file. (See also **ls -L *link*** to show the file that the symbolic link references.) Finally, as promised, you can link directories with symbolic links, which helps you to create shortcuts to "deep" subdirectories:

Step 5.43: Linking directories

```
unix> cd ~/Unix_work               Work somewhere logical.
unix> mkdir A1 A1/A2 A1/A2/A3                  Create tree.
unix> ln -s A1/A2/A3 A4          Create link A4 to A1/A2/A3.
unix> pico A4/test.txt           Create a file inside A4.
Hello!                                    Type something.
unix> ls A1/A2/A3                       List A3's contents.
test.txt                         You see the same test.txt.
```

Step 5.44: Changing directories with links

```
unix> cd A4                                Set CWD to A4.
unix> pwd                                     Report CWD.
/home/dis/Unix_work/A4               Unix uses the link's path.
unix> cd ..                           Go up one directory.
unix> pwd                                     Report CWD.
unix> /home/dis/Unix_work/A1/A2  Unix displays the real path now.
```

In the preceding example, anything you do inside A4 changes A1/A2/A3, because A4 points to A3. So, when you go to A4's parent, you are really going to A1/A2, which is A3's parent. If you wish to navigate directly with A4, investigate **pushd**, **popd**, and **dirs**, which many shells provide.

PRACTICE!

61. What happens if you delete b.txt? (See Section 5.9.2.)
62. How can you use a hard link to help avoid losing a file?
63. Using the tree in Figure 5.16, link f4 to f2.
64. Create a directory DirC inside DirB. Link DirC to DirA.

5.10 FILES: NAMES, TYPES, AND PERMISSIONS

This section ties together a number of concepts and develops some others more thoroughly in order to give you greater flexibility when you begin to organize your account and operate on files.

5.10.1 File-Matching Metacharacters (Wildcards)

Throughout the text, I occasionally use an asterisk (*) in the command line to indicate groups of files in a particular directory. For example, **ls *.txt** will list all files in the CWD that terminate with .txt. Unix shells provide *file-matching metacharacters* (sometimes called *wildcards*), which are characters that represent patterns of text in filenames. These metacharacters should seem similar to those used in regular expressions, but the symbols have different meanings, as follows:

- Asterisk (*): Represent 0 or more instances of any character. If the filename begins with a dot (.), the * will not match the name unless you say .*.

- Question mark (**?**): Match exactly one character.
- Square brackets **[]**: Select any character between the brackets. You can use a hyphen (**-**) to express a continuous range, as in **a-z**, **D-S**, and **1-5**. Backwards ranges are unpredictable. If you would like to provide a list of characters to exclude, use a caret (**^**) as the first character in the list (e.g., [**^a-z**] excludes all lowercase letters).
- Backslash ****: Interpret the next character as a literal character. For example, **more a\ b** will view a file called **a b** (which includes a blank space in the middle).

Here are some examples that you should try:

Step 5.45: Wildcard: *

```
unix> cd                                      Set CWD to HOME.
unix> ls *.txt                                List all files ending with .txt.
a.txt  b.txt                                  You'll have different files.
unix> ls .*                                   List all hidden files.
.aliases .csrch .login                        You will see files like these.
unix> ls A*.ps                   List all files that start with letter A and end with .ps.
Probably no output.                           I picked a rather restrictive criteria.
```

Step 5.46: Wildcard: ?

```
unix> cd Unix_work                            Work elsewhere.
unix> mkdir AAA ABA ACA                        Create 3 directories here.
unix> ls A?A                       List the contents of any directory with 3 letters,
                                                    beginning and ending with A.
AAA:                                      Unix matches all three directories
ABA:                                            and attempts to list each,
ACA:                                                   one at a time.
```

Step 5.47: Wildcard: [ ]

```
unix> ls A[AB]A                               List AAA or ABA.
Unix outputs AAA and ABA.                     You could also say ls A[A-B]A
unix> ls A[A-Z]?                    Match this pattern: A, any uppercase character,
Unix outputs AAA, ABA, and ACA.                            any character.
```

Step 5.48: Wildcard: \

```
unix> echo \\\*                               Echo text.
\*                                    \\ becomes \, and \* becomes *.
```

5.10.2 Oddball File, Directory, and Pathnames

Now and then, you will encounter odd characters in the command line. For example, to view something with a * you need to say *****. The backslash (****) tells Unix to interpret the next character literally. What if a file has a dash? As an experiment, run **pico** (no filename), type something, and then save your work to a file called -. That's right, just a hyphen. If you try to remove the file called - with **rm -**, Unix thinks that you have forgotten the command line arguments! Instead, you need to enter **rm - -**. Yep, hyphen, space, hyphen! For other weirdness, here are some common tips:

- Names beginning with -: Include an extra hyphen and space—for example, **rm - -test.txt**.
- Names with spaces: Use **\Spacebar**—for example, **rm My\ Data.txt**.
- Names with other characters: Use quotes and the backslash. For example, **mkdir '*&^;'** creates a directory called *&^; (which is an insane name). To remove it, enter **rmdir *\&\^\;**. See Chapter 8 for more quoting rules.

PRACTICE!

65. Create a text file that has a space in the middle of its name. Then, delete the file.
66. Why is naming a directory * an extraordinarily bad idea?
67. Show a command line that lists all unhidden files and directories that do not start with a number.
68. Show a command line that lists all files and directories with only three letters.

5.10.3 File Types Summarized

As you explore Unix, you will encounter various file types. **ls -F** indicates four common types:

- "Regular file": no trailing character
- Directory: / (e.g., Homework/)
- Executable: * (e.g., /usr/bin/ls*)
- Symbolic link: @ (e.g., A4@)

For more types, see **man ls** under the **-F** option.

5.10.4 File Listing Summarized

Table 5.1 summarizes various options for **ls**. For more options and information about each, see **man ls**.

TABLE 5.1 Various ls Options

Option	Description	Example
none	list all unhidden files in CWD	ls
	list all hidden files in CWD	ls .*
	list *path1* and *path2* and …	ls path1 path2
-a	list everything, including hidden files, ., and ..	ls -a ~
-A	list everything, excluding . and ..	ls -A ~
-d	list only a directory's name, not its contents	ls -as ~
-F	indicate file types	ls -adF ~
-h	show sizes in "human-readable" format	ls -h ~
-i	show i-node number	ls -il
-l	produce a long list: show lots of information	ls -al ~
-L	show the file that a symbolic link references	ls -L /usr/bin/*
-q	show nonprinting characters in a filename as a ?	ls -q ~
-r	list in reverse order	ls -raF ~
-R	list recursively: list everything in everything	ls -R ~
-x	list columns across instead of down	ls -x ~

5.10.5 File and Directory Permissions

Whenever you create a tree and manage the directories in your account, be mindful that you need to protect your work from prying and unscrupulous eyes. Section 4.10 introduces techniques to set file permissions but only touches upon directory permissions. All the commands and options that are used with **chmod** also apply to directories, but some have different features. As a reminder, **ls -l**'s first field (the file type) will show a hyphen (-) for "regular files," d for directories, and l for symbolic links:

Step 5.49: Show permissions

```
unix> cd ~/Unix_work                                    Don't clutter your HOME.
unix> touch a.txt                          A cool way to create a file if it does not exist.
unix> ls -alF                                        Long list everything in the CWD.
drwxr-xr-x  3 dis dis 4096 Apr 2 14:50 ./                               CWD.
drwx------ 49 dis dis 8192 Apr 2 14:16 ../                            Parent.
drwxr-xr-x  3 dis dis 4096 Apr 2 13:09 A1/                       Subdirectory.
lrwxrwxrwx  1 dis dis    8 Apr 2 13:10 A4 -> A1/A2/A3/          Symbolic link.
-rw-r--r--  1 dis dis    0 Apr 2 14:50 a.txt              Regular, but empty, file.
```

Setting the permission on a directory with the use of **chmod** follows the same pattern shown in Section 4.10. The following command removes all external access to your account, represented by the ~ for **HOME**:

Step 5.50: Remove external access to your account

```
unix> chmod go-rwx ~                       Remove group and world access to HOME.
```

To be extra safe, you can use **chmod -R**, which recursively sets permissions. You have seen a recursive call with **ls** and **rm**. So, you can change all permissions on everything in all directories for a specified path:

Step 5.51: Remove all access to all your files

```
unix> cd                                                             Go HOME.
unix> chmod -R go-rwx *          Remove all permissions (except hidden files in HOME).
unix> chmod -R go-rwx .*                         Remove access for hidden files.
```

After you learn more about configuring your shell, look up **umask** and setting permissions with numbers instead of letters. You can have **umask** automatically set permissions whenever you create files. (See Chapter 8 for discussion on customizing your sessions.)

Here is a handy trick for directories: You may choose to set only x. Why? Perhaps a trusted friend or teacher needs to see a particular file. So, you can grant only x permission to a particular directory. someone else who wants to **cd** to that location must know the name, as the disabled r prevents it from being listed:

Step 5.52: Grant only x permission for restricted access

```
unix> chmod go+x ~                      Allow directory access (but not listing) to HOME.
unix> mkdir ~/ReadmE1                                        Create new directory.
unix> chmod go-rw ReadmE1                    Prevent editing and listing of ReadmE1.
unix> chmod go+x ReadmE1                   Allow external user to cd ~you/ReadmE1.
```

You might prefer to keep r permission on ReadmE1 to make the external user's life easier. Why the strange filename for "read me?" README and readme are common filenames, so I use an obfuscated name.

5.11 ARCHIVING AND STORAGE

When the "old-timers" started with computers, memory was scarce and expensive. Nowadays, it seems that storage capacity keeps growing in leaps and bounds. However, with large image files, account restrictions, and the need to transfer large numbers of files, you will still find many archiving and compression commands useful.

5.11.1 File Size

Computers count your characters in terms of bytes (eights bits, each a 0 or a 1). You can use **ls -h** to see readable file sizes.

Step 5.53: File size

```
unix> cd                          Go home.
unix> ls -AFhl                    Long list of all files in readable sizes and types.
Lengthy output.                   Look for sizes with K, M, and other symbols.
```

5.11.2 Quota

Many systems place a **quota** on your account, or a limit on the amount of available memory for your files. To allow users to check their account usage, many systems employ the **quota username** command:

Step 5.54: Check quota

```
unix> quota dis                                         Check my quota.
Filesystem    usage quota limit timeleft    files quota limit timeleft
/home/dis      9835 15000 15050             1085  2050  2100
```

If **quota** reports nothing, you might have an unlimited quota. That, however, does not mean that the system has unlimited memory! Otherwise monitor the usage slot frequently. Usually, this quantity cannot exceed the quota slot.

5.11.3 Disk Resources and Usage

If you are worried about your system lacking physical memory, try **df**, which I like to call *disk free*. **df** will scan throughout the mounted file systems and report the space consumption:

Step 5.55: Report amount of remaining free space

```
unix> df -h                                    Use -h for human-readable sizes.
Filesystem        size  used  avail  capacity  Mounted on
/dev/dsk/c0t0d0s6 3.2G  1.7G  1.5G   53%       /usr
Many others listed.
```

To find out how much space your stuff consumes, use **du**, or disk usage. As with **df**, **du** has numerous options. In particular, use **-h** for human sizes and **-s** to sum all the sizes. Otherwise, **du** will show the size of every directory, recursively:

Step 5.56:   Report your space consumption

```
unix> cd ; du -hs                    Report my total consumption, in human-readable form.
3.2G  .                              I am using about 3.2 gigabytes as of today.
```

5.11.4 Compression

Various programs can compress a file's size by rearranging and encoding the file's contents. For simple compression, try **compress**, especially because of the easy-to-remember name. Note that **compress** *file* will append a .Z to *file*:

Step 5.57:   File compressions

```
unix> cd ~/Unix_work                              Work here.
unix> cp /usr/dict/words .                        Copy a big file to your CWD.
unix> ls -hl words                                Long list of files in readable form.
-r--r--r-- 1 dis dis 202K Apr 6 2002 words        202 kilobytes worth of words!
unix> compress words                              Shrink words to words.Z.
unix> ls -hl words.Z                              Check the compression of words.
-r--r--r-- 1 dis dis 103K Apr 6 2002 words.Z      Wow—the size is cut in half!
```

If you try to view words.Z, Unix will alert you that the file is *binary*, which means that the text characters were converted into possibly unrecognizable patterns of bits. To restore a compressed file, use **uncompress** *file.**Z**:

Step 5.58:   Uncompressing a file

```
unix> uncompress words.Z                          Restore words.
unix> ls -hl                                      Long list of files in readable form.
-r--r--r-- 1 dis dis 202K Apr 6 2002 words        words is restored.
```

You may also encounter GNU's **gzip** compression, which appends gz instead of Z to the filename. Use **gzip** *file* to compress a file and **gzip -d** *file* or **gunzip** to decompress a file. (See **man gzip** for more information.)

5.11.5 Archiving

To save account space, you can also pack particularly large files together into one file. Imagine packing boxes together into one big box: You rearrange contents and compress voids wherever possible. When you unpack the big box, you would then need to reassemble all the individual elements. There are three common "boxing" programs that you will likely encounter: **tar**, **zip**, and **gzip**. I am not sure how the name "zip" arose—perhaps in reference to zipping up luggage with stuff inside? First, I need you to create a small tree with which to work:

Step 5.59:   Some files to archive

```
unix> cd ~/Unix_work                              Back to work!
unix> mkdir A A/B Test1 Test2                      Create some subdirectories.
unix> pico A/B/c.txt                               Create a text file in B.
Hello!                                             Write something.
```

The **tar** (or *tape archiver*) packs files and directories together into a single file called a *tar file*. Technically, **tar** refers to storage on magnetic tape, but you may use **tar** to archive a file. Here is a summary of the common options and their syntax:

- Create tar file: **tar cvf *tarfile files*** (**c** for create, **v** for verbose mode, **f** to specify **tarfile**). You supply the name **tarfile** (e.g., **something.tar**). For example, **tar cvf work.tar *** will tar everything in the current working directory into a file called **work.tar**.
- Extract contents: **tar xvf *tarfile*** extracts the contents of **tarfile** (**x** for extract).
- Display contents: **tar tvf *tarfile*** displays a table of contents for **tarfile** (**t** for table of contents).

Now you can archive the tree you created in Step 5.59:

Step 5.60: **tar** example

```
unix> tar cvf stuff.tar A          Archive everything in A (including A) in stuff.tar.
a A/ 0K                            Unix reports each file being archived.
a A/B/ 0K                          To disable verbosity, don't use v.
a A/B/c.txt 1K
unix> mv stuff.tar Test1           Move the archive to another place.
unix> cd Test1                     Go to Test1.
unix> tar xvf stuff.tar            Extract the tree in Test1.
tar: blocksize = 6                 More verbiage.
x A, 0 bytes, 0 tape blocks        Unix is extracting the tree in
x A/B, 0 bytes, 0 tape blocks      its entirety at this CWD!
x A/B/c.txt, 4 bytes, 1 tape blocks
unix> ls -F                        Check new contents of Test1.
A/ stuff.tar                       Yes, the archive is here.
```

zip is another popular archiving program. In fact, **zip** works on many platforms outside of Unix:

- Create zip file: **zip *zipfile files*** will create a *zip file* from **files**. For example, **zip zipfile *** will zip all files in the CWD into **zipfile**.
- Unzip zip file: **unzip** file.

Now you can use **zip** to archive the same tree that you used in Step 5.60:

Step 5.61: Zip and unzip files

```
unix> cd ~/Unix_work              Return to work.
unix> zip -r stuff.zip A          Recursively zip all files from A.
unix> mv stuff.zip Test2          Move zip file.
unix> cd Test2                    Go to Test2.
unix> unzip stuff.zip             Unzip zip file.
creating: A/                      Unix extracts the tree
creating: A/B/                    in the CWD.
extracting: A/B/c.txt
```

For quick help on **zip**, enter it without any options or arguments. I will leave **gzip** as an exercise. **gzip** is GNU's zip program, which is quite popular because of Linux.

However, if you ever see a tgz extension (a ***tgz file***), then you likely have a tar file that has been compressed with **gzip** (i.e., file.tar.gz). You have two choices to unzip the file:

- Standard **tar**: Use **gunzip < file.tar.gz | tar xvf** - or **gunzip < file.tgz | tar xvf** -. The vertical bar (|) is a *pipe*, and the < is a *redirection operator*.
- GNU's **tar**: Use **tar xvzf file.tar.gz** or **tar xvzf file.tgz**. For me, GNU's **tar** has the path /usr/local/gnu/bin/tar. So, you might have to do some digging around.

You can get much more intensive information with **man tar**, **man zip**, and **man gzip**.

5.11.6 External Archiving

Although I doubt that you will be archiving anything to tape, you might very likely use a CD, a DVD, external memory, or even a floppy disk. Although floppy disks are pretty much antiquated, see **volcheck**. The **mount** command can be used by system administrators to mount devices. Look inside /dev, and you will see directories for mounted devices. I suggest that you consult with your local system administrators for available commands.

PRACTICE!

72. Store two text files, t1.txt and t2.txt, inside directory ~/Unix_work/ TEST.
73. Tar the directory TEST into a file called test.tar.
74. Show the contents of test.tar.
75. Extract the contents from test.tar.
76. If you have access to **gzip**, create a gzipped tar file (stuff.tgz) by using the tree in Step 5.59.
77. Unzip stuff.tgz.

5.12 APPLICATION: MORE DIRECTORY OPERATIONS

This section presents a few commands that can assist you with file management.

5.12.1 Comparing Directories

dircmp will compare directories side by side for any difference between them. For large amounts of output, you should use a pager:

Step 5.62: Directory comparison

```
unix> cd ~/Unix_work                                     Working from our favorite spot.
unix> mkdir DC DC/A DC/B DC/B/C                              Create a directory tree.
unix> pico DC/B/C/data.txt                                   Create file inside DC/C.
Hello!                                                                      Write text.
unix> cd DC                                                            Set CWD to DC.
unix> dircmp A B | less               Compare contents of A and B; page through results.
Apr  2 20:04 2005   A only and B only Page 1
./a.txt              ./C
                     ./C/data.txt
You might need to step through a bit more or use q or ^C to quit.
```

5.12.2 Searching for files

Just as you can search for text in files, you can search for files in a directory tree with the **find** command. The trouble is that the command's syntax is not as intuitive as other commands. Perhaps the most basic syntax is **find** *path*, which prints out the directory tree starting with *path*:

Step 5.63: Display directory path with find

```
unix> cd ~/Unix_work/DC                               Set CWD to DC.
unix> find.                                           Report directory tree for the CWD.
.
./A
./A/a.txt
./B
./B/C
./B/C/data.txt
```

To find a specific file, use **find** *path* **-name** *file*:

Step 5.64: Find a file

```
unix> find . -name data.txt                          Search directory tree for data.txt.
../B/C/data.txt                                      Unix reports the file's location.
```

With **find**, you can even run commands as you find certain files. With the **-exec** option, you specify certain commands to execute. For example, suppose that I want to delete all files ending with .txt in a tree. Then I might try the following:

Step 5.65: Remove specified files in a tree

```
unix> find . -name '*.txt' -exec rm {} \;            Remove all txt files.
unix> find .                                         Show current tree.
.                                                    Unix cannot show data.txt
./A                                                  because you deleted it!
./B
./B/C
```

Indeed, **find** can do much, much more! I will leave you to discover its power with **man find**.

PROFESSIONAL SUCCESS: REMEMBERING UNIX COMMANDS

Many people complain that Unix can be cryptic. After all, why couldn't the listing command, **ls**, be "list" instead? Well, it could have been—but more important matters dominated when the command was born. Recall that Unix was designed when saving memory was of supreme importance. A bit and byte saved here and there made all the difference. Now, many years later, too many applications have been built around the original command suite for sweeping changes to be made. But even if destiny chose another path, you probably would get sick of typing "list" anyway. People do invent easier operating systems, but few ever manage to thrive in the marketplace. Until one does, review these tricks to understand and memorize important Unix commands:

- *Translation*: Commands usually abbreviate longer names—**ls** abbreviates *list*, **mv** abbreviates *move*, **cp** abbreviates *copy*, and so forth. Always try to find such English equivalents.

- *Syntax*: Every command has syntax, which is a specific structure for command input and manner of usage. You must follow the syntax to obtain the results you desire. For example, you can distinguish two common uses of **ls** by their syntax: Entered alone, **ls** lists the contents of the current working directory, but entered as **ls** *directory*, **ls** lists the contents of *directory*. Similarly, the command **cp** follows the syntax **cp** *source target*, whereby **cp** duplicates the contents of *source* and places them into *target*—and the order of the pathnames cannot be reversed. Memorize the syntax for commands whenever possible.

- *Vocalization*: Do you notice how I try to translate command syntax into full sentences now and then? Try making the following sentence out of **cp** syntax: "Copy the contents of the original file, source, into a new file, target." Now repeat this sort of sentence for other commands until the meaning sinks in.

- *Memorization*: A full sentence aids in understanding but is difficult to memorize, so try shortening your vocalizations of commands. For instance, rather than plodding through the previous long sentence, say, "**cp** copies one file into another." Eventually, "**cp** duplicates files" should suffice.

- *Practice*: Practice the command **cp** with actual files. Try testing the results by viewing the contents of both files. (You should see no difference between them.) Practice using your commands by themselves and with options, especially right after learning them. Practice each method of comprehension until you feel comfortable. Keep trimming down your vocal translations until the commands become second nature. If you run into problems, you can access Unix's online help with the command **man** *command*. Soon you will impress your friends and family by deciphering "cryptic" Unix!

CHAPTER SUMMARY

- In Unix, directories are a special kind of file.

- Directories can store files and other directories. You can think of the Unix file system as a tree, starting at the root and terminating at files or empty directories at every level.

- Your account (variable **HOME**) exists in the Unix file system.

- The current working directory is set by going to a directory with **cd**.

- You can specify a directory path as relative (starting at CWD) or absolute (starting at *root*).

- You can use these directory shortcuts in a pathname: **.** (CWD), **..** (parent of CWD), **~** (**HOME**), and **/** (*root*).

- You should create directories (use **mkdir**) to organize your files and other directories.

- **cp** and **mv** rely upon the use of either relative or absolute pathnames. **mv** moves and renames files. It can also move and rename directories. **cp** copies files. To copy entire directories, use the **-r** option.

- **rm** deletes files. Do not use **rm** unless it has the **-i** option set. **rm** has some extremely dangerous options that should be used only with utmost caution. Unix lacks an undelete command!

- Every file has a unique internal number called the i-node number. Multiple files can link to the same i-node. When a file has no links to its i-node, Unix deletes the file from the system.

- You can link multiple names to the same file with **ln**. If you use **ln** **-s** (a symbolic link), you link multiple names to directories.

- Unix shells support file-matching metacharacters to assist with identifying groups of files at the command line. These metacharacters are different from regular-expression metacharacters!
- You should protect your directories, as well as files, with **chmod**.
- You can use **tar** and **zip** to create archive files that pack together groups of other files and directories.
- Besides searching for files, **find** has many other uses.

KEY TERMS

absolute pathname	hard link	root
backup	i-node	subdirectory
branch	leaf	symbolic link
current working directory (CWD)	link	tar file
deletion	pathname	tgz file
directory	quota	zip file
file-matching metacharacter	relative pathname	

COMMAND SUMMARY

cd	Change directory.
chmod	Change permissions.
compress	Compress file (.Z).
cp	Copy file or directory (**-r**).
df	Show free space in system.
dircmp	Compare two directories.
dtfile	Run GUI file manager.
du	Show your disk usage.
echo	Show variable value.
find	Search for a file (and much more).
gunzip	GNU unzip .gz files.
gzip	GNU zip (.gz).
ln	Make link.
ls	List files.
mkdir	Make a directory.
mv	Rename or move a file or directory.
pilot	Run 2-D text-based browser.
pwd	Print CWD.
quota	Show your account quota (if any).
rm	Remove a file or directory (**rm -r**). Use interactively! (**rm -i**, **rm -ir**).
rmdir	Remove an empty directory.
tar	Archive files and directories.
touch	Modify file's time stamp; create a new file.
uncompress	Uncompress .Z files.
unzip	Unzip .zip files.
zip	Archive files and directories (**-r**) into a zip file (.zip).

Problems

1. Name three examples of trees that provide a hierarchical structure to something you know. For example, I used a genealogy in this chapter. What else can you think of?
2. Can all filenames be directory names?

3. Is the directory name 1_2_3_4 acceptable in Unix? Why or why not?

4. What are two names for the uppermost directory in Unix?

5. What does *current working directory* mean?

6. Assume that your current working directory is /home/jre/Data. What is the absolute pathname of the parent directory?

7. Assume that your current working directory is /home/jre/Data. Which directory in this path is a child of jre? Specify a relative pathname.

8. What are two ways, not including absolute pathnames, of listing your current working directory?

9. Can you view the contents of a directory with **more**? Why or why not?

10. Assume that your working directory is **HOME**. What are three ways of listing the contents of **HOME**, using **ls** and only one command line for each?

11. Assume that your working directory is *root*. What is your working directory if you enter the command **cd ..**? Explain your answer.

12. What is the relative pathname of *root* for your system, starting from **HOME**?

13. What command line will change your CWD to a friend's **HOME** directory? Assume that your working directory is your own **HOME** and that your friend has the username rogil. Show both absolute and relative pathname methods of changing the CWD.

14. Assume that the text file info.txt has the path /home/dis/Unix_work/info.txt. Assume also that your working directory is your HOME, not dis. Show how to view the contents of info.txt, using just one command line with an absolute pathname.

15. Describe a sequence of command lines that use only relative pathnames with which you could view the same info.txt file described in Problem 14. (*Hint*: There are several ways to achieve the same goal. Assume that **dis**'s account allows access for **cd** and **ls**.)

16. Why does Unix lack a shortcut for going down a directory level?

17. This problem is for C Shell and Korn Shell users only: What are four ways of returning to your **HOME** directory from another directory with just one command line and one use of **cd**? Hint: Think of two ways in which the tilde (~) can be used.

18. Assume that you create an empty subdirectory, Empty, in **HOME**. First, you enter **cd ~/Empty** and then **rmdir ..**. Describe and explain what happens.

19. Make a subdirectory in your account called C. Now make a subdirectory B within C. Finally, make a subdirectory A inside B. What is the absolute pathname of A? Be sure to show the sequence of command lines you entered.

20. Show the command line for deleting an entire tree located at ~/Unix_work/something.

21. What does the command line **ls -aF** produce? Would entering **ls -Fa** change the output?

22. What is the difference between the Unix commands **cp** and **mv**?

23. Is the command line **cp test1 test1** valid for file test1? Why or why not?

24. Create a file called ._test.txt inside **HOME**. What command line would you enter to view the contents of ._test.txt? How would you view all of the contents of **HOME**?

25. Does **mv data1 data2** produce the same or a different i-node number for data2? Explain your answer.

26. Does **cp data2 data3** produce the same or a different i-node number for data3? Explain your answer.

27. Will the command lines **cp file1 file2** and **cp ./file1 ./file2** produce different results? Explain your answer.

28. Create a text file test1.txt and a subdirectory called TEST inside **HOME**. Set your current working directory to **HOME**. Move test1.txt inside TEST. Change your current working directory to TEST. Copy test1.txt to test2.txt in **HOME** without changing directories.

    The following information pertains to Problems 29–36: Suppose that your username is edemaitr and that all user accounts on your system are stored in /home. You want to obtain files from your instructor, whose username is jdelmar. All of jdelmar's files are stored in the parent directory /home/jdelmar/Class, and all files and directories are completely accessible for copying. Your system employs either a C or a Korn Shell.

29. Show the command line that jdelmar would have to enter to grant read and execute permission for the world for jdelmar's **HOME**.

30. What are three different command lines that will list all the contents of /home/jdelmar/Class, assuming that your CWD is **HOME**? (*Hint*: One is relative, one is absolute, and another uses a tilde shortcut.)

31. How would you set the CWD to /home/jdelmar/Class? How would you now list the contents of the CWD?

32. Working from **HOME**, how would you copy a file called /home/jdelmar/Class/vortex.ps to your **HOME** directory with the use of only one command line?

33. Working from the CWD /home/jdelmar/Class, how would you use a relative pathname to copy the file vortex.ps to your **HOME** directory?

34. Working from CWD of ~jdelmar/Class, how would you copy the file called /home/jdelmar/Class/vortex.ps to your ~/Unix_work subdirectory?

35. What does the command line **cp ~jdelmar/Class/vortex.ps ~/** do?

36. What does the command line **cp ~jdelmar/Class/vortex.ps ~/v1.ps** do?

37. Show the command lines that create a a tree with the following pathnames, starting from ~/Unix_work as your CWD: A, A/B, A/B/C, A/B/D, A/B/D/E. You will use this tree for Problems 38–40.

38. Show the command line that creates a symbolic link from A to E.

39. Show the command lines that create a tar file and a zip file for this tree.

40. Show the command line that searches for a file called stuff.txt in the entire tree.

41. Suppose that you are coordinating a project to design widgets. As project manager, you need to organize various tasks, including research, scheduling, analysis, and inspection. What other tasks might be associated with a large design project? Identify several categories of project work, and think of at least two other subtasks associated with each. For instance, analysis might involve choosing software, developing test cases, and determining results. Create directories and subdirectories for these tasks and subtasks. Provide thorough examples of your command-line sequences, and edit your report with a text editor. Draw a

directory tree that depicts your organization. Use **dtfile** (or a similar file manager) to display the tree.

42. Organize your account such that the pathname ~/Unix_work/A/B/C is viable. Store three text files called a1, b1, and c1 in subdirectory C. Now, store three text files called a2, b2, and c2 inside ~/Unix_work. Move a1 and a2 to A, b1 and b2 to B, and c1 and c2 to C. Write a list of all your command lines.

6

Communication and the Internet

6.1   COMMUNICATION

All projects require communication, because they are completed by teamwork (and your supervisors' instructions). Whether talking to coworkers, sending updates, or writing reports, your interaction with other people is essential. Traditional means of communication include memos and telephones. Computers have enhanced such communications with data transfer, Web browsing, and e-mail. Unix provides a wide variety of tools well suited to these and related tasks. For teaching introductory Unix, I prefer to classify the three kinds of communication that you need to learn:

- *Communication with your computer* via devices, programs, and processes. In Unix, you spend a great deal of time communicating with a shell. You can learn this kind of communication in Unix with this book and by consulting a users' manual.

- *Communication with other users* by chatting, writing, e-mailing, and researching information about local users. We cover these programs in this chapter.

- *Communicating with the world* by searching or surfing the Internet, publishing Web pages, e-mailing (again), and more. Many of these tasks overlap with communication with other users, so we'll examine some helpful programs in this chapter, too.

To orient you, this chapter presents a slimmed-down, high-level view of networking. If the concepts strike your interest, I strongly recommend checking out other sources as well.

OBJECTIVES

After reading this chapter, you should be able to:

- Determine the IP address of your local system and other hosts.
- Obtain news on the state of your Unix system.
- Use tools for dates and times, which can help you manage your schedule.
- Chat with someone online.
- E-mail other users.
- Log onto a remote system.
- Run a command on a remote system.
- Transfer files between local and remote systems.
- Use USENET.
- Browse the Web.

6.2 NETWORKING

To communicate with one another, computers require a ***network***—a collection of connected computers. Networks of connected computers exist on local and global scales. This section provides a high-level description of networks, extending to the Internet.

6.2.1 LAN

A ***local area network*** (LAN) connects a group of computers that are in relatively close proximity to one another. Each computer connected to the LAN "listens" for *packets*— small bursts of electronic data. *Protocols* govern how networked computers interact while transferring such information. Many protocols feature common programs, such as `ftp` and `telnet` (explained later in this chapter), although more modern tools can replace these programs because of security concerns. Unix employs *transmission control protocols/Internet protocols* (TCP/IP). Fully describing TCP/IP is beyond the scope of this text, but you should know that Unix shares these protocols with the Internet. In fact, one of Unix's greatest strengths is this "natural understanding" of the Internet.

6.2.2 WANs and The Internet

A ***wide area network*** (WAN) connects a geographically dispersed conglomeration of computers that share information. The ***Internet*** is the largest of all WANs, with millions of nodes, or connected computers. Sharing TCP/IP protocols with the Internet has enhanced Unix's utility in local and global communication, enabling Unix to provide efficient programs for e-mail, file transfer, chatting, and browsing the World Wide Web. Most computers, in fact, share common protocols for transmitting, receiving, and translating information.

The Internet evolved out of the ARPANET, a communications network devised by the United States military to survive a nuclear attack. Today, commercial, educational, and private organizations dominate the Internet, which has rapidly become a necessity for research, information, commerce, advertising, and entertainment. Who's in charge? Technically, no one controls the Internet. However, several organizations, such as the *Internet Engineering Task Force* (IETF, *http://www.ietf.org*), the *Internet Architecture Board* (IAB, *http://www.iab.org*), and the *Internet Society* (ISOC, *http://www.isoc.org*), help set standards.

6.2.3 Hostnames

To communicate across networks, computers need to know each other's addresses. Each ***host*** on the Internet is a computer that can communicate with other connected computers. System administrators give hosts specific ASCII names, called ***hostnames*** (also called *domains*), to help humans identify the different machines. For example, when I access my network remotely, I can use `devildog.cs.cornell.edu`. Anyone who has accessed the World Wide Web has seen many commercial hostnames, such as `www.google.com` and more. You could look at a host's hostname as *computer.server.organization.domain*, although this is a simplification. The last portion, the *domain*, is formally called a ***top-level domain*** (TLD). Common top-level domains are com, edu, gov, mil, net, org, and two-letter country abbreviations. For example, the island nation of Tuvalu scored big time because it was assigned tv! *The Internet Network Information Center* (InterNIC, *http://www.internic.net*) currently assigns TLDs and hostnames. In recent years, InterNIC has added new top-level domains, including *aero, biz, coop, info, museum, name,* and *pro*.

6.2.4   IP Addresses

For hosts connected to the Internet, the human hostnames have numerical equivalents called **IP addresses**, based on the "IP" portion of TCP/IP. Current IP addresses have 32 bits, taking the form *n.n.n.n,* where *n* is a number between 0 and 255. The decimal values help humans, because the underlying values are binary. This standard is called *IPv4.* To see a particular IP address associated with a hostname, try **host *hostname*:**

Step 6.1:   Hostname

```
unix> host www.prenhall.com            Look up IP address of Prentice Hall's website.
www.prenhall.com has address 165.193.123.253
```

How does Unix know that IP address? There is a system called *DNS,* the domain name system, that the host calls.[1] You can see the *nameservers* (programs that try to resolve IP addresses and hostnames) that your system calls in /etc/resolv.conf. To assist with nameservers, your system should have a list of hosts in /etc/hosts. You can view both of these text files. My system even provides help on them with **man -s4 hosts**. See also **man dig**—domain information groper—for "deeper" DNS analysis of a hostname.

6.2.5   IPv6

An important aspect of the current IP address standard is that we're running out of addresses. A new standard (IPv6) of 128-bit addresses is slowly being adopted, providing 2^{128} addresses. (On your system, try **man -s 7p ip6**.) To get a handle on this size, imagine a trillion. Now, multiply that by a trillion. Then do it again. You're still a "bit" under how many unique addresses we will have. For the sake of comparison, IPv4's 32 bits gives over 4 billion addresses.

PRACTICE!

1.   What is one of the hosts of your system?
2.   What's the IP address of the host you're using? Hint: Start with **echo $HOST**

6.3   SYSTEM NEWS

Daily computer work demands communication. Among other things, monitoring system changes, warnings, and upgrades helps maintain your account. Staying abreast of important information isn't too difficult. Learn to communicate with system administrators. You can rely on them to fix account problems and dispense advice. Take the time to check site announcements. Sometimes site administrators post daily announcements in /etc/motd ("message of the day"), which your shell displays after you log in. Some systems might even provide a **motd** command to view that file. A standard command, **news**, relays important system updates. Try entering **news -s** to produce a count of unread updates on your account:

Step 6.2:   System news

```
unix> news -s              How many news announcements have accumulated?
No news.                   ...is good news! Enter news if Unix shows a number.
```

---

[1]Check out *http://en.wikipedia.org/wiki/Domain_Name_System* for more information.

6.4   DATE, TIME, AND CALENDAR

Part of the communication process is keeping track of dates, times, and schedules. Although sophisticated programs, such as Outlook, provide great assistance in scheduling your day, Unix has some extremely handy text-based commands. For example, Unix can help you keep track of times and dates.

Step 6.3:   Date and Time (`date`)

```
unix> date                                      What is the current date and time?
Sun Apr  3 18:45:42 EDT 2005                              Default format.
```

You can modify the output. **date** allows you to use the formats from **strftime** with **date +*formats***. You will need to see **man strftime**, however, for explanations of all the formats. If you want spaces in the output, surround ***formats*** with single quotes (`'`). For example, **man -s1 date** demonstrates date `'+DATE: %m/%d/%y%nTIME:%H:%M:%S'`, but I can tweak it as follows:

```
unix> date '+Date: %m/%d/%Y%nTime: %r'          Show formatted date and time.
Date: 04/03/2005                                         Date: %m/%d/%Y.
Time: 06:54:47 PM                                        Time: %r.
```

Step 6.4:   Monthly and yearly calendar (`cal`)

```
unix> cal 2005                                   Output the entire calendar for 2005.
Output not shown.                                For a specific month, use cal month year.
```

You can even use Unix to alert you about upcoming events with **calendar**. First, create a text file called `calendar`. Each line should have a date, like `4/3` or `Apr. 3`. See **man calendar** for a complete list of formats. When you invoke **calendar**, it looks for dates in each line corresponding to today's and tomorrow's dates. For each match, **calendar** displays the line:

Step 6.5:   Your Schedule

```
unix> pico ~/calendar                                   Create calendar file.
4/3   Work on Chapter 6                                      My first entry.
Apr 4   CIS300 meeting                                      My second entry.
unix> calendar                                               Run calendar.
4/3   Work on Chapter 6                                  It reports today's task
Apr 4   CIS300 meeting                                      and tomorrow's task.
```

By adding the command **calendar** to one of your login files (`.login`, `.cshrc`, `.profile`, ...), you can be alerted every time you log in.

PRACTICE!

3. Write the command line that will show the current day and date in the format *Day, Month* (abbreviated), *Date, Year* (four digits).
4. How does **calendar** treat the weekend?

6.5 FINDING PEOPLE AND ACCOUNTS

Unix has a variety of commands to find information about yourself and your system's users.

6.5.1 Who Are You?

Unix knows quite a bit about you. Try **logname**, **echo $USER**, or **who am i**:

Step 6.6: Finding current information about yourself

```
unix> who am i                                Report current information about yourself.
dis  pts/14  Apr 1 16:19  128.253.161.179)        User, terminal, date, time, hostname.
```

6.5.2 Who's Online?

Used alone, **who** provides a list of everyone currently logged on to your network:

Step 6.7: Output list of people logged on

```
unix> who                                              See who's online.
List of users and their hosts.
unix> w                                          Alternative commands.
List of users and what they're doing. Yes, Unix let's you spy a bit!
```

Actually, Unix seems to have many commands for keeping track of everyone. For a list of just users logged on, try the BSD command **users**. You can also run **finger**, as shown in Step 6.9. In addition, you can see a list of people logged in remotely with **rusers**. In these examples, you might see yourself listed multiple times if you are using multiple windows.

6.5.3 Who Has an Account?

For a list of all users who have system access, you could dig around the parent directory of **HOME** with **ls ~/...**, but **listusers** will save you some effort:

Step 6.8: List everyone

```
unix> listusers | less                      Access all user account information.
Likely very long if your system supports this command.                Use a pager!
```

To check on a certain person, you can use **finger**. Without any arguments, **finger** resembles **who**. If you know part of the name, **finger** *string* will look for all users who have names that contain *string*. The **finger** command supports many options, such as **-m**, which forces **finger** to treat *string* as a username.

Step 6.9: Look up information about users

```
unix> finger                              Check everyone currently on your system.
List of current users.
unix> finger Schwartz                  Look up anyone with Schwartz in their name.
Login name: dis                    In real life: David Schwartz
Directory: /home/dis               Shell: /usr/local/bin/tcsh
On since Apr 14 22:28:14 on pts/8 from 172.23.16.76
18 hours Idle Time
No unread mail
No Plan.
unix> finger -m dis                           Look up user dis on your system.
```

If you would like someone to see a message whenever they finger your account, set `r` and `x` access to **HOME** and create a text file called `.plan`. Whatever you enter will be seen, so be nice! However, because of security concerns, **finger** may act differently, depending on your host system's settings.

PRACTICE!

> 5. How can you quickly find the number of users logged into your system?
>
> 6. Finger all people named June on your system.

6.6   CHATTING

Once you know someone else on a Unix system, you can chat, writing back and forth in a command window! (Yes, Unix provides an early precursor to "Instant Messaging" someone.)

6.6.1   Talk with Others

The **talk** command enables you and another user who is currently online to write messages inside a command window. If you both login to the same system, use **talk *username***. For "long-distance" chatting over different, but connected, systems, use **talk *username@hostname***. Acting as a telephone, **talk** "rings" a user's session by flashing a message on their monitor, indicating your desire to "talk." The other person can respond with **talk *yourusername***. The following sequence illustrates this procedure:

Assume that someone named Aaron with username `ajw` is currently logged in. To "call" Aaron, enter **talk ajw**. For the sake of the exercise, assume that your username is `dis`. As a result of your running **talk**, Aaron gets a message that `dis` wants to talk. To respond, Aaron would enter **talk dis** if `dis` is on the same system. Aaron could also enter **talk dis@*hostname*** if `dis` is logged on to a different system:

Step 6.10:   Talk with another user currently logged on

```
unix> talk ajw                                          Call Aaron (ajw) to talk.
```

Step 6.11:   Responding to someone with talk

```
ajw would see this message suddenly flash somewhere on his computer monitor:
Message from Talk_Daemon@somwhere.edu at 23:10 ...
talk: connection requested by dis@somewhere.edu.
talk: respond with: talk dis@somewhere.edu
unix> talk dis                                  ajw enters this command in his screen.
```

At this point, each user's screen will split in half. Each person types in *his* top half, while the messages from the other person appear in the bottom half. Whether or not you initiate contact, you will always enter text in the top:

Step 6.12:   talk session

```
Hi Aaron. What's up?                                          You type up here.
----------------------------------------------------------------------------------
Not much. How's your Unix book going?            ajw's messages appear down here.
```

If the boxes become cluttered, clear the screen with `^L`. To exit **talk**, enter `^C`.

6.6.2   Block Messages

Sometimes you just need to be left alone. To block incoming calls, enter the command line **mesg n**. Entering **mesg y** will permit your account to accept messages again. See also Chapter 8 for customizing your sessions. You can check your blocking status with **mesg**:

Step 6.13:   Check your message status

```
unix> mesg                              Does your account disable talking?
is y                                    My account allows people to talk to me.
```

6.6.3   Write

You can also write a message directly on a user's terminal with **write**. I think that **talk** is a bit easier to use, but you might find this command fun. Here is how I write myself, so that I can show you what the other user sees:

Step 6.14:   Write a message to yourself

```
unix> write dis                                     Write a message to yourself.
dis is logged on more than one place.
You are connected to "pts/21".
Other locations are:
pts/23
Message from dis on mortiis cornell.edu (pts/21) [ Fri Apr 15 20:04:34 ] ...
hello                                               This is what I write.
hello                                   This is what the other user (myself) sees.
<EOT>                                   Use ^C or ^D to exit. EOT means "end of text."
unix>                                              The Unix prompt reappears.
```

To prevent people using **write** from communicating with you, enter **mesg -n**, just as you would with **talk**. If you eventually become a system administrator, you will learn **wall**, which will write a message to *all* users who are logged on. I doubt that your system allows you to use that command!

6.6.4   IRC

Inter Relay Chat (IRC) provides a larger-scale "chat session" in which you can join a "channel" to write to others currently on that same channel. My own system does not support the **irc** command, but maybe yours does. Check out *http://www.irchelp.org* for more information. Although I include this section for completeness, I recommend that you avoid IRC and concentrate on your schoolwork. Don't say I didn't warn you!

PRACTICE!

7.   Use **talk** to talk with someone online.

8.   Use **write** to write to someone online.

6.7   E-MAIL

Why are regular letters sent via the post office called "snail mail"? Because electronic mail, or *e-mail*, arrives much more quickly and with far less effort. E-mail messages are composed of electronic data sent to and collected by people on networked computers. To deliver your snail mail, the postal service requires an address that specifies the person and place to whom and where you wish to send your mail. With e-mail, you must do much the same only with an **e-mail address**, which typically is expressed as **username@hostname**. Many programs will automatically append the "**@hostname**" portion when **username** exists locally.

6.7.1 Accessing Your Mailbox

You receive mail in a unique **mailbox** assigned to your account. The mailbox is a file typically found in /var/mail or /usr/mail, stored as your username. Although you actually view the file (for me, **less /var/mail/dis**), e-mail programs provide more convenient access and allow you to send your own messages. You should check with your system administrator to see what your system supports. In this section, we will explore two text-based programs: **mailx** (a Unix standard) and **pine** (not universal, but extremely popular). If you are an **emacs** fan, you can indeed use it for e-mail. I recommend that you investigate GUI programs, however, such as **dtmail** and Netscape's mail tools.

6.7.2 Checking for Mail

If you have received new e-mail since your last Unix session, your system will often report You have mail when you log on. If your system supports the BSD command **biff**,[2] you can set **biff y** so that Unix will alert you in the command window when you receive e-mail. (Your start-up files might already set this option. See Chapter 8.) I prefer GUI programs, such as **xbiff**, which I set to beep when mail arrives during a session. **xbiff++** is even fancier, allowing you to show pictures of people mailing you. For a quick check of *new* e-mail, try another BSD command called **from**:

Step 6.15: Checking for new mail

```
unix> biff                                    Check current biff setting.
is n                              I have disabled biff, because I use xbiff.
unix> from                             Check sender and date of new e-mail.
```
Unix will display information about new e-mails. After you look at them, they no longer count as new.

6.7.3 E-mail Programs

mailx is a more advanced version of Unix's **mail**. However, I prefer PINE, which I find vastly easier to use. PINE is not standard for Unix, but I will bet that your system supports it. To test whether it does, enter the command **pine**. If I were to explain all of PINE's multitude of features, I would need another book. Instead, PINE has a terrific online tutorial under "Getting Started with PINE" at the official PINE website: *http://www.washington.edu/pine*. If you wish to run PINE on your own computer, you can even download Macintosh and Microsoft Windows versions! Adventurous students may wish to explore **emacs**'s mail facilities. Yes, **emacs** might seem like it does everything. Unix GUIs also provide useful programs, notwithstanding Internet browsers, such as Netscape and Mozilla, which have wonderful mail programs.

6.7.4 E-mailing a Message

To e-mail a message, enter **mailx username**. **mailx** usually prompts you for a Subject, a label that describes the contents of your message. After typing a subject line (leaving the Subject blank is often considered rude) and pressing **Return**, you

---

[2]Named after a dog. One day, you may also get to name your own Unix command!

are in *input mode*. Begin typing your message, but be forewarned: In standard input mode, you cannot edit lines after pressing **Return**. Why? If you have investigated **ed** or **ex**, you will recognize that **mailx** uses a *line editor*. When you are through typing, press **^D** at the beginning of a new line to transmit your message. For example, try e-mailing a message to yourself:

Step 6.16: **mailx**—send e-mail to yourself

```
unix> mailx you                              Mail yourself a new message.
Subject: test1                                    Give a simple subject.
This is test #1 of mailx.                                Type this line.
^D                                                    Enter ^D to exit.
EOT                                                   EOT: end of text.
unix>                                                    Back to Unix!
```

Your message has now been sent to yourself. Had you chosen another person, the message would have been sent to that user. Remember, write with care! Once sent, e-mail cannot be recalled.

6.7.5 Tilde Escape Commands

You can avoid making errors by taking advantage of some of **mailx**'s advanced options, such as the *tilde escape commands*. Entered as **~command**, these commands operate inside input mode and perform some handy tasks. For example,

- **~r filename** will load a text file **filename** into the e-mail you are sending.
- **~v** will invoke **vi** or the default visual editor (which might be something like **emacs**),[3] so that you can edit messages before sending.

In the following example, you invoke a text editor to create your message:

Step 6.17: **mailx**—edit an e-mail message before sending

```
unix> mailx you                                      E-mail yourself again.
Subject: test2                                         Pick another subject.
~v                            To invoke the default editor, enter ~v and then press Return.
If your system uses vi, you will need to enter insert mode to start editing. Refer to Section 3.3.
To: you                                            You can change the recipient.
Subject: test2                                       You can change the subject.
This is test #2 of mailx.                                 Write your message.
:wq                                             Enter last-line mode (assuming vi).
Now, mailx returns to standard mail editing with a line editor.
^D                                                         Exit the editor.
EOT                                                 End of text. Message sent!
unix>                                                        Back to Unix.
```

To see the complete list of tilde escape commands, enter **~?** in the *message body* in **mailx**.

---

[3]Check **echo $VISUAL** and **echo $EDITOR** to see if your system has a setting. You can set these values in your start-up files for more convenience, as explained in Chapter 8.

6.7.6   Quitting E-mail

If you decide to cancel a message, enter `^C` twice:

Step 6.18: `mailx`—cancel a message

`unix>` `mailx dis`	*Mail yourself yet again.*
`Subject:` `test3`	*Another silly subject.*
`^C`	*Enter* `^C`.
`(Interrupt -- one more to kill letter)`	*Enter* `^C` *again.*
`unix>`	`mailx` *cancelled your e-mail.*

6.7.7   Reading E-mail

To read e-mail, enter the command `mailx` with no arguments. When you do, `mailx` will indicate that you are in command mode by displaying the query prompt (`?`). Each message is shown with a *header*. (See Figure 6.1.)

At the prompt, pressing **Return** will display the message marked with a >, whereas entering a message's number will cause that message to be displayed. Try accessing the two mail messages that you sent to yourself earlier:

Step 6.19:   Reading E-mail

`unix>` `mailx`	*Access your mail.*
`mailx version 5.0 [date] Type ? for help`	`mailx` *reminds you it's* `mailx`.
`"/var/mail/dis": 2 messages 2 unread`	*Alert about new e-mail.*
`>N 1 david i schwartz Wed Oct 26 00:03 16/667 test1`	*A new e-mail.*
` N 2 david i schwartz Wed Oct 26 00:13 16/657 test2`	*Another new e-mail.*
`?`	*The* `?` *is the command prompt*
Enter **Return** *to read the message denoted with* > *(message 1). Or you can enter the specific message number (*`1`*).*	
`?q`	*When finished, enter* `q` *to quit.*

6.7.8   Mailbox

The first time you use `mailx`, Unix creates a file called `mbox` inside your **HOME**. Unless you specifically delete messages that have been read, they will be appended to `mbox`. Unread messages will be listed with status U when you run `mailx` again.

6.7.9   More `mailx`

I have only scratched the surface to get you started. Table 6.1 lists some tilde escape commands. (See also **man** `mailx`.) As with many other Unix programs, you can modify `mailx`'s behavior with a run-control text file, which is called `.mailrc`. For example, if

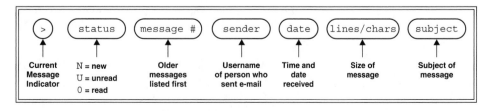

Figure 6.1   Message Headers in `mailx`

TABLE 6.1 Some `mailx` Commands

Command	Description
`?`	Show all commands and descriptions.
`h`	List all current messages.
`s` *filename*	Save message by appending to filename.
`d`	Delete message.
`u`	Undelete message.
`R` *message*	Reply to sender of message (specify with number).
`q`	Quit **mailx**. Remove messages that have been read or deleted.
`x`	Exit **mailx** without removing any messages.

you include the line `set askcc`, **mailx** will always prompt you to enter a list of usernames that will receive copies[4] of the message. For a complete list of **mailx** settings, see the `Internal Variables` section in **man mailx**.

6.7.10 Mail Forwarding

You can set Unix to forward your mail automatically to another address. To do so, create a text file called `.forward` in your **HOME**. Inside, enter the e-mail addresses to which you want your e-mail sent. You should either separate each address with a comma or enter it on a new line. To keep a copy of each message in your current address, enter `\`*username* as one of the addresses. For example, you might consider the following if you want all e-mail forwarded to a private Internet service provider (ISP):

Step 6.20: Forward your e-mail

```
unix> pico $HOME/.forward                          Edit .forward in HOME.
\dis                                   Keep a copy of each e-mail in your account.
myaccount@somewhereelse.com           Forward a copy of each e-mail to another account.
```

Your system *might* require access to your `.forward`. (Test your `.forward` by mailing a message to yourself and checking the remote system.) So, you might need to set permissions, as follows:

- Directory access for **HOME**. Use **chmod a+x $HOME**, which allows access, but not read permission, to your files. That way, you can "hide" your files from the public.
- Read permission on `.forward`. Use **chmod a+r .forward**.

Be careful with forwarding your mail! Never create a mail *loop*. If your remote system forwards mail back to the current system, your mail will bounce back and forth.

6.7.11 Vacation

When you know that you will not read your e-mail for an extended period, you should probably let everyone know. Unix supports the **vacation** program that will automatically alert people. On Unix, **vacation** is interactive. When you run the program, it will prompt you to answer some questions:

- What message do you want Unix to mail to people? **vacation**'s standard message to people who mail you is as follows:

---

[4]Actually, cc stands for *carbon copy*, which only Generation X and older folks will likely remember. If you're curious about the history, look up "carbon paper" on the Internet. When I was a kid, I actually used this stuff!

```
Subject: away from my mail
I will not be reading my mail for a while.
Your mail regarding "$SUBJECT" will be read when I
return.
```

The $SUBJECT line will extract the sender's subject and insert it *inside* the mail that **vacation** sends in response. If you would like to change the message, you can simply edit $HOME/.vacation.mesg, which is the file that **vacation** creates.

- Do you want to activate the program, which requires creating a special .forward file. If you already have a .forward file, **vacation** will prompt you to disable it. Why? **vacation** wants to create the following .forward file, which keeps a copy of each e-mail for you and responds to each sender:

```
\username, "|/usr/bin/vacation username"
```

So, in advance, you should rename your current .forward file. If you do not, Unix will disable **vacation**. You may also need to set permissions on the preceding files, as you did in Section 6.7.10. For more information and options, see **man vacation**. Note also that many system administrators have set up websites that will create the necessary files for you.

6.7.12 Other Mail Tools

Given the scope of this book, we have only scratched the surface of Unix's e-mail programs. If you wish to discover more programs, I suggest that you start with the **man** pages for **procmail**, **formail**, and **sendmail**.

6.7.13 Responsibilities

Check with your system administrators about proper e-mail use. In general, treat your e-mail as you would regular snail mail. Here are some rules for you to follow:

- Never threaten or harass people!
- Do not spam people; we get enough junk already!
- Never continue chain mail "just in case." Listen up, people—it's insipid! Break the chain![5]
- Never send anything that will embarrass you or someone else; you cannot "unsend" a message once you have sent it!

For more pointers, investigate ***netiquette*** (Internet etiquette) guides, such as the one found at *http://www.fau.edu/netiquette/netiquette.html*.

PRACTICE!

9. E-mail a friend. Say hello.

10. E-mail two people the same message, using **mailx *person1 person2***.

11. You can e-mail a text file with the command line **mailx *username* < *file***. Try e-mailing a file called info.txt to yourself.

12. Send yourself an e-mail. Save the message to a file called saved.txt in **HOME**.

---

[5]A popular website, *http://www.snopes.com*, tries to provide evidence that debunks (or proves) urban legends, many of which chain mail perpetuates.

No one writes "good" or "really good," let alone the abominable "goodly." You must aspire to write well—to convey your thoughts and feelings in a clear and cogent fashion. Too many students excuse their poor writing by arguing that they are "just engineers." Writing follows rules of *grammar* and must have *semantic* meaning. Writing requires creativity and structure. Writing has form and flow. Writing demands concept and precision. Writing employs books and computers. I say, "Writing is engineering!"

Foremost in writing is *communication*. Clear expression is crucial: Anyone who muddles a concept will not be understood by others. Lately, however, e-mail has come to dominate written communication, and sloppiness pervades the medium. Don't fall prey to it; consider some of these tips for proper e-mail communication:

- *Subjects*: The subject line of an e-mail should convey the message's purpose. Consider the subject line READ IMMEDIATELY for a message saying hey mike, what happened to sam's toenails last night? These subject lines

and messages do not inform; they just annoy. Also, when replying, consider whether the subject is still appropriate. The salutation Yo dude or Hey babe or hi boss-person! is certainly cozy and perhaps even appropriate in certain circumstances. However, first try correctly identifying your addressee.

- *Spelling*: Consider the choice—and know the difference—between homonyms, such as affect/effect, hear/here, it's/its, than/then, to/too/two and you're/your. Also, many e-mail programs have built-in spell-checkers. TRY using one occasionally.

- *Grammar*: *i am fed up with people who simply cannot bother to punctuate capitalize insert articles and define sentences inside email like this sample see what i mean its really annoying and ti getz wurss whan i statr missspelign wurds*

Proofreading your own work is tough, but the effort pays off. (Have I caught all mistakes?) Consider investing some time and energy in developing better communication skills. Communication is essential for *all* professions.

6.8   REMOTE SESSIONS

One of the great advantages that networking provides is the ability to communicate with different computers throughout your LANs and WANs. For example, you might work at a home machine and wish to connect to a work machine so that you don't end up living at work (although your work will live with you). Unix provides several programs to connect to other machines. In this section, I will review some older, or "classic," commands that you will often see referenced in Unix books. Then, I will have you focus on a program called SSH (*secure shell*), which supersedes these commands.

6.8.1   Older Commands

The **rlogin** (*remote login*) command is still quite handy for internal networks. When you enter **rlogin *hostname***, your machine will begin a login procedure for you to log onto that host. You can also enter **rlogin -l *username hostname*** in case ***hostname*** does not "know" about you.

Step 6.21:   Remote login

Pick a host that differs from your current host. Your system may or may not prompt you for a password.
```
unix> rlogin -l dis gregarious.cs.cornell.edu
```
Log onto a remote host.

How could the remote system "know" about you? Your system might have a file called /etc/hosts.equiv, which contains trustworthy remote hostnames. Your own account may also have a text file `.rhosts` in your **HOME** that lists hostnames and your usernames on separate lines in this format:

> *hostname username*

Be sure to set only user *read* and *write* permission. Assuming that you attempt to access a known remote system, you should not have to provide your username or password.

A once-popular program called *Telnet* (derived from *terminal emulation*) also connects you to another host. However, Telnet sends data as *clear text*, which means that Telnet does not encrypt the characters you type. So, if you enter your password, a program called a *sniffer* could intercept the packets and easily convert them back into their original text characters. I would explain more about Telnet, but you should concentrate on SSH, which I explain in Section 6.8.2. To risk using Telnet, try **telnet** *hostname* to access another system in your network:

Step 6.22: Telnet

unix> **telnet somewhere.edu**	*Connect to a remote host.*
Trying 999.999.9.999…	*Telnet reports the IP address.*
Connected to somewhere.edu	*You have successfully accessed the host.*
Escape character is '^]'	*To quit Telnet, enter ^].*
UNIX(r) (somewhere.edu)	*Your host.*
login: **dis**	*Your host will prompt you for a username.*
Password:	*Send an unencrypted password.*

If you need to run only a few commands on a remote system, you do not have to log onto that system. Unix has commands to run other commands on a remote host: **rsh** and **remsh** (*remote shell*) and **uux** (*Unix-to-Unix execute*). Again, you can use SSH instead. Following is a brief example of **rsh**, using **rsh -l** *username host command*:

Step 6.23: Execute command on remote shell

unix> **rsh -l dis somewhere.edu ls**	*List my* **HOME** *on another account.*
Unix will list your files on somewhere.edu, *assuming that you have an account there.*	

As with **rlogin**, if your system has a /etc/hosts.equiv file that includes the remote host, you do not need to provide your username or password. You can also use your .rhosts file for these commands.

6.8.2   Secure Shell (SSH)

SSH is a versatile and (you guessed it!) *secure* program for remote access and command entry. In fact, **man ssh** indicates that **ssh** is designed to replace **rlogin** and **rsh**. I would include **telnet** as well. For remote access, **ssh** provides different forms of syntax:

- **ssh hostname**: Your system and the other system must "know" about each other via .rhosts files.
- **ssh -l** *username hostname*: Log in with a specified username.
- **ssh** *username@hostame*: alternative to preceding syntax.

SSH will encrypt your information so that you can safely log on:

Step 6.24: Use SSH for remote login

```
unix> ssh dis@somewhere.edu                  Remote login to somewhere.edu.
dis@somewhere.edu's password:                              Enter password.
                                   SSH will log you on to the remote system.
unix> hostname                                        Report current host.
somewhere.edu
unix> exit                               To log out, use exit or logout.
Connection to somewhere.edu closed.    You will return to your original host.
unix> hostname                               Confirm your original host.
You should see your original host.
```

Like **rsh**, SSH can also remotely execute a command, except with encryption. All you need to do is append a command to the remote-access command line. For example, suppose I wish to list my remote system's **HOME**. Then I can do the following:

Step 6.25: Execute remote command with SSH

```
unix> ssh dis@somewhere.edu ls                 Run ls on your HOME elsewhere.
dis@ira.cs.cornell.edu's password:                    Enter your password.
              Unix will list your files on somewhere.edu, assuming that you have an account there.
unix> hostname                        Confirm that you have not left your original host!
You should see your original host.
```

When running a GUI from a remote host, you may need to use the **-X** option. Your **ssh** manpage may recommend the **-f** option instead. You should check with your system administrator concerning your system's configuration of SSH if you need these options. You can also configure **ssh** in a file called $HOME/.ssh/config so that it includes the line **ForwardX11 yes**, as described in **man ssh**.

6.8.3 Logout Display

If you find that you frequently connect to different accounts, you can have some fun with the logout process depending on your login shell. When logging out, you can have your shell display a message that you create inside $HOME/.logout. **csh** and **tcsh** use .logout. **bash** uses .bash_logout. **zsh** uses .zlogout. Each line in the .logout file is a Unix command. Unix will run each line in the file, starting at the top.[6]

Step 6.26: Set a logout display (**csh**, **tcsh**)

```
If you are using a GUI, open a new window. Enter the following commands and text in that window:
unix> pico $HOME/.logout                        Edit a logout file in HOME.
clear                                   This instruction will clear the window/screen.
echo 'My work here is done!'                         Output a message.
echo ' '                                             Output a blank line.
unix> exit                                                Quit the shell.
My work here is done!           The window/screen will show this message before quitting.
```

A logout file is helpful when you access a remote system because that that system has your .logout, your screen will display the logout message when you exit.

---

[6]When you learn about programming, you will discover that the .logout file resembles a *program*: a series of statements that a computer will execute. In this case, your program is *script*.

Step 6.27: Leaving a remote session

```
unix> ssh dis@somewhere.edu                    Remote login to somewhere.edu.
dis@somewhere.edu's password:                           Enter password.
SSH will log you on to the remote system.
unix> exit                                      To log out, use exit or logout.
My work here is done!                                   Your logout message!
Connection to somewhere.edu closed.         You will return to your original host.
unix>                                                   Your prompt returns.
```

See also **man printf** for a more rigorous printing command.

PRACTICE!

13. Run SSH such that it shows a summary of all its options.
14. Find another system on which you have an account, and connect to it.
15. Rewrite your logout file from Step 6.26, using **printf**.

6.9 FILE TRANSFER

You will often discover that you need to transfer files to and from various systems. You might need to either download *from* a remote site or upload *to* a remote site. In modern times, people usually just go to a website and click on links. However, Unix and other operating systems support programs specifically designed for file transfer. In this section, I review some older commands (primarily **rcp** and **ftp**) that you will still occasionally need. I will also discuss their more modern and secure versions (**scp** and **sftp**).

6.9.1 UU Commands

A "long time ago," Unix users might have seen **uucp** (*Unix-to-Unix copy*). There are still several UU programs that you might occasionally see (**uux**, **uuencode**, **uudecode**, and others). Your system's manpages should still have explanations of these commands.

6.9.2 Remote Copy (**rcp**)

Remote copy (**rcp**) provides a quick, nonsecure way to copy files from one remote system to another. The basic syntax, **rcp *sourcepath targetpath***, is akin to that of **cp**, except that each path may include a hostname or username (or both). The following examples illustrate how to use **rcp**:

- **rcp *localfile remotehostname:file***
- **rcp *remoteuser@remotehost:remotefile localfile***
- **rcp *localfile remoteuser@remotehost:remotefile***

Just as with **cp**, **rcp** supports a **-r** (recursive) option for copying entire directories.

Step 6.28: Remote copy

```
Copy an entire directory (DataDir) in your CWD to your HOME on somewhere.edu:
unix> mkdir DataDir                                Create a test directory.
                              You should create some files and put them inside DataDir.
unix> rcp -r DataDir somewhere.edu:~    The -r option causes all contents to be copied.
unix> rsh somewhere.edu ls ~/DataDir        List DataDir on the remote account.
Unix will list DataDir on somewhere.edu, assuming that you have an account there.
```

Because **rcp** will not prompt you for a password, the program is convenient for copying your own files. However, for more security, you should consider using **scp**. (See next section.)

6.9.3   Secure Copy

Like **rcp**, **scp** (*secure copy*), will copy files between hosts. But unlike **rcp**, **scp** uses **ssh** for data encryption and password authentication. The syntax, **scp *options user@host1:file1 user@host2:file2***, is essentially the same as that of **rcp**, although **scp** provides additional options. For example, **-o *option*** lets you call an **ssh** option. Since you are still new to Unix, I recommend using the more basic version of **scp**:

Step 6.29:   Secure copy

```
unix> scp dis@somewhere.edu:~/pic1.jpg ~            Copy remote file pic1.jpg to
                                                    HOME on current host.
dis somewhere.edu's password:                       Enter your password.
pic1.jpg            100%  113KB 113.2KB/s    00:01  scp reports the data transfer.
```

For more examples of **scp**, use the syntax examples in Section 6.9.2.

6.9.4   FTP

FTP (*file-transfer protocol*) was a popular program for uploading and downloading files across the Internet. However, because FTP sends information in clear text, it suffers from the same security flaw that other older Unix session/transfer programs had. So, if you need to upload and download files, I recommend that you use **sftp** (secure FTP), as discussed in Section 6.9.5. Alternatively, many locations still allow for *anonymous* access to download publicly available files safely. The process of ***anonymous FTP*** refers to accessing an FTP site and logging in with **anonymous** as your username. First, you must know the essential commands. To start **ftp** without a particular host in mind, just enter **ftp**. At the prompt (ftp>) enter **?** or **help** to see the complete list of commands.

Step 6.30:   FTP and help

```
unix> ftp                                                       Start FTP.
ftp> help                                               Show list of commands.
Commands may be abbreviated.   Commands are:       FTP shows list of commands.
Long list of commands follows.
ftp> help dir                       Enter help command to get help on command.
dir         list contents of remote directory
ftp> bye                                                         Quit FTP.
unix>                                                        Back to Unix!
```

As Step 6.30 shows, **ftp** supports many commands. I list some common commands in Table 6.2. **ftp**'s manpage provides comprehensive descriptions.

I will demonstrate anonymous FTP for *GNU* ("Gnu's Not Unix") software, which you will find useful if you run Linux or another variant of Unix on your home computer. Before downloading any files, however, you should learn the following common rules of FTP:

- *Site access*: You can enter **ftp *ftpsite*** or **ftp** followed by **open *ftpsite*** at the ftp> prompt. If the site is protected, you will need a username and

TABLE 6.2 Common FTP Commands

Command	Description
!	Escape to shell; enter **exit** to return to FTP.
ascii	Set ASCII to download text files.
binary	Set binary to download general (non-ASCII) files.
bye, quit	Quit FTP.
cd *remdir*	Change remote directory to *remdir*.
cdup	Change remote directory to parent of remote CWD.
dir	List remote CWD. (See also **ls**.)
get *remotefile*	Copy remote file to local host in your CWD. You can also specify a new filename.
glob	Toggle *globbing*. When globbing is on, FTP will understand filename wildcards, such as *****. See Sections 4.2.3 and 5.10.1.
help, ?	Show list of commands. **help command** shows help on *command*.
lcd	Change directory on local system. (Change local CWD.)
ls	List contents of remote directory. Supports options such as **-a**, **-l**, and **-F**.
mget *remotefiles*	Get multiple files; e.g., **mget *.jpg**.
mput *localfiles*	Put multiple files on remote host (e.g., **mput *.data**).
open *host*	Open an FTP site (e.g., at the ftp> prompt, enter **open ftp.gnu.org**).
prompt	Toggle between interactive prompting modes. Entering **prompt** will turn interaction on or off. I prefer *off* for **mput** and **mget**.
put *localfile*	Copy local file to remote host at the CWD you've set in FTP. You can also specify a new filename.
pwd	Show remote CWD.
status	Show FTP's current status.

password. For anonymous FTP, enter **anonymous** as your username. You might be prompted to enter a real username as the password.

- *File information*: Look for a file called README (or something similar). Download that file with **get README** and then quit FTP (**bye**). The file should explain the directory structure and availability of files on the site.
- *File locations*: Inside an FTP site, the directory structure follows the hierarchical structure that you learned for Unix. So, you can use **cd** to change directories and **pwd** to show your CWD at the remote site. To move up a directory, use **cdup**. To generate a listing, use **dir** or **ls**, as described in Table 6.2.
- *Canceling a command*: Use **^C** to cancel a command in FTP.
- *Local directory*: To change your CWD on your local system, use **lcd**. Do not confuse **lcd** with **cd** (which changes the directory on the FTP site).
- *File type*: If you want to download strictly text files, enter **ascii**. For non-ASCII files, such as images and zip files, enter **bin**. You can check the current type mode with **status**. If the file type is ascii, you will garble nontext files! For text files, **bin** will still work, but FTP might not properly convert DOS and Unix text formats. (See **man dos2unix** in Unix for an explanation).
- *Download a file*: To download a specific file, you first need to find the file in the remote hierarchy. To retrieve the file, enter **get filename**. You can

also specify **get *filename localname*** to change the name on your system.

- *Download many files*: To download a group of files, you need to ensure that *globbing* (Section 4.2.3) is on, so that FTP understands filename wildcards. You can check the current globbing mode with **status**. Use **glob** to turn globbing on and off. Also, I recommend that you turn prompt off with **prompt**. (Check the state with **status**.) Once you have identified the location, you can use **mget**. For example, **mget *.jpg** will download all files with extension jpg in the remote CWD.

- *Uploading files*: Refer to the rules for **get**. Now, however, you will use **put** and **mput** to copy files *from* your local system *to* the FTP site. Note that **lcd** will change for local CWD. See also **!**, which gives you access to your local shell to run regular Unix commands, helping you to work on files before uploading them. To return to **ftp** and entering **!**, enter **exit**.

You are now ready to use FTP! The following FTP session downloads one file from GNU:

Step 6.31: Anonymous FTP Session

`unix> `**`ftp ftp.gnu.org`**	*Access GNU's FTP repository.*
`Connected to ftp.gnu.org.`	*You aren't logged in yet.*
`220 GNU FTP server ready.`	*FTP prepares to log you in.*
`Name (ftp.gnu.org:dis): `**`anonymous`**	*Use anonymous FTP.*
GNU's FTP now shows a legal notice.	*Most sites show a welcome message.*
`230 Login successful.`	*FTP lets you know that you have logged in.*
`Remote system type is UNIX.`	*Sometimes FTP will check your system.*
`Using binary mode to transfer files.`	*The site already has* `binary` *set.*
`ftp> `**`cd /gnu/units`**	*Change the remote directory to* `/gnu/units`.
`250 Directory successfully changed.`	*FTP keeps you informed.*
`ftp> `**`ls`**	*List contents of remote CWD.*
`200 PORT command successful. Consider using PASV.`	*PASV is more secure.*
`150 Here comes the directory listing.`	*You may enter* **quote PASV**.
`units-1.53.tar.gz`	*Directory listing follows.*
`units-1.54.tar.gz`	*GNU archives older version of the program.*
`units-1.55.tar.gz`	*Ignore this one.*
`units-1.74.tar.gz`	*Ignore this one, too.*
`units-1.80.tar.gz`	*Aha! We want this one.*
`226 Directory send OK.`	*FTP reports* `ls`*'s success.*
`95 bytes received in 0.0076 seconds (12.17 Kbytes/s)`	*FTP alerts you about data rates.*
`ftp> `**`get units-1.80.tar.gz`**	*Get the latest version of* **units**.
`200 PORT command successful. Consider using PASV.`	*Another successful command!*
`150 Opening BINARY mode data connection for units-1.80.tar.gz (206483 bytes).`	
`226 File send OK.`	*Note that you didn't need to enter* **bin**,
	since the site already set the `binary` *file type for you.*
`local: units-1.80.tar.gz remote: units-1.80.tar.gz`	*Local name, remote name.*
`206483 bytes received in 0.26 seconds (775.06 Kbytes/s)`	*File was downloaded!*
`ftp> `**`bye`**	*Quit FTP.*
`221 Goodbye.`	*FTP is a polite protocol.*
`unix>`	*Back to Unix!*

As intimated earlier, FTP actually works for pretty much all operating systems. The similarity of FTP commands to Unix commands derives from the fact that the Internet protocols were developed "hand in hand" with Unix. Actually, you can skip the text-based interface if you use a Web browser.

6.9.5   Secure FTP (`sftp`)

When accessing a nonanonymous FTP site (a site that requires a real username and password), you should use *Secure FTP* (`sftp`) if possible. As with `scp`, `sftp` builds upon `ssh`, providing an interface and command set similar to those of FTP. The following session demonstrates how downloading and uploading work on my system, which is restricted (the commands will seem familiar, as many FTP commands work in Secure FTP):

`unix> `**`sftp ftp.cs.cornell.edu`**	*Secure FTP on my system.*
`Connecting to ftp.cs.cornell.edu...`	*Unix attempts to contact the FTP site.*
`dis@ftp.cs.cornell.edu's password:`	`sftp` *requires my password.*
`sftp>`	*I connected!*
`sftp> `**`pwd`**	*Where am I?*
`Remote working directory: /`	*I start at the remote root.*
`sftp> `**`cd dis`**	*I go to my remote directory.*
`sftp> `**`ls *.html`**	*Look for files with extension* `html`.
`index.html  topics.html`	*Two files found.*
`sftp> `**`get topics.html`**	*Download* `topics.html`.
`Fetching /dis/topics.html to topics.html`	`sftp` *reports progress.*
`/dis/topics.html   100% 1473    0.0KB/s    00:00`	*Done!*
`sftp> `**`put ex.c`**	*Upload* `ex.c` *from my* **HOME** *to the remote CWD.*
`Uploading ex.c to /dis/ex.c`	`sftp` *reports progress.*
`ex.c              100% 1428    0.0KB/s    00:00`	*Done!*
`sftp> `**`ls -l ex.c`**	*Long list uploaded* `ex.c`.
`-rw------- 0 0 0 1428 Apr 22 22:26 ex.c`	*Long listing.*
`sftp> `**`bye`**	*Quit* `sftp`.

I list some commonly used commands in Table 6.3, which I adapted from `sftp`'s `help` listing. Note that the complete list often uses square brackets (`[]`) to indicate an optional form of syntax. For example, `help` shows `lls`'s complete syntax as `lls [ls-options  [path]]`, where both `ls-options` and `path` are optional. For more information, see **`man sftp`**.

PRACTICE!

16. Use **`scp`** to copy a file on the same system.
17. Download a package called *Octave* from GNU's FTP site. What is *Octave*?
18. Determine whether your system has an FTP site to which you can upload files. Should you use **`ftp`** or **`sftp`**?

6.10   USENET

When I first encountered the Internet, I was obsessed with reading a whole bunch of *newsgroups* on *USENET*. Depending on your school, system, and courses, you might not encounter these terms. However, Unix users should be savvy Internet users, due to Unix's wide range of Internet programs. This section provides an overview of USENET and some popular programs for accessing and posting messages.

TABLE 6.3 Common `sftp` Commands

Command	Description
`cd path`	Change remote directory to `path`.
`lcd path`	Change local directory to `path`.
`chmod mode path`	Change permissions of file `path` to `mode`.
`help`, `?`	Display this help text.
`get remotepath`	Download file.
`lls path`	Display local directory listing.
`lmkdir path`	Create local directory.
`lpwd`	Print local working directory.
`ls path`	Display remote directory listing.
`mkdir path`	Create remote directory.
`progress`	Toggle display of progress meter.
`put localpath`	Upload file.
`pwd`	Display remote working directory.
`exit`, `quit`	Quit `sftp`.
`rename oldpath newpath`	Rename remote file.
`rmdir path`	Remove remote directory.
`rm path`	Delete remote file.
`!command`	Execute `command` in local shell.
`!`	Escape to local shell.
`^C`	Cancel/quit.

6.10.1 Background

So, what is **USENET**? USENET is an interconnected network of servers that allows users to post messages and files, which the servers will share with each other. You can post a message (called an *article*) to a particular forum (called a **newsgroup**) via your local NNTP (*network news transport protocol*) server. Typically, the article looks like an e-mail message, but you do not address the message to a user. Instead, you address your message to an entire newsgroup. You can think of a newsgroup as a public forum, containing articles posted to that forum. Except in the case of special groups that require moderation, you can also respond to messages in a newsgroup.

6.10.2 Newsgroup Names

Newsgroup names have the form *name1.name2*..... Currently, there are thousands of different groups, with one or more focusing on almost every imaginable topic. Newsgroup names follow a hierarchical structure. The first name (*name1*) dictates the most general category, like `comp` (*computers*), `sci` (*science*), `talk` (*discussion*), and others. When you learn how to read newsgroups in the sections that follow, you can investigate which groups your system carries.

6.10.3 Newsgroups

I occasionally read `comp.text.frame` to look for advice on using FrameMaker. Would your news server carry that group? Some groups are strictly *local*, whereas others are considered *global*:

- *Local newsgroups* are forums that your system does not distribute to other servers. For example, `cornell.class.cis300` is a newsgroup local to Cornell and lacks relevance and access elsewhere.

- *Global newsgroups* are forums with worldwide appeal. For example, nearly every news server carries `news.announce.newusers` to assist *newbies* (newcomers to the system) with USENET.

When users on your system post messages to a global newsgroup, your NNTP server will inform other news servers about the messages. Those news servers pass along the new articles to other servers, and so forth. Thus, USENET can provide relatively quick global communication. Although USENET lacks centralized control, the distribution model allows for global communication.

6.10.4 Unix Newsreaders

A *newsreader* accesses a particular news server, which carries a variety of newsgroups. By default, your newsreader will attempt to access your local news servers, although you can specify others. If your system supports **newsetup**, I suggest that you run it before trying to run a newsreader. **newsetup** will create a file called `$HOME/.newsrc`, which contains a pre-determined (and likely small) number of newsgroups:

Step 6.32: **Preparing for reading news**

```
unix> newsetup                                          Set up .newsrc in HOME.
Welcome to trn.  Here's some important things to remember:
Many helpful descriptions follow. I show the last few lines.
Creating /usr/u/dis/.newsrc to be used by news programs.
Saving your current one as /usr/u/dis/.newsrc-old...
Done.
To add a new group, use "a pattern" or "g newsgroup.name".  To get rid of
newsgroups you aren't interested in, use the 'u' command.
```

newsetup relies on **trn** (*threaded newsreader*), which displays collections of messages according to common *threads*. A threaded newsreader is akin to a modern web forum, which groups messages together on the basis of certain criteria, such as subject lines.

Step 6.33: **Threaded newsreader (trn)**

```
unix> trn                                               Run threaded newsreader.
Unread news in news.announce.newusers     6 articles
Unread news in news.newusers.questions    88 articles
Unread news in misc.test                  49 articles
Unread news in news.announce.newgroups    6 articles
Unread news in news.answers               783 articles
etc.
======   6 unread articles in news.announce.newusers -- read now? [+ynq]
```

As Step 6.33 shows, using your `.newsrc`, **trn** (and other news programs) accesses each newsgroup that you have stored inside the file. **trn** prompts you to select a particular group.

Besides **+**, **y**, **n**, and **q**, you can enter **h** to see all the commands you may enter. For example, entering **=** accesses the group and lists the subjects of articles. Once you have accessed a group, you can read each article—and yes, entering **h** will display even more commands. Of course, starting with something as complex as **trn** might seem overwhelming, so you might wish to try **xrn**, which provides a GUI interface.

6.10.5 PINE

PINE provides a vastly simpler interface than **trn**, does, although **trn** is vastly more powerful (no pain, no gain!). If you have started using PINE (see Section 6.7.3 for a link to an online tutorial), start the program (**pine**) and select **L** to see the list of folders. Assuming that you have a news server specified, select that folder to access your newsgroups, as shown in Figure 6.2. If you do not have a news server, do the following:

- Determine the local NNTP server. See your system's local homepage.

- Run **pine** and enter the following selections: **M** (main menu), **S** (setup), and **C** (config).

- Move the cursor down to nntp-server and enter **C** (change value).

- At the bottom of the window, enter your NNTP server. If you need to access it with a different username, include **/user=username**. For example, I have my server set to newsstand.cit.cornell.edu/user=dis9.

- Press **Enter** and then **E** (to exit). You may be prompted to accept the changes. If so, enter **Y** (yes).

- You might also need to set a *collection list*. If so, you can consult your local documentation, as this step is a bit more complex.

After you have selected the proper news server, PINE will let you select a particular newsgroup. What makes PINE great is the reminder of commands at the bottom of the screen or window. To add a group, just enter **A**. PINE will then prompt you to enter a name. You can enter a full newsgroup name (such as **comp.text.frame** in Figure 6.3) or just a partial name (like **furry** in Figure 6.4) to see what PINE can find. As shown in Figure 6.4, PINE will look for all group names that match the pattern you enter.[7] For only one match, just press **Enter**. For multiple matches, select the name with the cursor and press **Enter**. When you add a group, PINE subscribes you, which simply means that it will add the group to $HOME/.newsrc. PINE shows only subscribed groups in a news folder.

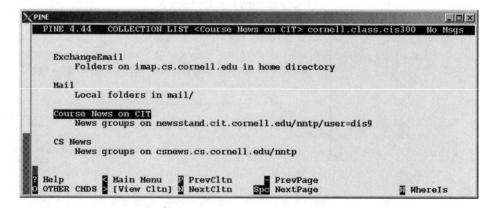

Figure 6.2 PINE News Folder

---

[7]Lest anyone think I have a *furry* fixation, I wanted to pick something odd for the book. In all my years of USENET, I never actually looked at the furry hierarchy. I'm now glad that I didn't.

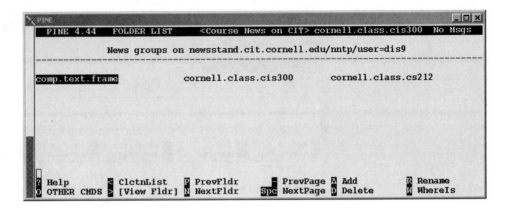

Figure 6.3 PINE Newsgroups

To get a feel for posting a message, look for a local group with `test` in its name. For example, Cornell has a local group called `cornell.test`, whereby local people can post test messages. After subscribing to such a group (possibly even to the global `test.test`), enter **C** to compose an article, as shown in Figure 6.5. You should give a subject line. In a regular message, you also should include a body just as you would write an e-mail. I am relying on you to review PINE's tutorial on sending e-mail. Note that you can address your articles to multiple newsgroups, a process known as *cross-posting*. Do not cross-post unless absolutely necessary. You can also include usernames, which I do now in `CC` (and `Bcc`, using `^R`) and then to alert a particular person about my news post. Enter `^X` to send your message.

To read newsgroup messages, simply select a particular group with your mouse or your arrow keys and press **Enter**. You can scroll up and down the list just as if you are reading e-mail. In fact, you can simulate threaded listing by entering `$` (listed under **O** for `OTHER` commands), which sorts the messages according to various criteria. For example, select **A** for the arrival date.

PINE supports many, many features. I have only barely scratched the surface. I strongly recommend that you investigate PINE's online tutorial.

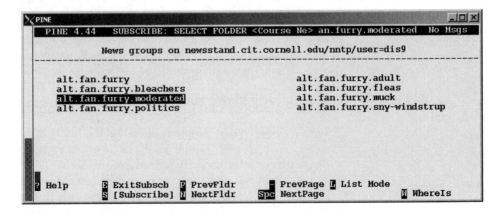

Figure 6.4 Furry Newsgroups

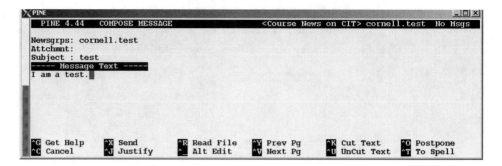

Figure 6.5 PINE Test Message

PRACTICE!

19. How many newsgroups on your system use the name `metal`?
20. Subscribe to a global newsgroup that deals with Unix.

6.10.6 USENET History and Humor

I suspect that entire history books can be written on the early insanity of USENET. *Wikipedia* (*http://en.wikipedia.org/wiki/Usenet*) currently has an excellent collection of historical references. My greatest amusement is "Serdar Argic," once referred to as the "Zumabot." (see also "It's Always September.")

6.10.7 The Future of USENET

Due to excessive spamming, many people have shifted communication to Web-based forums, private chat rooms, and *blogging* (posts on web logs). However, USENET is still alive! In fact, *Google Groups* (*http://groups.google.com*) provides web-based access to a variety of newsgroups. See also *USENET II* (*http://www.usenet2.org*), which proposes to redo USENET.

6.11 THE WORLD WIDE WEB AND BROWSERS

All throughout this chapter, I have mentioned various websites, assuming that you actually know how to access a web browser and visit a website. If your K–12 schooling did not teach you these skills, you can use this section to get a quick overview. I also provide a few "inside" details that you might not have encountered before.

6.11.1 Gopher and Other Programs You Probably Never Heard Of

Before web browsing, people realized that the Internet could provide an excellent infra-structure for sharing documents. Each program, such as *Gopher* or *Archie*, facilitated file search and retrieval. Today, variants of *Archie* (*Veronica* and *Jughead*) exist and retain a small, but dedicated, group of followers. Although few *Gopher* sites remain, try entering `gopher://gopher.floodgap.com` inside a web browser such as Netscape. If you want to be really "old school," enter `lynx gopher.floodgap.com` for the "real" experience.

6.11.2 The World Wide Web

The **World Wide Web** is a grand agglomeration of electronic information accessible over the Internet and features text, graphics, and, often, an interactive capability. Accessing and viewing documents here is frequently referred to as "browsing the web," as shown in Figure 6.6.

6.11.3 Browsers

In Figure 6.6, I ran a program called *Mozilla* (`mozilla`) and entered `http://www.cs.cornell.edu` in the white bar near the top of the window. Your system will likely support *Netscape Navigator* (`netscape`) and possibly other GUI browsers. As hinted at in Section 6.11.1, `lynx` is a text-based web program that strips out graphics and leaves pure text. Why bother with such a primitive program? If your modem connection is slow, you can greatly accelerate web accessibility! Investigate *http://lynx.isc.org* for more information.

6.11.4 URIs and URLs

A **uniform resource identifier** (URI) is an name that can identify a resource. Although you will most often use URIs in the context of naming an Internet resource (e.g., a file that you wish to download), a URI could name any resource, including local data. When you wish to specify a resource location and a method (or *scheme*) by which to download

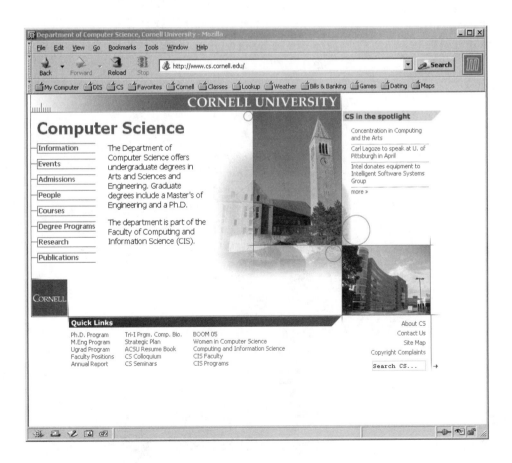

Figure 6.6 Sample Website

the resource, use a ***uniform resource locator*** (URL). If you learn more about the web, you will discover that URIs encompass URLs, although many people still refer to URLs. The simplified syntax of a URL can be considered as

> `scheme://location`

For example, entering **http://www.cs.cornell.edu** in a web browser accesses the document located at `www.cs.cornell.edu`. Try **host** to obtain the IP address `128.84.97.36`, which is the formal location. The `http`, or *hypertext transfer protocol* scheme, instructs your browser to process the website as a *hypertext markup language* (HTML; see Section 6.12) document. Most browsers will assume an **http** scheme if you do not specify it. However, URLs (and URIs) support many other schemes. You can use **mailto** for e-mail, **ftp** for FTP, **news** for accessing a USENET server, and others. See *http://www.iana.org/assignments/uri-schemes* for the complete list.

6.11.5 Browser Tools

Since URIs support a variety of schemes, most browsers provide options for accessing a variety of tools. For example, you can actually use Netscape and Mozilla to browse a file system on Unix. Either open a particular file or directory or enter a URL with the **file** scheme, as shown in Figure 6.7. For e-mail and USENET, you may use their schemes, or simply select **Windows** (in Netscape).

PRACTICE!

21. Use a web browser to load *http://www.asce.org*. What site have you found?
22. Is *www.aaes.org* in the form of a URL?
23. In Figure 6.7, the URL for my **HOME** is `file:///usr/u/dis`. Why does Netscape use three forward slashes (/) in the URL?

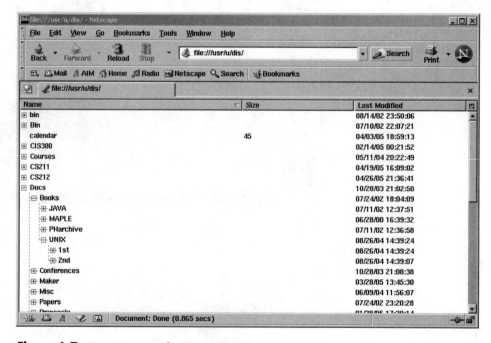

Figure 6.7 Using Netscape for Browsing a Directory Tree

6.12   APPLICATION: CREATING A WEBPAGE

Many students maintain personal webpages (or just *homepages*) to communicate with people, blog (post a we**b** **log**), and even assist potential employers by showcasing their work and promoting themselves. Although I do not have the space to teach web design, we can do some rudimentary work. First, you need to find your system's webserver, which should be posted by your system administrator. You will need to post your files there.

6.12.1   Development

You should first develop your site in **HOME**, as you probably want to delay unveiling your work when you have finished. After all, a homepage is a personal expression of yourself, and most artists do not display their work until they finish! You should also access an actual tutorial online. You might want to start with *http://www.xhtml.org*.

6.12.2   HTML

Many websites and tutorials extensively discuss HTML. For example, you can create a simple file with a basic structure that I demonstrate in Step 6.34. Each line starts with a *tag*, which is text that has the syntax **<name>**. The hypertext protocol instructs your browser to start at the top left corner of your text file, reading each tag and the text that follows it. The following are three basic tags:

- **<html>**: an indication that the document contents are HTML format
- **<body>**: The main portion of the document that you want displayed
- **<p>**: a paragraph

To distinguish elements, you need to close each tag with **</name>**. Step 6.34 gives an example:

Step 6.34:   Create an HTML File

```
unix> cd                          Start in HOME.
unix> pico hello.html             Edit a text file.
<html>                            Start HTML.
<body>                            Primary display.
<p>Hello!</p>                     Paragraph to display.
</body>                           Close body.
</html>                           End HTML.
```

Step 6.35:   View an HTML File

```
unix> netscape &                  Run Netscape.
```
Inside Netscape, either use the **File→Open File...** *menu sequence or enter the URL* **file://HOME/ hello.html***, using the absolute pathname for your* **HOME***. You will see a webpage like that in Figure 6.8.*

There are many more tags that you can use. HTML can be rather fun once you get the hang of it. You may also want to use Netscape's Composer tool, which is a GUI-based webpage editor.

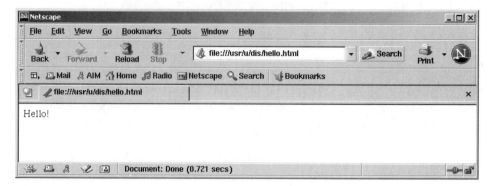

Figure 6.8 View HTML File

6.12.3 XHTML

If you review *http://www.xhtml.org*, you will learn that many Internet developers feel that HTML needs vast improvements, which have been implemented in *XHTML*. Why the new markup language? With HTML, browsers tend to be forgiving, allowing you to be sloppy and inconsistent in your syntax. So, browser developers have a difficult time making their displays consistent. In fact, if you do any real web development, you will learn that you need to test your documents in many different browsers due to the incompatibilities among them. Moreover, HTML has tags, such as **<b>** (bold) and **<i>** (italics), that indicate a font style. Modern development philosophy dictates that you should separate style from content and structure. Strict XHTML disallows mixing, although standards for style are still being developed. If you would like to learn more, visit *http://www.xhtml.org*, which has links to many tutorials and examples.

CHAPTER SUMMARY

- Unix provides many tools for local and global communication.
- Networked computers have the ability to transfer information over LANs and WANs.
- The Internet is a WAN. Hosts on the Internet have IP addresses.
- Humans use hostnames, which are strings that represent IP addresses.
- To communicate with another user, you need to know that person's username. On the local system, you usually do not need to include the hostname. Otherwise, use the syntax ***username@hostname***.
- Enter **mesg n** to block chatting. Otherwise, enter **mesg y**.
- You can read and send e-mail with a variety of programs. (See *http://www. washington.edu/pine* to keep abreast of new versions of PINE.)
- *CC* refers to carbon copy, meaning others whom you wish to receive a copy of your e-mail.
- You must be responsible with e-mail and other postings on the Internet. Follow rules of "netiquette."
- To access a remote site, avoiding using commands like **rlogin** and **rsh**. Instead, use **ssh** (secure shell), which prompts you for a password and encrypts your data.
- To transfer files between systems, anonymous FTP will suffice for public files and for a site that does not require confidential information. Otherwise, use **sftp** (secure FTP).

- USENET is a collection of local and global newsgroups to which you can post articles. Programs, called newsreaders, resemble e-mail programs, although you send messages to newsgroups, not users.
- The World Wide Web is a vast connection of linked documents. With Netscape and Mozilla, you can browse the web. When accessing a site, you use a URI, which has the syntax ***scheme://resource***, where ***resource*** denotes the web address and ***scheme*** is usually **http**.

KEY TERMS

anonymous FTP	Inter Relay Chat (IRC)	top-level domain (TLD)
clear text	Internet	uniform resource identifier (URI)
e-mail	local area network (LAN)	uniform resource locator (URL)
e-mail address	mailbox	USENET
host	netiquette	World Wide Web (WWW)
hostname	network	wide area network (WAN)
IP addresses	newsgroup	

COMMAND SUMMARY

biff	Set alert for incoming e-mail.
cal	Show calendar.
calendar	Remind you about things to do.
date	Show current date.
dtmail	GUI e-mail program.
exit	Exit from a shell. Could log you out if you exit your login shell.
finger	Find information about users.
from	Display listing of new e-mails.
ftp	Access a remote site for file transfer. (See **sftp**.)
host	Determine IP address.
hostname	Show local system's hostname.
listusers	Display list of all users on your system.
logname	Show your username.
logout	Logout. See also **exit**.
lynx	Text-based browser.
mailx	Standard Unix e-mail program.
mesg	Activate or deactivate talk and write for your account.
motd	Show message of the day.
mozilla	Run Mozilla.
netscape	Run Netscape Navigator.
news	Show system news.
newsetup	Set up newsgroups in $HOME/.newsrc.
pine	Popular e-mail program.
rcp	Copy files between systems (possibly remote).
remsh	Run a remote shell. (See **ssh**.)
rlogin	Remote login. (See **ssh**.)
rsh	Run a remote shell. (See **ssh**.)
rusers	Show information about remote users.
scp	Secure remote copy.
sftp	Secure version of **ftp**.
ssh	Run a secure shell for remote access, to execute commands, and more.
talk	Chat with another user.

`telnet`	Run a remote session. (See **ssh**.)
`trn`	Run threaded newsreader.
`users`	Show information about users.
`vacation`	Set vacation program for e-mail.
`who`	Show information about users.
`write`	Write a message to another user.
`xbiff`	GUI version of **biff**.

Problems

1. What is a computer network?
2. What is the minimum number of computers required to create a network?
3. Distinguish between a LAN and WAN.
4. Why is the Internet a WAN?
5. What is your e-mail address for global communication?
6. Write the command line that will output the date using two digits for day, month, and year (DD/MM/YY).
7. Are you using this book for a class? Create a calendar that has all due dates for the course.
8. What are two ways to find out information about yourself on your account? (*Hint*: Use **finger** and **who** with options.)
9. How many users on your system have the first name `Chester`? Write the command line that will report the result.
10. Write the command line that will count how many users exist on your system.
11. E-mail yourself and your instructor a message about your educational goals.
12. E-mail a message to yourself, and send a copy to your instructor by using Bcc (blind carbon copy).
13. How do you find a full list of tilde escape commands from within **mailx**?
14. How would you e-mail a file using **mailx** with a line that starts with a tilde (~)?
15. Sometimes e-mail you send "bounces" back to you; that is, you receive notification that your message could not be delivered. Discuss some reasons e-mail might bounce.
16. What is an e-mail alias? How do you create an alias in PINE? (*Hint*: See **T** for *Take*.)
17. What is a mailing list? How do you use *Take* to create a mailing list in PINE?
18. How do you attach a file to an e-mail message in PINE?
19. Does your system support an FTP site? If so, access the public directory with **sftp**.
20. If you wish to transfer an image, what file type should you set **ftp** to?
21. When is using **ftp** appropriate?
22. Write the command line to log onto a remote site called `blurgle.moppy.do`. Assume an account name `firzam`.
23. Write the command line to run the command **ls** in your **HOME** on a remote site called `blurgle.moppy.do`. Assume an account name `firzam`.

24. Subscribe to an engineering-oriented newsgroup. Name at least five other engineering-oriented groups.

25. Post a message in your local `test` newsgroup. Save that message after it has been successfully posted. Print it out.

26. Is **gopher** a recognized scheme?

27. What is a FAQ?

28. Use your Web browser to locate the Unix FAQ FTP site. Download all FAQ files contained therein.

29. Project 1: Find the main URLs of the World Wide Web homepages of the following engineering organizations:

    - American Institute of Aeronautics and Astronautics
    - American Institute of Chemical Engineers
    - American Society of Civil Engineers
    - American Society of Mechanical Engineers
    - American Society for Engineering Education
    - Institute of Electrical and Electronics Engineers
    - Institute of Industrial Engineers

    Draft a one-paragraph, double-spaced essay about the nature of each organization. Use a text editor to type your report.

30. Project 2: What other engineering organizations can you find on the World Wide Web? Draft a one- to two-paragraph, double-spaced essay about the nature of each. Use a text editor to type your report. (Hint: Find the American Association of Engineering Societies [AAES] website.)

31. Project 3: Create a homepage on your network.

7

Processes

7.1 UNIX PROCESSES

As you have learned, everything in Unix is a file. So, when you run a Unix command, you are running a program that exists somewhere in the Unix file system. Since running a program causes your system to do something, you will consume system resources. Most often, you do not need to worry, but occasionally you will need to investigate system status, programs that have mysteriously halted, or "hogs" that you have (inadvertently?) created. This section provides tools for you to manage your programs.

7.1.1 What Is a Process?

Each program that you run is called a **process**, or a *job*. From logging in to logging out, processes encompass nearly everything you activate. Basic tasks such as routine file management consume very little resources, whereas big software applications can eat up large portions of memory. Microsoft Windows users might have experience using the *Task Manager*, which is a GUI program that helps to manage processes. In Unix, there are useful commands that encompass similar management capabilities.

7.1.2 Multiprocessing

Simultaneously running several programs is called **multiprocessing**, or *multitasking*. GUIs provide a good example of multiprocessing. Different windows and utilities appear on your screen, running continuously even while you perform other tasks. You can conceptualize multiprocessing as the **forking** illustrated in Figure 7.1. Why *forking*? You can run other processes during a process. For example, you can run **ls** at your command prompt, which indicates a shell process. Thankfully, the system does not shut down or log

OBJECTIVES

After reading this chapter, you should be able to:

- Display a basic listing of your processes.
- Display a customized listing of your processes.
- Place a process in the background.
- Move a process to the foreground.
- Kill a process and its zombies (if any).
- Use the job shell for process management.
- Report the time a process takes.
- Schedule a periodic process.
- Schedule a nonrepeating process.
- Schedule a batch of processes.

PROFESSIONAL SUCCESS: HOW TO TAKE A COMPUTER-SKILLS TEST

Have you done as well as you expected on your tests? Do you experience test anxiety? If so, does the anxiety occur before or after the test? Or perhaps at both times? In any case, stop! Take a deep breath and pause for moment…. Instructors give tests, in part, to motivate study. Unfortunately many students would skip studying if reproducing material were not mandatory. Tests measure and compare student performance, producing internal and external pressures on students to succeed. Nevertheless, you can alleviate test anxiety.

Computer tests are tricky and have many forms. Whatever the case, never even think about cramming for a computer-based test. Using software involves skill, and skill always requires practice. To study, I offer the following advice:

- Sit in front of a computer with this book.
- Try each command and step.
- Train with practice and homework problems.
- Obtain solutions to your homework after you've submitted your assignment.
- Seek help when you become stuck.
- Do additional problems from this book and others as well.

I recommend that you start studying at least one week before your test. If you have the time, create study sheets that combine and summarize lecture notes, homework, and the text. Writing and organizing your own notes drums material into your mind and helps break the tedium of reading. (And just from finishing the notes, you will gain a sense of accomplishment as well.) Sometimes classes even permit "cheat sheets" during tests, and concocting great cheat sheets yields terrific comprehension. In developing study sheets, write a list of all commands and options, always note syntax, and show how options affect each command. Give examples that demonstrate command usage.

Be advised that engineering and science tests require you to apply your knowledge. Can you use your acquired knowledge to solve problems and draw conclusions? Yes, sometimes teachers test you on material that you have never seen, but you will be ready to handle this situation if you know not only *what*, but *how* and *why* as well. So, first memorize the what—basic commands and syntax—as a safety precaution; at a minimum, memorization typically produces passing grades. Next, study the how and why for a better grade. Finally, practice applying this knowledge to sample problems for the best grade.

If you still perform poorly, pick yourself off the ground, shake off the dust, and try again. Meet with your teacher to discuss ways to improve. Everyone has bad days. Understanding the material is more important in the long run. You will do better next time. Success is not always doing well: Success is also fighting in the face of defeat. Never give up! A bit more effort will frequently give you the world.

you out when you run **ls**! Both processes continue. In fact, you can spawn many more processes. If you think of a process as a line, then many processes splintering off one another begins to look like a fork. If you want the complete scoop on forking, check out **man -s2 fork**.

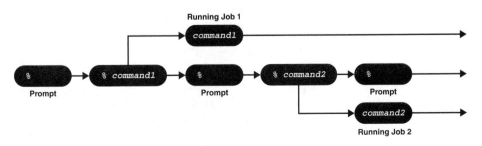

Figure 7.1 Multiprocessing as forking

7.1.3 Process Status

To obtain a current list of your processes and information associated with them, use the **ps** (*process status*) command. Although **ps** has options, for now I will show the basic version of the command.

Step 7.1: Report current processes (basic)

```
unix> ps                              Report processes with basic listing.
   PID TTY      TIME CMD              Types of information.
   894 pts/17  0:00 ps               Process information for ps!
 28607 pts/17  0:00 tcsh             Process information for my login shell.
```

The information from **ps** includes each process' unique process identification number (PID), the location of the terminal (TTY), the duration of the process (TIME), and the command name (CMD). You will see these items in further detail in Section 7.1.5. For a complete listing of all processes on your system, including those of other users, use **ps -e**.

7.1.4 Child and Parent Processes

Processes fork each time a new process is activated while another still runs. For example, your login shell is the *parent process* for all processes created by commands that you run. Each *child process* begins when you activate commands and programs at the prompt. In Figure 7.1, the prompt indicates the parent process, the middle "prong" on the fork.[1] The processes from **command1** and **command2** activate new child processes: Job 1 and Job 2. These children fork off of their parents, running separately and simultaneously with each other and their parents.

You can view your parent–child process relationship with **ptree username** (or **pstree** on Linux). The **ptree** command will display children below and indented from their parents. **ptree** will indent sibling processes at the same level.

Step 7.2: Show parent–child process relationship

```
unix> ptree dis                       Show my current parent–child process tree.
28606 xterm -display 999.99.99.99:0.0
  28607 tcsh
    5380 xterm -sb -geometry 80x52+0+0 +ut -title PINE -e /usr/bin/pine
      5381  /usr/local/pine/bin/pine.bin -d0
    12212 ptree dis
```

In the preceding example, my remote connection (PID 28606), which is a terminal window displayed on my home machine, is the ancestor of all my other processes. One child of **xterm** is my login shell (**tcsh**) which has two children: another terminal with its own child (**pine**, my e-mail program) and the **ptree** command itself.

7.1.5 Full Process Listing

Now and then, you will discover that **ps** might abbreviate command names and lack needed detail. For a tabular view of your parent and child processes, use **ps -u user**. I recommend that you include the **-f** (*full*) option, which produces the columns described in Table 7.1.

---

[1]A fork's prongs are called *tines*. You can now impress your friends and family with your knowledge of table utensils.

TABLE 7.1 Full Process Listing Fields

ps **Field**	**Description**
UID	User ID number. Every username has an associated number. You can see your own with **id**. The **-f** option will force the display of the username. Enter ps -o uid to see the associated UIDs.
PID	Process ID.
PPID	PID of parent process.
C	Obsolete information.
STIME	Starting time of the process.
TTY	The controlling terminal (window/screen/computer) for the process. **ps** shows ? when the process lacks a controlling terminal.
TIME	Cumulative execution time.
CMD	Full command name and arguments, up to 80 characters.

Step 7.3: Full process listing

```
unix> ps -fu dis                                      Full process listing for me.
UID    PID  PPID  C    STIME TTY       TIME CMD
dis 28607 28606  0 21:50:34 pts/17   0:01 tcsh
dis  5381  5380  0 22:04:28 pts/2    0:00 /usr/local/pine/bin/pine.bin -d0
dis  6919 28607  0 23:15:50 pts/17   0:00 ps -fu dis
```

You can see that my execution of **ps** is a child of **tcsh** because **ps**'s PPID is **tcsh**'s PID. Besides "full user," I have another handy trick for remembering the **-fu** options, which I cannot write here. For more details, see **man ps**. Some systems also support a similar BSD version: **ps -aux**.

7.1.6   Custom Process Status

To customize the output of **ps**, use **ps -o item1,item2,…**, where you separate each format item with a comma. For example, **ps -o user,pid,comm** will show the user, PID, and command name:

Step 7.4: Show custom process status

```
unix> ps -o user,pid,comm                          Username, PID, command.
  USER   PID COMMAND                               Custom process listing.
  dis  28607 tcsh                              Only parents shown because
  dis  11409 ps                                I did not request children.
```

For a full list of options, enter **man ps**.

7.1.7   Process Commands

In addition to **ptree**, Unix supports many other process tools. For example, **pwdx PID** will display the CWD of **PID**. Check out **man proc** for a complete list of these tools.

7.1.8   System State

If you are curious about the state of the system, perhaps the most useful command for you (and for new Unix users in general) is **uptime**, which displays how long the system has been up:

Step 7.5:   Display how long your system has been working

```
unix> uptime                                        How long has your system been up?
11:58pm  up 38 day(s), 20:29,  20 users,  load average: 1.02, 1.12, 1.16
```

There are a variety of other useful commands that system administrators might use: **vmstat**, **mpstat**, **iostat**, **sar** (*system activity reporter*; likely restricted), **sag** (*system activity graph*; also likely restricted). For fun, you can see when your system administrator last booted the system with **who -b**.

PRACTICE!

1. What is your user ID?
2. List your processes. Which one is your login shell?
3. Show a full process listing for everyone on your system.
4. Show a process listing for the cumulative time and command name for all your processes.
5. When is the last time your system was rebooted?

7.2   MANAGING YOUR PROCESSES

With any computer, sooner or later something will go wrong, usually inadvertently or inexplicably. Something you do will cause an errant process. Or maybe something will "hang." Either way, you are responsible for managing your processes. Your system administrator, however, monitors the system in case something goes *really* wrong. This section covers commands for helping you manage your process in less drastic situations.

7.2.1   Killing a Process

In Unix, life is brutal. If you no longer need or desire a process, you destroy it! More formally, you *kill* the process. **Killing** a process involves stopping its execution. You cannot restart the program from the point you quit. There are several ways to kill a process:

- Enter **^C** while a program runs.
- Enter **kill** *PID* for a particular process.
- Close the window in which a program runs.
- Exit (or log out) from the shell in which a program runs. Use **exit** or **logout**. Try also **^D**, which usually works.
- Exit your GUI entirely.
- Log out from your session.

Following are some examples:

Step 7.6:   Kill a process

```
unix> grep e /usr/dict/words                        Find all lines with the letter e.
```
Enter ^C! Otherwise, **grep** *will list thousands of words, because* e *is the most common letter in the English language. You can even make this step a game. How quickly can you quit* **grep** *after pressing* **Return***? So far, the quickest I can stop is at* absorptive.
```
unix> xclock &                                      Run a GUI clock and return control to the shell.
[1] 16940                                Unix reports process information: job number (Section 7.2.7), PID.
```

If you see an icon, such as ⊠ *, select it to kill the window. You can also try selecting the title bar with the right mouse button.*

```
unix> xdaliclock &                          Run another kind of clock and return control to the shell.
[2] 16946                                    New clock process started.
[1]   Done      xclock                       Old clock process is done.
unix> ps                                     Display processes.
   PID TTY     TIME CMD                       Let's see if ps shows the clock process.
 28888 pts/2   0:00 tcsh                      My shell.
 16957 pts/2   0:00 ps                        The process status display.
 16946 pts/2   0:00 xdaliclo                  xdaliclock runs in the background.
                                              ps abbreviates long names unless you use option -f.
unix> kill 16946                             Kill xdaliclock, using its PID.
unix> ps                                      Display process status.
   PID TTY     TIME CMD
 28888 pts/2   0:00 tcsh
 16978 pts/2   0:00 ps
[2]  - Terminated      xdaliclock             kill worked!
unix>                                         Your Unix prompt returns.
```

In the foregoing step, I used an ampersand (**&**) with the GUI clock commands. The **&** allows you to keep working at the prompt. I will explain the reason in greater detail in Section 7.2.5. Note that you should not kill your primary shell process—the parent for all your other processes after logging in. Otherwise, you will log yourself out! For more information, see **man -s1 kill** and **man shell built_ins**.

7.2.2   Zombie Processes

Now and then, the approaches for killing processes may not work. In extreme cases, supposedly killed processes may still linger. For example, an abrupt interruption in your system access might leave a process running, which **ps** will show when you log on again. Such processes are called *zombies*. In zombie movies, the dead return to life looking for brains to eat. Unlike movie zombies, Unix zombies eat system resources. To see if a process is indeed "zombified," use **ps -o pid,s,comm**, where **s** gives a *process state* (S). If the value shown under S is Z, you've got a zombie! To kill Unix zombies, try **kill PID**. If you absolutely cannot kill a process, read the next section.

7.2.3   Process Signals

If you have trouble killing a process, someone might recommend to you that you enter **kill -9 PID**, which is one of Unix's most classic (and cryptic) commands. Why **-9**? If you enter **kill -l** (lowercase *L*), you will see a list of *signals* that you can send to a process:

Step 7.7:   List of signals for processes

```
unix> kill -l                               Show list of signals for kill. Use lowercase L.
HUP INT QUIT ILL TRAP ABRT EMT FPE KILL BUS SEGV SYS PIPE ALRM TERM and more.
```

A signal is a special value that can be sent to and from a command. Counting from left to right, the ninth signal is KILL, which tells a process to die immediately. So, instead of **kill -9**, you can actually enter **kill -KILL PID** to obliterate a process without allowing it to shut down other resources. You may cause drastic results if other processes rely upon the one you kill with KILL. But when you enter **kill PID**, by default you are entering **kill -TERM PID**, which gives the process a chance to clean up resources and then stop.

In fact, you can send a variety of signals to a process, including some signals that don't kill! For a complete list of signals, I enter **man -3HEAD signal**. On your system, maybe you will find the process signals in **man kill** or **man signal**. For related commands, see **pkill** and **pgrep**.

7.2.4 Suspending a Process

If you prefer not to kill a process, but only temporarily suspend it, enter **^z** during the process execution. ***Suspending*** tells Unix merely to interrupt the process. If you suspend a process at the command line, the shell's prompt will reappear, allowing you to enter more commands and fork more processes. Once you suspend a process, you can leave the job on hold, restart it, or destroy it. Below, you will practice suspending a process with **^z**.

Step 7.8: **Start process**

```
unix> pico avb.txt                          Edit a file.
Pointless verbiage.                         Your text does not matter.
unix> less avb.txt                          View the file.
Pointless verbiage.                         Contents of file.
avb.txt line 1/1 (END)                      less is running.
```

Step 7.9: **Suspend (stop) process**

```
Do not quit from less! Enter ^z to suspend less:
Suspended                                   Unix alerts you that you suspended a process.
unix> ps -o pid,s,comm                       Show current primary processes:
PID S COMMAND                                PID, State, Command.
28888 S tcsh                                 S: sleeping (not complete yet).
27987 O ps                                   O: running.
23495 T less                                 T: stopped.
```

I will explain how to reactivate a suspended process later in Section 7.2.7. If you want to stop viewing avb.txt, you can kill that process with **kill**:.

Step 7.10: **Kill suspended process**

```
unix> kill 23495                            Hasta la vista less avb.txt!
unix> ps                                    Check processes.
  PID TTY    TIME CMD                        Do you see less in what follows?
28888 pts/2  0:01 tcsh                       Not here...
 4865 pts/2  0:00 ps                         Not here...
[1]  - Terminated      less avb.txt          You are terminated!
```

In the sections that follow, you will learn about other ways of manipulating and killing processes.

7.2.5 Background

As discussed in Section 7.1.2, a number of processes run simultaneously, or fork off the shell, in any Unix session. Although you may see nothing but a prompt, there's a lot going on, as evidenced by **ps -fe**. Why don't you see so many processes? Besides the fact that numerous processes belong to other users, the system runs many commands "below the surface." Processes that continue to run simultaneously with other programs run in the ***background***. Background jobs continue working without command-line input, happily running elsewhere—in other memory locations—while you continue to work on the task at hand. Thus, background processes leave your Unix prompt free to accept more commands.

Appending an ampersand (**&**) to a command line pushes the associated process into the background. Be sure to place the ampersand at the end of the command. GUIs provide a good example of background processes. In a GUI, windows simultaneously perform different tasks, each with its own command prompt accepting separate command lines. When running GUI programs, you should enter commands as **command &** to free up the terminal window for further entry of commands. Step 7.11 uses **xclock** to demonstrate a background process:

Step 7.11: Background processes

```
unix> xclock &                                        Run xclock in the background.
[1] 16959              Unix reports process information: job number (Section 7.2.7), PID.
unix>                                                  Your prompt returns for you to use!
```

Besides GUIs, you might wish to execute intensive commands in the background. For example, I am curious as to whether any of my system's GNU ("Gnu's Not Unix") distribution has files with sex in their names. The command **find *path* -name *pattern*** will search for filenames that match ***pattern*** at ***path***. Step 7.12 searches for files and sends their pathnames to a text file called sex.txt in my **HOME**. On my system, GNU is located in /usr/local/gnu. To send the output of a command to a file, I use ***cmd > file***.

Step 7.12: Search for "sex" on your Unix network

```
unix> cd                                                          Work at HOME.
unix> find /usr/local/gnu -name 'sex*' > sex.txt &             Search for files.
unix> ps                                              Work while find searches.
26696 pts/2  0:00 find                                   Portion of ps's output.
```
Wait a little while, or do some other work while **find** *works on finding* sex.
```
unix> less sex.txt                                        What did find discover?
/usr/local/gnu/emacs-20.5/share/emacs/20.5/etc/sex.6              A result!
/usr/local/gnu/emacs-21.2/share/emacs/21.2/etc/sex.6         Another result!
```

In the preceding example, putting an intensive process into the background (see Figure 7.2) allowed you to keep working—and yes, **emacs**'s standard distribution usually includes a joke file called sex.6.

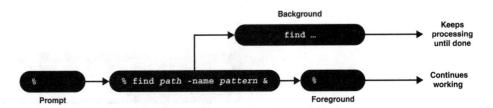

Figure 7.2 Putting process in background

7.2.6   Foreground

What happens to the primary process, your shell, in Step 7.11? You can still interact with a process in the ***foreground***. A foreground process is "up front," taking over as the primary program that you run at the command prompt. For example, consider a GUI in which windows are processes. In that case, you can think of a foreground window as the active window, perhaps residing on top of a background window. You must finish working with a foreground process before you may regain control of it's parent process. Thus, before you enter new command lines, you must wait for the previous command line to finish. Step 7.13 demonstrates this principle.

Step 7.13:   Dealing with a foreground process

```
unix> xclock -d                                    Run a digital clock in the foreground.
The cursor will just sit here. You can't enter another command line!         See Figure 7.3.
```

As shown in Figure 7.3, the digital clock runs in the foreground, which means that the previous process—the shell—must wait. Unfortunately, to return control to the shell, you must kill the clock! You can enter **^C** at the command line or use a GUI action with the mouse. Note that you can still type text in the shell—the text just won't do anything. I hope that you now see why putting GUI programs in the background with an **&** is so handy.

7.2.7   Job Control

Most shells provide a further means of managing your processes, enabling you to run, suspend, restart, or destroy them as necessary. The **jobs** command produces a numbered list of background and suspended processes. Like the PIDs provided by **ps**, job numbers help you access your jobs.

Step 7.14:   Access jobs

```
unix> xclock -d &                                  Run a digital clock in the background.
[1] 16959                              Unix reports process information: job number, PID.
unix> jobs                               Access my background and suspended processes.
[1]   + Running      xclock -d                           The clock is in the background.
```

Above my background process is the clock, which is labeled internally as job 1. On your system, you may already have several programs running, giving you more jobs and several

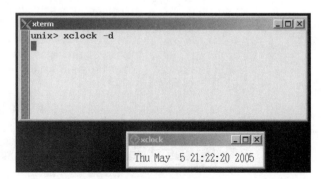

Figure 7.3   The command prompt waits for a foreground process to finish.

job numbers. Those job numbers provide access for you to control their corresponding processes. For a particular job number *job*, you can do the following:

- Run a job in foreground: Enter **fg** %*job* or just %*job*.
- Run a job in background: Enter **bg** %*job*.
- Suspend a job: Enter **stop** %*job*.
- Destroy a job: Enter **kill** %*job*.

Step 7.15 demonstrates the various actions you can perform with job control commands:

Step 7.15: Manage a process with job number

```
unix> cd                                    More clutter for HOME.
unix> pico sjz.txt                          Create another text file.
Mindless rambling.                          No words of wisdom here.
unix> less sjz.txt                          View your silly text.
Mindless rambling.                          It's still silly.
sjz.txt line 1/1 (END)^Z                    Suspend less with ^Z.
Suspended                                   Unix alerts you.
unix> jobs                                  Show background and suspended processes.
[1]   - Running     xclock -d              I still have a clock running.
[2]   + Suspended   less sjz.txt           less is still suspended.
unix> fg %2                                 Move less to the foreground.
Mindless rambling.                          less sjz.txt is active again.
sjz.txt line 1/1 (END)^Z                    Suspend less again.
Suspended                                   Unix obeys.
unix> kill %2                               Terminate less sjz.txt!
unix> jobs                                  Check your jobs again.
[1]   - Running     xclock -d              I still have a clock running.
[3]     Terminated  less sjz.txt           less sjz.txt is toast.
```

For more information, see **man jobs** and **man stop**.

7.2.8   Notification

If you are running a shell that has the **notify** command (**csh**, **tcsh**), then your shell can alert you immediately after you change the status of a job. For a particular job, enter **notify** *job*. Otherwise, **notify** will use the most recent job.

Step 7.16: Set notification for a job

```
unix> xclock &                              Run a clock in the background.
[1] 29528                                   Unix lets you know that the clock is job number 1.
unix> notify 1                              Notify you if the clock process changes.
unix> kill %1                               Kill the clock.
[1]   Done      xclock                      Unix alerts you about the change.
```

PRACTICE!

6. Kill any clocks you might already have running.

7. Run **xclock** in the background.

8. Determine the job number of the clock.

9. Put the clock in the foreground. What happens to your shell?

10. Suspend the clock in the shell. What happens to your shell?

11. Restore the clock to operation without interfering with command input in the shell.

7.2.9 **Control**-Key Sequences for Processes

The following are **control**-summarize sequences having to do with processes. I believe you will find it helpful if I summarize these sequences in one place:

- `^C`: Kill a process. Try also `^\`.
- `^D`: Exit a shell.
- `^S`: Suspend display of input (pause).
- `^Q`: Restore input from `^S` (continue).

I tend to forget about `^S`, because other programs give it a different use, such as *save*. I inadvertently enter `^S`, which causes my screen to hang. So, I must remember to enter `^Q`:

Step 7.17: Suspend and Continue

On a new command line, enter the following sequence of inputs: `ls^S` **Spacebar~Return**`^Q`. *Before you enter* `^Q`, *all you will see is* `ls`. *But Unix remembers the keystrokes you type after* `^S`. *Entering* `^Q` *will activate your input and resume display:*

```
unix> ls                         See preceding instructions for commands to enter after ls.
Output HOME's listing.
```

To see a list of all **Control**-key sequences for your shell, enter `stty -a`.

7.2.10 General Resource Management

If you discover that you enjoy this journey into the "guts" of Unix, you might want to try `plimit`, which can get and set a process' resources. See also `preap` to "reap" (as the *Grim Reaper* brings death!) a zombie process. Section 7.1.8 also hints at many such commands.

7.3 TIMING A PROCESS

If you find that a Unix command which you enter "hangs" (doesn't seem to finish), perhaps the process simply takes a long time to finish. Unix provides tools for measuring process times with `timex` (an updated version of `time`). To time a process, enter `timex commandline`. Unix will display how long `commandline` takes in terms of real elapsed time (hours/minutes/seconds), user's CPU time, and system CPU time.

Step 7.18: Measure process time

```
unix> timex ls                      Time the ls command. These times are in seconds.
    real    0.01                    Output from ls not shown. These times are in seconds.
    user    0.01                    Focus on the real time.
    sys     0.00                    The process is quite quick.
unix> timex ls -R ~ > mystuff.txt   Time a recursive list of everything in HOME.
    real    34.20                   The > sends the output to
    user     0.31                   a file called mystuff.txt.
    sys     13.94                   As expected, this command takes more time, which is shown in seconds.
```

In the preceding example, the recursive listing (and subsequent dumping of results in **mystuff.txt**) takes much longer to process than just **ls**. Why? After years of work, I have accumulated a lot of files! I suspect that you are curious what user and system times are and why they are different. These times reflect the time that the CPU takes for you and for itself internally. For a formal explanation of the measurements, see **man -s2 times**. For more precise timing, try **ptime**.

7.4   SCHEDULING PROCESSES

If you start using Unix for programming, managing your schedule, or doing large-scale computations, you may want to schedule a process to occur at another time. Otherwise, your work may enslave you. (Do as I say, not as I do!) This section gives you a brief overview of how to schedule processes.

7.4.1   Be Nice

Niceness is the degree to which a process will let the system handle other processes first. Essentially, niceness is priority. For example, suppose that on a shopping trip you fill your cart with items. To be nice, you allow people with only a few items to "cut" in front of you. With Unix, you may let other processes have more attention from the system by setting their values higher than their default niceness values. More important processes have *low* nice numbers, whereas less important processes have *high* nice numbers, which might seem counterintuitive, so be careful. You can use **ps -l** or **ps -o nice** to view the niceness of processes. Step 7.19 displays all system processes. Note that I use *cmd* | **less** to send results of **ps** into **less**, to allow for paging.

Step 7.19:   Display the niceness of processes

```
unix> ps -eo user,nice,comm | less          View all system processes:
   USER NI COMMAND                            user, niceness, command.
A long display ensues, a portion of which is follows:
   root 10 /opt/SUNWut/lib/utsessiond
   root 20 dtgreet
   dis  20 ps
```

Your system administrator will likely assign some system processes higher priorities with corresponding lower numbers. To *increase* a niceness level, use **nice *commandline***:

Step 7.20:   Increase niceness of process

```
unix> nice xclock &                         Run a clock with less priority.
[1] 22850                                    Clock runs in background.
unix> ps -o nice,comm                        Check process status.
   NI COMMAND                                Niceness, command.
   20 tcsh                                    My shell runs normally.
   24 xclock                           The clock runs with more niceness.
```

There are two forms of the **nice** command. If you do not use **csh** or **tcsh**, your default *increment* in niceness should be 10. To select your own increment, use **-*n*** (standard) or **+*n*** (**csh** or **tcsh**), where *n* is a positive number less than or equal to 19. Anyone with some competitiveness should now be curious as to whether you can grant a process higher priority and thus *less* niceness. After all, isn't your work more important than everyone else's? Probably not, as your system might require root (system administrator) access. If you could reduce niceness, you would enter **-m** (standard; e.g., **--10**) or **-n** (**csh** or **tcsh**; e.g., **-10**). For more information, see **man nice**.

7.4.2 Keep Something Processing

Suppose you need to log out for a little while, but you have a long process running, and it is really important. Unfortunately, if you log out, the system will likely terminate the process. However, if you invoke the *no-hang-up* command, **nohup commandline**, your process will continue running after you log out. For example, suppose you want to dump the listing of everything you own into a single file. Normally, you would enter **ls -R ~ > stuff.txt**. You don't need to use the **&**, but it does let you use the terminal until you do log out. But suppose you are like me and have zillions of files. If you do not wish to wait around, you can let **nohup** do the work, running **ls** in the background.

Step 7.21: Keep a process going after you log out

unix> **nohup ls -R ~ > stuff.txt &**	*Store listing of* **HOME** *in* stuff.txt.
unix> **logout**	*Log out.* **ls** *will still run in the background.*
After taking a break, log on again.	
unix> **ps -fu dis**	*Check processes.*
If you see **ls** *still running, it's not done yet. For me, I let a few more minutes go by, so* **ls** *does not appear.*	
unix> **tail stuff.txt**	*Look at the last few lines of* stuff.txt.
If **ls** *finished writing out everything you own, the last few lines should be the last directory's contents, in alphabetical order.*	

nohup has some options and other features, which **man nohup** explains.

7.4.3 Schedule Something to Happen Periodically

In Unix, you can create a calendar, which Unix will scan, using a ***daemon*** to send you reminders. Unix daemons are processes that lie dormant, providing service when requested.[2] The **cron** (*chronological*) daemon (on some systems, **crond**) is a process that allows users to schedule processes to run periodically or at specified times. To use the **cron** facility, you create a text file called $HOME/crontab.cron (*cron table*; often referred to as just *crontab* or *cronfile*) that contains one or more lines with a date/time and command line.

First, you may wish to check your system to see if your administrators have granted users this capability. Either in /var/spool/cron or /etc/crond.d, you should see a file called cron.deny, which should *not* list your username. If a file called cron.allow includes your username (or doesn't exist at all), then you should have access to **cron**. After checking, you are ready to create your file. Your crontab.cron may have multiple lines. Each line has five fields with time/date information and a sixth field with a command line to run:

- Field 1 = *minute* (0–59).
- Field 2 = *hour* (0–23).
- Field 3 = *day of the month* (1–31).
- Field 4 = *month of the year* (1–12).
- Field 5 = *day of the week* (0–6, with 0 = Sunday).
- Field 6 = *command line*.

---

[2]A *daemon* is named after special creatures from Greek mythology who did tasks for the gods. Many Unix daemons have command names that end with **d**.

The time/date information can be multiple values (e.g., **1,3,10**), a list (e.g., **0-4**), a combination of multiple values and ranges (e.g., **1-3,6**), or *****, which matches to any time/date. If a line begins with **#**, the line is called a *comment*, which is ignored. Inside the command line, **%** is treated as a new-line character. In order for the **cron** daemon to activate your crontab, you must register it via **crontab crontab.cron**. Step 7.22 demonstrates a simple example that creates a rudimentary alarm clock for your shell from Monday to Friday:

Step 7.22:   Schedule a periodic process

```
unix> cd                              Work in HOME.
unix> pico crontab.cron               Edit a crontab file.
0,30 * * * 1-5 echo '\nBeep!'         Schedule an "alarm" for every 30 minutes.
unix> crontab crontab.cron            Register your crontab.
unix>                                 Wait for the next half hour or hour.
Beep!                                 Your "alarm" sounds.
unix> date                            Check the current time soon afterward.
Fri May 6 22:00:05 EDT 2005           The time for the alarm worked!
```

Note that if you include a **%** inside the command line, **crontab** will treat the characters to the right of the **%** as an *input file* to the command to the left of the **%**. So, if you use **mailx mom %Happy Mother's Day!**, the system will mail a user called mom an e-mail with Happy Mother's Day! in the body.

In fact, if you run the crontab in Step 7.22, you will already be sending e-mail— to yourself! To disable e-mail when displaying output to the screen, use the following command:

```
0,30 * * * 1-5 echo '\nBeep!' > /dev/console 2> /dev/null
```

The **>** *redirects* the output of a command to another destination, such as a file. Here, **/dev/console** is the terminal, which displays the alarm. You might need to enter **/dev/tty**. You should check **ps** or **tty** to see the actual pathname of your terminal:

Step 7.23:   Check terminal name

```
unix> tty                   What's my terminal name?
/dev/pts/20                 I have a weird name because of remote access.
        Actually, you will see that it seems to shift, as I've worked on this chapter at different times.
```

I direct all other output (something called *standard error*, indicated by the **2**) to **/dev/null**, which is the "black hole" of data. Anything directed to /dev/null is ignored.[3] If you prefer to see no output *and* not receive any e-mail, use **> /dev/null 2>&1**, which sends both output and errors to /dev/null. (By default, crontab uses **sh**. Chapter 8 covers this syntax in greater detail.) For example, with the following command I could copy all my text files to a special directory every morning at 1:17 A.M. without being notified:

```
17 1 * * * cp *.txt Data > /dev/null 2>&1
```

---

[3]Unix users typically use "dev-null" (as it is pronounced) as part of everyday lingo. For instance, to tell someone that you do not think their advice is worthy, say that they should save it for /dev/null.

If you find that you need to start over, you can disable your crontab by unregistering it:

Step 7.24: Unregister your crontab

```
unix> crontab -r                                        Disable your crontab.
```

You could also edit it (**crontab -e**) and comment out the lines. (Use **#**.) Note that you must re-register your crontab. For more information see **man crontab**.

PRACTICE!

> 12. Show a line for your **crontab.cron** that will e-mail you a New Year's greeting immediately after each New Year has started.
>
> 13. Write a crontab that will e-mail your friends a reminder about meeting to study every Sunday at 5 P.M. They should receive the e-mail every Thursday and Friday at 9 P.M.

7.4.4 Schedule Something to Happen Once

To schedule a process for just one execution, you might wish to use **at**, which pretty much does what it sounds like: **at** a *date*, do *task*. The **at** command relies on the **cron** daemon, just as **crontab** does. So, you inspect /usr/lib/cron/at.allow and /usr/lib/cron/at.deny to see if you have permission to use **at**. If at.allow does not exist, you should not see your name listed in at.deny.

The **at** command has a variety of options and forms of syntax. In this section, I demonstrate the basic, interactive form: **at** *time*. When you enter this command, the **cron** daemon will prompt you with at>, upon which you enter your commands one at a time. (Press **Return** after each.) When you are done, enter **^D** (EOT, or *end of text*) to exit:

Step 7.25: Schedule a command with **at**

```
unix> at now + 1 min              At 1 minute from now, execute the following commands....
at> echo Hello!                                              Say "Hello!" and
at> echo Buh-Bye!                                     say something more irritating.
at> <EOT>                               Enter ^D to exit. Unix will display <EOT>.
commands will be executed using /usr/local/bin/tcsh    at will use your default shell.
job 1115782319.a at Tue May 10 23:31:59 2005              You're at job's schedule.
```

The form I used in Step 7.25 is *time+increment*. You could have picked a specific date or time, such as **10:23 am Oct 22**, but that's harder to test. **man at** shows many examples of times and increments you can use: **today**, **tomorrow**, **next week**, and others.

Step 7.26: Specific date for **at**

```
unix> at 10:13am Oct 22, 2027                             Do something later.
at> echo Hello from the past!                          Send a "time capsule!"
at> <EOT>                                                  Exit at with ^D.
commands will be executed using /usr/local/bin/tcsh         Use default shell.
job 1824214380.a at Wed Oct 22 10:13:00 2027   Years from now you will get a message.
```

To access job information and remove various entries, use **at -l** (list) and **at -r** (remove). Your system may also have **atq** and **atrm**, which are respectively similar:

Step 7.27:   List and remove `at` jobs

```
unix> at -l                                              List pending at jobs.
1824214380.a   Fri Oct 22 10:13:00 2027          A message to your future self.
unix> at -r 1824214380.a                         Remove the pointless message.
unix> at -l                                            List at jobs again.
unix>                                                     Nothing to list!
```

If you prefer to schedule a bunch (or *batch*) of commands to run as soon as the system has the resources, use **batch**. Running CPU-intensive jobs during peak hours could slow down the system. By queueing up your processes with **batch**, you enable the system to perform each big process one at a time. A *queue* is a line that forms under the motto "First come, first served." Imagine lining up for tickets to enter a concert or check-out line. Those lines are queues, unless you are extremely courteous.[4] In fact, the **batch** command is a shortcut for running one or more **at** jobs. **batch** places the jobs into the system's **queue**:

Step 7.28:   Use `batch` to queue up `at` jobs

```
unix> batch                                       Run a batch of at jobs ASAP.
at> echo hello                                             One of the jobs.
at> echo bye                                                 Another job.
at> <EOT>                                               Exit batch with ^D.
```

As soon as the system has resources, it will run your batch of jobs. You can use **at -l** and **at -r** for listing and removing batch jobs.

By the time you have entered Step 7.25 with **now + 1 min**, you might wonder why your screen doesn't show the output. If your **at** works as mine does, you just received an e-mail from yourself with the output of the two commands, hello and bye, on separate lines. If you did not receive e-mail and wish to, use **at -m** (mail). I do not like to receive such e-mail, and I expect you feel the same. I suggest that you use **at -s** (Bourne shell), which gives you the same output options as you have with **crontab**. Then, enter the command syntax as follows:

- To send output to the screen and no report by e-mail, enter
  command > terminal 2> /dev/null.

- To send no output or report, enter
  command > /dev/null 2>& 1.

In both cases, **at** will still perform **command**. For more information, refer to **man at**.

PRACTICE!

14.   Show a command line that will e-mail your homework (`$HOME/hw1.txt`) to your instructor (mohan) next week at 2 P.M. Allow **at** to mail you a confirmation.

15.   Show a command line that will store the number of unhidden files in your entire account in a file called `filecount.txt`. The command should run immediately and neither e-mail you any result nor report an answer to the screen.

---

[4]If you let everyone cut in front of you because they are more important, that kind of line is a *priority queue*. For example, if you visit an emergency room because you stubbed a toe, I will bet that the doctors will see the truly urgent patients before you, regardless of how soon you arrived.

7.4.5   Sleeping

Although computer users today expect blazing speeds, deliberately slowing down or pausing your command line provides some useful tricks. The **sleep** command has the syntax **sleep** *seconds*. The command finishes *seconds* from the time you enter the entire command. For example, supposed you would like to remind yourself about something an hour from now. You could **sleep 3600** and then echo a message. Since you would like to keep working, you need to put both commands together in the background. To group commands together, use **(command; command;...)** . To assign background processes, use **&** (Section 7.2.5):

Step 7.29:   Quick-and-dirty alarm

```
unix> ( sleep 3600; echo Dinner time! ) &        Alert yourself about dinner 1 hour from now.
[1] 14932                                         Unix indicates job number and PID.
                                                  You may want to try a shorter sleep time to test the command.
unix>                                             Do something for an hour.
unix> Dinner time!                                Unix alerts you!
                                                  Press Return to get the prompt.
unix> [1] Done    ( sleep 1; echo Dinner time! )  Unix reports the finished process.
```

7.5   APPLICATION: HAPPY BIRTHDAY!

This section explores some brief applications for scheduling processes that may assist with managing your personal life. Suppose you wish to send birthday messages to everyone you know so that you never forget any of their birthdays—well, technically never. How can Unix rescue you from forgetfulness? You have a few options. Instead of **at**, I recommend **crontab**. Inside a crontab file, you could either type generic messages or create separate files. I will demonstrate both forms, so you will need at least one external file:

Step 7.30:   Create birthday file

```
unix> cd                            Work from HOME.
unix> pico ead_bday.txt             Eugene's birthday file.
Dear Gene, happy birthday!          Pick someone you know.
Love,                               If you are lonely, pick yourself.
Crontab                             Unix is your friend!
```

Next, you will edit a `crontab.cron`. For Gene, I will send my birthday file by redirecting `ead_bday.txt` with **mailx** *user* **<** *file*. For other people, I can write messages directly in the crontab. In each line, a **%** indicates a new line. The first **%** in each line is special: All subsequent lines before the next crontab entry are sent into the current command as an input file. For instance, the crontab entry

    * * * * * mailx dis%Hello!%How am I doing?%Fine, I hope!

will mail three lines of pointless self-analysis to myself every minute. Step 7.31 creates a crontab file for mailing Gene via an external file. For comparison, I show how to directly mail someone named JEFF:

Step 7.31:   Create birthday crontab

```
unix> pico crontab.cron                      Create a crontab file.
0 8 1 2 * mailx ead@somewhere < ead_bday.txt Every February 1 @ 8 A.M.,
```

mail Gene the file **ead_bday.txt**.

```
0 9 3 6 * mailx jec@somewhere %Hi Jeff,          Your crontab redirects input into mailx.
                             %Where's the pickle?
                             %Well, happy birthday!%Dave
0 4 10 2 * mailx dis %Happy Birthday to me!%Me          Mail myself every year.
                                                Well, not really. I scrambled all the dates.
```

Don't forget that Unix's **cron** daemon will not know about your edited **crontab.cron** unless you register the file:

Step 7.32: Register your crontab

```
unix> crontab crontab.cron          Register your new crontab.
```

I recommend that you change your birthday messages now and then. In fact, somewhere on your system you likely have emacs installed, and if you do, you should also have the following file:

less /usr/local/gnu/emacs-21.2/share/emacs/21.2/etc/yow.lines

If you learn how to program, you could write a small program that generates a random integer, which corresponds to a line number in yow.lines. You could then copy and send that line to someone, providing amusement for many years.

CHAPTER SUMMARY

- When you run a command, you create at least one process.
- Unix can run multiple processes simultaneously.
- You can view the status and other important information concerning your processes, including those of the system and other users. Use **ps -o** to customize the listing.
- A parent process may spawn multiple child processes.
- PIDs are numbers that label each process.
- You can kill a process with **kill**, which has many kinds of signals that you can send to the process. To stop a process without gracefully shutting it down, use the **-9** signal, but with caution.
- To put a process in the background, enter **command &**. You will commonly see this syntax with GUI programs.
- If you suspend a process, you can restart it at the prompt (move the process to the foreground) or continue it in the background.
- The job shell provides an alternative to managing jobs. You can access background or suspended jobs with **jobs**. The job shell assigns job numbers to these processes. The job shell commands, such as **fg** and **bg**, use the job numbers.
- Increasing the niceness of a job allocates less system resources to your process.
- You can continue processing a job while bogged out with **nohup**.
- Unix daemons are primarily dormant programs that activate processes as necessary.
- You can schedule commands to run periodically in a crontab file. To register your file, use **crontab del -r**.
- You can schedule commands to run once with **at** and **batch**.

KEY TERMS

background	killing	queue
daemon	multiprocessing	signal
foreground	niceness	suspending
forking	process	zombie

COMMAND SUMMARY

`^C`	Kill a process. Try also `^\`.
`^D`	Exit a shell.
`^Q`	Restore input from `^S` (continue).
`^S`	Suspend display of input (pause).
`at`	Perform a process a certain time.
`batch`	Place one or more processes in the system queue.
`bg`	Place a process in the background.
`crontab`	Manage scheduled processes.
`echo`	Display a string or variable value.
`fg`	Place a process in the foreground.
`jobs`	List background and suspended processes.
`kill`	Kill a process; send a signal to a process.
`nice`	Modify the niceness level (the importance of a process).
`nohup`	Keep a process running even if you exit a shell or log out.
`notify`	Send an alert if the process changes.
`ps`	Display the process status.
`ptree`	Display the process tree (parents and their children).
`sleep`	Pause for a period of time.
`stop`	Suspend a job.
`stty`	View and/or modify terminal information.
`timex`	Display how long a process takes.
`tty`	View terminal information.
`uptime`	Display how long the system has been working.
`xclock`	Run a GUI clock.
`xdaliclock`	Run a GUI clock.

Problems

1. What is a Unix process?
2. Explain the difference, if any, between a job and processes.
3. Explain why Unix allows you to place commands in the background.
4. Write a command line that displays the basic process listing for user `jre`.
5. Write a command line that displays the user, elapsed time (days, hours, minutes), and full command name for user `svendsen`.
6. What is the difference between killing and suspending a process?
7. Does a suspended job run in the background? Explain your answer.
8. What are three ways of killing a process? What are two ways of suspending a process? (Other than using a GUI menu selection or clicking on a title bar icon.)
9. Assuming that you are using a GUI, how would you activate **xman** from a command line such that you can use your shell prompt? Does **xman** run in the foreground or background?

10. Describe the series of steps that places two processes in the background by using job shell commands.

11. What happens if you kill the shell process that was created when you logged in?

12. Write the command lines for the following steps: (a) Place the process **finger kcm > kcm.txt** in the background; (b) Show your process and job listings; (c) Kill the process, using the job number.

13. If, after you've typed several characters, you still do not see your cursor move on the screen, what do you think might be the problem? Suggest some remedies.

14. Write a command line that will measure how long **sleep 10** takes to finish. Does the reported time match exactly 10 seconds? Explain your answer.

15. Write a command line that sets the niceness of a program called **maze** to the nicest level.

16. Write a line that you would include in a crontab file to alert you by e-mail each Sunday at 10:00 P.M. about a meeting you have every Monday at 11 A.M.

17. Write a line that you would include in a crontab file for deleting all files that end with `.###` throughout your entire account. This process should occur every night at 1:23 A.M. You should not be e-mailed anything.

18. Write a sequence of commands and their output for an interactive session of **at** that mails you a reminder next week at the same time about whatever is happening that day.

19. Does your system support **atq** and **atrm**? If so, generate several **at** requests. List the requests and remove them. How does the default behavior of **atrm** differ from that of **at -r**?

20. As a project, explain how to schedule a sequence of commands using a file with **at** instead of the interactive interface. Provide an example that performs three separate and different actions.

8

Shells

8.1   UNIX SHELLS

As you learn about Unix you will encounter references to shells. I introduced shells early on in Figure 1.1, which depicts the layers of Unix. A Unix shell is a program that provides interface between you and the kernel's low-level programs in the operating system. In fact, the name *shell* derives from the fact that it covers, or hides, the internal OS layers. To become proficient in Unix you need to master a variety of shell features. Since I lack a couple thousand pages to detail every aspect and nuance, I use this chapter to review the fundamental features to start your path to Unix wizardry.

8.1.1   Types of Shells

Just as Unix provides a multitude of programs with similar purposes, it also offers you a choice of shells. This "shell game" involves deciding which Unix shell to choose. I summarize common shells in Table 8.1. Many Unix textbooks tend to focus on **csh** (*C Shell*), **ksh** (*Korn Shell*), **sh** (*Bourne Shell*), and **bash** (*Bourne-Again Shell*). To see which shells your system supports, enter **more /etc/ shells** and **man shells**. When discussing shells, the classification of features follows two primary shells (**sh**, **csh**) and their newer (and more robust!) "descendents," as shown in Figure 8.1:

- **ksh** and **bash** descend from **sh**.

- **tcsh** descends from **csh**.

- **zsh** descends primarily from **sh** but borrows heavily from newer shells, like **bash** and **tcsh**.

OBJECTIVES

After reading this chapter, you should be able to:

- Identify and change your login shell.
- Specify the responsibilities of a Unix shell.
- Redirect input and output to and from files.
- Connect commands together with pipes.
- Form command sequences.
- Access, set, and change local and environment variables.
- Set your command path.

TABLE 8.1   Common Unix Shells

Shell	Command	Website	Comments
Bourne Shell (or just *shell*)	`sh`	*en.wikibooks.org/wiki/Bourne_shell*	• Ancestor of Unix shells. • Used by many Unix scripts.
Bourne-Again Shell	`bash`	*www.gnu.org/software/bash*	• Updated Bourne Shell. • Incorporates many popular features of other shells. • Popular with Linux users.
C Shell	`csh`	*en.wikipedia.org/wiki/C_shell*	• Modeled after the C programming language. • Fallen out of favor—see the website for details.
Korn Shell	`ksh`	*www.kornshell.com*	• An updated Bourne Shell. • Modern versions (`ksh93` and `pdksh`) are available for free.
TENEX C Shell (T Shell)	`tcsh`	*www.tcsh.org*	• Improved C Shell. • Commonly set for new users by system administrators.
Z Shell	`zsh`	*www.zsh.org*	• Resembles Korn Shell, but updated. • Multitude of features—`man zsh` lists several other manpages with features.

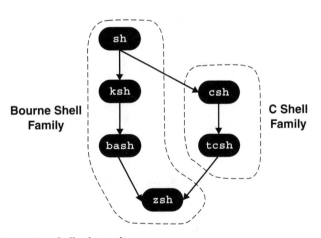

Figure 8.1   Basic Unix shell relationships.

All shells continue to influence each other as they develop. Thankfully, you can find online information on each shell on your system: `man sh`, `man csh`, and so forth. `zsh` is so expansive that it takes several mapages to explain its features (start with `man zsh`).

8.1.2   Interactive and Login Shells

All throughout this text you have entered command lines at a shell prompt. You have been using an ***interactive shell***, a shell that accepts command lines and provides feedback.[1] When logging in, you must use a special kind of interactive shell called a ***login shell***. The login shell sets certain kinds of information (usually variables). Fortunately,

---

[1]A noninteractive shell refers to a program that you run composed of statements, which is called a *script*.

Unix system administrators do not saddle newbies with choosing a login shell, though it might be fun to watch them squirm. When your system administrator created your account, a `passwd` file containing your username and other fundamental information was created. (I discuss the settings in Sections 8.4 and 8.9.) The last entry in your `passwd` file is the name of your login shell. To see the shell, you can view the **SHELL** value with **echo**. Your process status (**ps**) will also list your shell:

Step 8.1: Check your login shell

```
unix> echo $SHELL                                    Check my login shell.
/usr/local/bin/tcsh              I use a T Shell. I am toying with switching to zsh.
unix> ps                                          Check basic process status.
   PID TTY      TIME CMD                    Process ID, terminal, time, command.
  2758 pts/32  0:01 tcsh                         My login shell. Yours may differ.
Other processes listed. (Not shown.)
```

With a GUI, opening a new window (**xterm**, **dtterm**, …) will usually spawn the same type of shell as the login shell inside the window. Try entering **xterm &** a few times and then **ps -fu** *username*. Each window allows you to interact with a shell—you can think of each window as mini-session.[2]

If you dislike your login shell, I recommend experimenting with interactive shells, though you might lack robust start-up files. To experience the "flavor" of another shell without commitment (no carnal sin involved), simply enter the shell name at the prompt. Your parent shell process will spawn a child shell process as an interactive shell.[3] The parent must await the child's termination, so practice using this new shell:

Step 8.2: Temporarily change your shell (run a child shell)

```
unix> zsh               Run a child shell process. Do not put it in the background.
%                                    See man zsh for unique commands you can try.
% exit                            Quit this child shell to return to parent shell.
unix>                                              Back to your original shell.
```

You can also change your default login shell! On some systems, you must contact your system administrator. Your system may also support **chsh** (*change shell*).[4] For now, I do *not* recommend changing the default shell that your administrator set for you. If you do decide to change the shell, you need to know the full pathname of the shell. For example, to set **ksh** for my default shell on my system I would enter **/usr/bin/ksh** when prompted by **chsh**. You can find full pathnames in /etc/shells or by entering **which** *shellname*. On some systems, your **chsh** might be equivalent to **passwd -r nis -e**, which I demonstrate in the following step:

Step 8.3: Permanently change your login shell (do not attempt this yet!)

```
unix> which zsh                                             Where is zsh?
/usr/bin/zsh                                       Full pathname of zsh.
```

---

[2]The GUI windows might not be running login shells. If you have a ~/.xinitrc, see if you have an **xterm** process modified with **-ls**. See section 8.9.3.

[3]You can run an interactive shell as a login shell with command options, e.g., **tcsh -l** and **bash --login**.

[4]Before changing your shell, I recommend reviewing *www.faqs.org/faqs/unix-faq/shell/shell-differences* and Table 8.1.

```
unix> /usr/bin/passwd -r nis -e
Enter existing login password:
Old shell: /usr/local/bin/tcsh
New shell: /usr/bin/zsh
```

*Use **passwd** to change login shell.*

Enter your Unix password.

Your current shell.

*I decide to change to **zsh**.*

To access your new login shell, you must log out from the current window. I also suggest logging out entirely by exiting all shells before logging in again. After you login again, check **echo $SHELL** to confirm the change.

PRACTICE!

1. How do **sh** and **ksh** differ?
2. Demonstrate that each new window you run spawns a new shell.
3. What happens if you kill the process corresponding to your login shell?
4. Run a child shell. Explain the result of entering **echo $SHELL**.

8.1.3   Shell Language

As discussed in Section 2.2, operating system and programming languages tend to model human communication. To command someone to do something quickly you must be concise and lucid. *Shave your armpits!* is certainly clearer than *Garple flooput yeck!* Computers don't usually shave your body hair but they *do* respond to correct commands. Shells provide robust methods for writing command lines. Recall that the interactive shell splits, or *parses*, your command line into individual tokens and checks their syntax. If you use correct semantics (Section 2.2.5), the shell should produce meaningful results.

As you become skilled with writing complex command lines, you might become interested in **scripts**, which are collections of command lines. Why write a script? If you find that you are repeating the same group(s) of command lines, it would certainly be easier to write them just once in a file and then run *that file* as a program!

8.1.4   Shell Features

You will discover that shells differ, but many newer shells (**bash**, **tcsh**, **zsh**) share many features, which I summarize in Table 8.2. As you will note, other sections of this book cover more details. This chapter covers the remaining features. As you learn about the Unix shells and their components, I strongly recommend that you remember to review your shell's document (or just *manpage*). I agree that it's long, but I guarantee that you will continue to find useful information to help Unix become more familiar.

8.1.5   Parsing the Command Line

You might find the listing of common shell features in Table 8.2 rather daunting;[5] but each shell follows a sequence of steps in parsing, interpreting, and executing all of the tokens you enter. I listed each feature in the approximate order in which the shell processes your command line. Because you do not yet know all of these features, I suggest that you focus on this simplified sequence:

- Parse the tokens.
- Substitute and expand special symbols and other words.

---

[5]Although I have deliberately neglected *functions*, I provide a short introduction in Section 8.8.5. Functions resemble mini-scripts, or small collections of commands that you provide a name for.

TABLE 8.2 Common Shell Features

Element	Description	Example	Reference
History	Access or enter a previous command.	Enter **history** to display a list of previous command lines.	Steps 2.13 and 2.14, Section 8.6
Tokenizing	Parse command line into tokens.	Commands use hyphen (−) to separate a command from its options.	Section 2.4.6
Quoting	Interpret characters and words literally with **"**. **/**, and ****.	**more test|.txt** views a file called test|.txt.	Section 8.7
Aliases	Define your own commands.	**alias ll 'ls -al'** allows you to enter **ll** instead of **ls -al**.	Step 2.15, Section 8.8
Redirection	Change sources of command input, output, and errors.	**mailx user < file** mails *file* to *user*. **cat f1 f2 > f3** appends the contents of **f2** to **f1** and sends the output into **f3**.	Section 8.2
Pipes	Send output of a command into another command.	**command	less** sends the output of **command** as the input of **less**.	Sections 2.8, 8.2.13, 8.2.14
Processing	Handle execution of programs.	Enter **xeyes &** to place **xeyes** in the background. You now have "googly-eyes" watching your mouse.	Chapter 7
Variables	Define words to store values.	**echo $HOME** shows the full pathname of your home directory.	Sections 2.4.8 and 8.4
Command Substitution	Replace a command with its result in the command line.	**mkdir Backups`date +%d_%m_%Y`** replaces the **date** command with the *value* it produces.	Section 8.7.1
Wildcards (Globbing)	Use special characters to match patterns of filenames.	Enter **ls *.txt** to list all files with suffix .txt.	Section 5.10.1
Subshells	Group commands together to run as a child shell.	Enter **(ls > stuff.txt) ; more stuff.txt** to store a CWD's contents and then view the resulting file.	Section 8.3
Sequences	Combine command lines.	**cd ; ls** will change your CWD to **HOME** and then list the contents.	Sections 2.7.1 and 8.3
Built-in commands	Shells provide some commands that are literally built "inside" the shell.	**man shell_builtins** provides a complete list for **csh**, **ksh**, and **sh**. See also shell manpages.	Section 8.5

- Look up command names.
- Stop if shell encounters error; otherwise, run the command.

For a more rigorous explanation, refer to *Unix Shells By Example* in the Bibliography and your shell's manpage.

PRACTICE!

> 5. What are shell metacharacters?
> 6. Where can you learn about how **bash** sets up your login shell?

8.1.6 Command-Line Editing and Spelling

One feature I did not list in Table 8.2 is your ability to edit a command line. You might ask why I consider this notion worthy of an entire sub-section. If you use only left and right arrow keys, **Backspace**, **Del**, and **^C** for editing, you definitely need to learn about the tools which modern shells provide: *editing* and *spelling*.

While editing a command line, you can use **emacs** or **vi** style commands and shortcuts to jump around, fix mistakes, and often recall commands from your history. To see a complete list of keystrokes (which are called *bindings*), enter either **bindkey** (**tcsh**, **zsh**) or **bind -P** (**bash**). (See also **man zshzle**.) I really like **emacs**'s **^A** [(a)head of line)] and **^E** (end of line). You can also use **bind/bindkey** to change keystrokes. To establish greater "coolness" (and introduce shell programming), you can create a separate script that contains key bindings that your start-up files call.

If you frequently misspell words, you can allow the shell to suggest spelling corrections. Many shells sport spell checking, usually with shell variables that you can set. Below, I demonstrate **tcsh**'s **M-$**, which attempts to correct the entire command line:

Step 8.4:   Spell check

Below, type **mna shred***, followed by* **M-$***. But don't press* **Enter***!*

```
unix> mna shredM-$                         Type a command and then run a spell checker.
unix> man shred                tcsh displays the corrected command line, don't re-enter it.
```

All you need to do is press **Enter** *or* **Return** *if you like the correction. Otherwise, you may continue editing it.*

Note also that modern shells provide two other ways to assist with editing:

- *Aliases*: Assign meaning to names you frequently misspell (Section 8.8).
- *Filename completion*: Press certain keys to force the shell to attempt/suggest ways to complete filenames, like commands, files, and directories (Section 8.5.7).

Consult your shell's manpage for specific information on editing and spelling.

PRACTICE!

7. How do you skip entire words with **emacs** shortcuts?
8. What does **shopt -s cdspell** do? Give a demonstration.

8.2   I/O, REDIRECTION, AND PIPING

Unix commands can accept input and output, or ***I/O***, from a variety of sources, as shown in Figure 8.2. Typically, you enter a command, press **Enter**, and Unix reports results (if any) at the prompt. But you can change the sources of input and the targets of output. Each shell has slightly different syntax, which the shell's manpage will explain. I show common forms and highlight important distinctions in this section.

8.2.1   File Descriptors

When you begin to write your own programs, you will learn about I/O *streams*, which are the bytes that go into and out of programs. The kernel labels open files and I/O streams with ***file descriptors***, which are special integers that indicate the particular files or streams. For example, in Chapter 7, you might have used **> /dev/null 2>&1** as part of a command. The **2** and **1** are file descriptors that refer to important kinds of I/O. So, why **1** and **2**? See the next section.

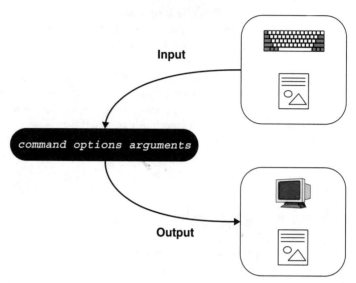

Figure 8.2 Examples of standard I/O: input from keyboard or file; output to terminal or file.

8.2.2   Standard I/O and Error

When you run a command, you have three kinds of I/O streams that Unix treats as files for all commands:

- stdin (*standard input*): Input into the command.
- stdout (*standard output*): Output from the command.
- stderr (*standard error*): Error messages that the shell may report.

Why files? Remember, in Unix, everything is a file, which is a collection of bytes stored in memory. For more efficient command-line parsing, Unix associates stdin, stdout, and stderr with **0**, **1**, and **2**, respectively, as shown in Table 8.3.

Note that most shells assign a default device for these forms of I/O. I use these typical defaults throughout this book to demonstrate standard input and output via the keyboard and terminal, respectively. Although you might have lumped error messages with "command output," they belong to standard error. I strongly suspect that your shell sends standard error to the terminal (/dev/tty), appearing as command output. You can test the default target of stderr by deliberately making a mistake, as in the next step:

Step 8.5:   Standard error

```
unix> /usr/local/gnu/bin/make love          Run command make on file love.
make: *** No rule to make target 'love'. Stop.    Standard error sent to terminal.
              OK–Stop! (This example is a classic Unix joke. Yes, a bit geeky, but I still think it's funny.)
```

TABLE 8.3   Standard Input, Output, and Error Files

Filename	Explanation	Descriptor	Typical Source/Target
stdin	Input to a command	0	Keyboard
stdout	Output from a command	1	Terminal
stderr	Error message(s) from a command	2	Terminal

PRACTICE!

8.2.3   Redirection

You might be curious if you can change a default I/O source or target. Well, yes you can! Changing the source and/or target of standard input, output, and/or error is called ***redirection***. The remaining sections demonstrate a variety of approaches.

8.2.4   Output Redirection

The operator for output redirection is **>**. The basic command-line syntax is **command > target**. The output of **command** will be sent to **target**. So, Unix will not report the results of **command** to the terminal. To help remember the direction of the streams, I like to pretend that **a > b** is $a \rightarrow b$, where **a** sends results to **b**. For example, suppose you wish to store a list of users currently logged on. Try the following step:

Step 8.6:   Redirect output to a file

```
unix> who > users.txt          Create a file containing current users.
unix> less users.txt           View the target file.
```

You now have a record of everyone logged onto the system at the time of the command entry. Pointless, yes (unless you like spying), but at least you understand **>**. (Actually, system administrators occasionally need to do this.)

Some commands, like **cat**, allow for delayed output. For example, **cat > out.txt** tells **cat** to send it's output to a file called out.txt. But, I did not supply an input file to **cat**, as in **cat in.txt > out.txt**. So, **cat** allows you to enter text from the keyboard until you finish with ^D, after which **cat** stores your input in out.txt.

Step 8.7:   Using **cat** and output redirection

```
unix> cat > out.txt            Prepare to store input in out.txt.
Domo arigato, Mr. Roboto!      stdin comes from the keyboard.
^D                             Finish entering text. Send signal to exit.
unix>                          The Unix prompt returns.
```

Why bother with **cat > out.txt**? This command line provides a quick and dirty text editor!

If you use **sh** or its descendents, you can specify stdout in the output redirection using its file descriptor (**1**), as thus: **command 1> output**. The **1>** (no space between **1** and **>**) indicates command's stdout goes into file **output**.

Step 8.8:   Specify file descriptor in output redirection (**sh, ksh, bash, zsh**)

```
unix> bash                     Use sh or one of its descendents.
$ ls 1> mystuff.txt            Redirect listing output to mystuff.txt.
$ more mystuff.txt             View mystuff.txt.
```

Unix will show you the CWD listing you stored in `mystuff.txt`.

`$ exit`   *Exit your shell (if necessary).*

In general, you do not need to specify the file descriptor for `stdout`. But when you wish to redirect `stderr` along with `stdout`, you will need to know them. In some cases, you can use other file descriptors, but I will leave you to discover that concept on your own. (I can't cram *everything* about Unix into this book!)

PRACTICE!

11. If you cannot figure out how to use **find** for finding a particular file, how can you use output redirection to assist with the search?
12. Use **cat** to append **file2** to **file1** and store the resulting file in **file3**.
13. Can you specify a file descriptor with **csh** or **tcsh**?

8.2.5   Using Output Redirection to Erase a File

When using output redirection, you need to be careful when sending output to an existing file. What happens if you do? **csh** and **tcsh** users may encounter the following scenario:

Step 8.9:   Existing file with output redirection (csh, tcsh)

```
unix> ls > L1.txt                                    Send output listing to L1.txt.
unix> pwd > L1.txt                              Try to send other output to L1.txt.
L1.txt: File exists.                                       I cannot overwrite a file!
```

Actually, your shell may exhibit different behavior. My shell (**tcsh**) has a special variable called **noclobber** set in my start-up files. If you lack **noclobber**, entering **pwd > L1.txt** erases the previous contents of L1.txt and stores the CWD inside.[6] Rather than bogging you down with tangential conversation, I will explain variables in greater detail in Section 8.4. To see if your shell sets **noclobber**, enter **set | less**, which pages through all of your variable settings.

Unix lets you obliterate files and output in a variety of ways! You can also deliberately send output to "nowhere" with `/dev/null` (Section 7.4.3). `/dev/null` will "eat" whatever file you send there, effectively deleting the stream. You can demonstrate the obliteration of a stream with any command that has output:

Step 8.10:   Sending output to /dev/null

```
unix> ls > /dev/null                                                List your files.
        Unix shows no output, because you sent the output listing to the "black hole" of /dev/null.
```

As shown in Section 7.4.3, `/dev/null` is particularly useful for target output that you do not need to see.

If you wish to completely obliterate the contents of a file without deleting it, use **sh** (or a descendent) and enter **> *file***:

---

[6]Clobbering an existing file happens because redirection of `stdout` to an existing file sets the *next byte pointer* (NBP) in that file to 0, or the first byte. To visualize this pointer, imagine that an arrow points at the *next* free line inside a file, which is below the last line. With >, Unix always moves the NBP to the first line, forcing Unix to overwrite the old contents from the beginning. Worse yet, Unix has no undelete command, so be careful when clobbering a file.

Step 8.11:   Obliterate file contents without removing the file (**sh** or descendent)

```
unix> pico kcm.txt                              Edit a text file.
Carrot seeds.                       Enter something you don't mind deleting.
-rw-r--r-- 1 dis dis 14 May 20 23:59 kcm.txt       14 bytes of senselessness.
unix> sh                                    Use sh or descendent shell.
$ > kcm.txt                           Do not specify a command before >.
$ ls -l kcm.txt                          Long list kcm.txt to see size.
-rw-r--r-- 1 dis dis 0 May 207 23:55 kcm.txt       kcm.txt has 0 bytes now!
$ exit                                     Return to my default shell.
unix>                                         Back to tcsh for me.
```

If you wish to override **noclobber** and rewrite output to the same file, you can use **>!** (**csh**, **tcsh**, **zsh**) or **>|** (**ksh**, **bash**, **zsh**). If your shell has **>!**, you must put a space between the **!** and the output file, otherwise Unix might treat the file as a history command (Step 2.14). Below, **noclobber**'s setting does not affect the redirection:

Step 8.12:   Redirect output to an existing file (**csh**, **tcsh**, **zsh**)

```
unix> ls >! stuff.txt                        Send listing into stuff.txt.
unix> ls -l >! stuff.txt                  Send long listing into stuff.txt.
```

8.2.6   Appending Output

If you would like to *append* the output of a command to an existing file, use **>>**, which has pretty much the same syntax as **>**, as thus: ***command >> output***. You might wonder why you should bother, since **cat** already facilitates concatenation, as with **cat f1 f2 > f3**. To skip creating the third file ***f3***, you can directly append the contents of ***f1*** to ***f2*** with **cat f1 >> f2**:

Step 8.13:   Append output with **>>**

```
unix> pico f1.txt                                Edit a text file.
def                                              Type something.
unix> pico f2.txt                                Edit another file.
abc                                          Type something else.
unix> cat f1.txt >> f2.txt                   Append f1.txt to f2.txt.
unix> less f2.txt                              Check the results.
abc                                           Hooray for Unix!
def
```

PRACTICE!

> 14.   Create a file called home_stuff.txt that contains the contents of your **HOME**.
> 15.   Put two more copies of everything in your **HOME** inside home_stuff.txt.

8.2.7   Writing Output

Although many commands incorporate output as part of their execution, you might wish to report additional values or messages to the user. Such output is common with scripts, though you have seen examples herein that use command-line output. For instance, if you need to check the value of a variable, like **HOME**, you could enter **echo $HOME**. In general, you can use two output commands: **echo** and **printf**.

Each shell differs in treatment of **echo**. Some shells allow certain escape characters (**\a**, **\b**, **\f**, ...), and others require certain options. As usual, check out **man echo**. To use your shell's **echo**, simply run **echo *output***. Otherwise, use **/usr/bin/echo *output***. Below, I use **tcsh**'s **echo** to output two lines. Note that I use forward quotes (**'**) to indicate the new-line escape character (**\n**). Section 8.7 provides more information about quoting:

Step 8.14: Write output with `echo`

```
unix> echo hello'\n'good-bye          Output a multi-line message.
hello                                             First line.
good-bye                                        Second line.
```

On my system, **man echo** actually recommends using **printf** to provide consistent behavior across shells. Moreover, **printf** has extensive formatting abilities. You can supply *format labels* in a string using **printf *format output***. Refer to **man -s1 printf** and **man formats** for the complete (and extensive) listing of available format labels.[7] For example, inside **printf "%'.2e\n" 10.3**, the label (**%1.2e**) modifies **10.3** using exponential notation (**e**). The **2** instructs **printf** to use two decimal digits after the dot (**.**). More concisely, **%'.2e** means **d.dd**, according to **man formats**. After printing the number, the **\n** instructs **printf** to start a new line. I demonstrate this example, below:

Step 8.15: Write output with `printf`

```
unix> printf "%'.2e\n" 10.3           Express 10.3 in scientific notation.
1.03e+01                                      10.3 = 1.03 × 10¹.
```

Note that **printf** supports escape characters, as shown above.

PRACTICE!

16. Write a command line with **echo** that does not place a newline character at the end of the output string.
17. Fill in the blanks in the command line, below, to produce the following session:
    ```
    unix> printf _____   _____
    I graduated in 1.99e+3.
    unix>
    ```

8.2.8 Error Redirection

New Unix users might have trouble distinguishing between stdout and stderr because both file streams tend to appear on the terminal. But, they truly differ. For example, suppose you try to store the listing of a nonexistent directory called Money in file savings.txt. Unix will create savings.txt but give you an error:

---

[7]The **printf** formats strongly resemble C-style formats, which a multitude of languages have adopted. I recommend trying a few of the examples from **man printf** get a feel. Trying a few now will definitely help you get a head start on learning how to program! In fact, you might even wish to try **man C**.

Step 8.16:   Generate standard error

```
unix> ls Money > savings.txt
Money: No such file or directory
unix> more savings.txt
No contents shown.
unix> rm savings.txt
```
Send listing of Money *directory to* savings.txt.
Because I have no Money, *I get an error.*
Unix still makes an empty file!
There's nothing in savings.txt *because I had no directory contents.*
I want to reuse this filename, so I delete it. See also Step 8.12.

When using **sh** and its descendents, you can direct stderr with its file descriptor as **command 2> file**. The syntax **n> file** tells the shell to take stream **n** and send it into **file**:

Step 8.17:   Redirect standard error (**sh** and descendents)

```
unix> bash
$ ls Crapperroo 2> crud.txt
$ more crud.txt
Crapperroo: No such file or directory
```
Run **bash**.
I don't own a directory called Crapperroo.
View crud.txt.
The error message was redirected there.

If you would like to direct output (**1**) and errors (**2**) to different files, use the syntax **command 1> output 2> errors**, though the **1** is optional:

Step 8.18:   Redirect stdout and stderr to different places (**sh** and descendents)

```
unix> bash
$ ls Test 1> listing.txt 2> errors.txt
```
Run **bash**.
Send output of ls **Test** *into* listing.txt
and (possible) errors into errors.txt.

csh and **tcsh** use a different syntax: **(command > output) >& errorfile**. The parentheses **()** create a child process (*subshell*, Section 8.3), which runs *before* the rest of the command line executes. The output of the subshell process is then sent to **errorfile**. However, the process inside the subshell may redirect their own output elsewhere. Below, I send the output of an erroneous listing and its **stderr** to the same file errors:

Step 8.19:   Redirect stdout and stderr to different places (**csh, tcsh**)

```
unix> (ls Doodlydo > /dev/tty) >& errors
unix> more errors
Doodlydo: No such file or directory
```
Redirect stdout *of* ls *to terminal.*
and **stderr** *to errors.*
stderr *was directed here.*

You should wonder about the meaning of **>&**. I sure did when I first saw it. The **&** signifies that the redirection uses an *and*, which assists sending output and errors to the same file. Why would you use the same file? Suppose that you really prefer seeing only stdout. You could redirect stderr somewhere else, like /dev/null (Section 8.2.5), which prevents alerts from reaching you. To receive alerts for scheduled processes (e.g., **crontab**), having just one message by e-mail might be handier than two. So, to direct stdout and stderr to same file, use **>&** (*"redirect* this *and* that*"*) in the following forms of syntax:

- **csh/tcsh** use **command >& file**. You can think of the **>&** as saying "send the output of **command** to the same **file** as the errors." Or, "send errors and output to **file**."

- **sh** and descendants use `command 2> file 1>&2`. You can think of this syntax as "send the errors of **command** to **file**, and send the output to the same file." Or, "redirect both the errors and output to **file**."

With the above syntax, Unix will first write `stderr` in **file**, followed by `stdout`, as depicted in Figure 8.3. You can test both forms of syntax with `ls Dir1 Dir2`, which attempts to list two directories. Assume that **Dir1** exists and **Dir2** does not:

Step 8.20: Redirect `stderr` and `stdout` to the same file

```
unix> tcsh                                   Use csh or tcsh.
% ls Unix_work Bwack >& testA.txt            List two directories.
% exit                                       Return to default shell.
unix> bash                                   Use bash (or related).
$ ls Unix_work Bwack 2> testB.txt 1>&2       List two directories.
$ exit                                       Return to default shell.
unix> diff testA.txt testB.txt               Check if the results differ. They do not.
unix> less testA.txt                         Look at one of the identical files.
Bwack: No such file or directory            The redirection first stored stderr.
Unix_work:                                   stdout was redirected next.
Listing of my Unix_work directory not shown.
```

There are even more variations, such as `>>&`, `>&-`! Check out the shell manpages.

PRACTICE!

18. Explain the syntax `command 2> file 1>&2`. How do the results of this command-line differ from `command 1> file 2>&1`?
19. Demonstrate how to append errors to the end of a file that you created by listing **HOME** and a missing directory in the same command line.

8.2.9 Input Redirection

Unlike output redirection, you probably will not spend too much time redirecting input, as least explicitly. What does that mean? Suppose I ask you to list something called **whatever**. You would enter `ls whatever`. Now suppose I ask you to redirect the input of **whatever** into `ls`. You would enter `ls < whatever`. Guess what? These commands have the same effect! So, you can indeed formalize your input with `command < input`. If you have trouble remembering which angle bracket to use, think of `d < c` as $d \leftarrow c$, where **c** is the input for **d**.

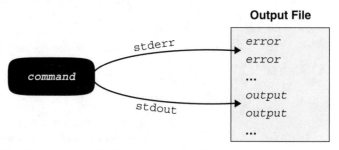

Figure 8.3 Redirecting errors and output to same file.

You will usually encounter **<** when needing to mail someone a file without bothering with attachments and browsers and whatnot:

Step 8.21: Input redirection

```
unix> mailx you < something.txt                    Mail a file to yourself.
```

Another common example is sending a data file into a program, as **program <data.txt**. In this case, you have typed all of **program**'s input data in the exact order and format that **program** would prompt you to enter. If you delve into scripts and **tr** (*translate*), you will see even more input redirection.

8.2.10 Combining Input and Output Redirection

You can combine both input and output redirection methods. The syntax to provide input and output files to a command is **command < infile > outfile**. This command sends the data inside **infile** into **command** for processing, which sends the output to **outfile**.

8.2.11 Appending Input ("Here Document")

When comparing output and input redirection, you can consider each operation as the opposite of its counterpart. As you have learned, **>** and **<** redirect files out and in, respectively, to a command. So, what is the input counterpart to **>>**, which appends output? Input redirection with **<<** is called a ***here document***, which has always sounded weird to me. So, I prefer to consider a *here document* as the *input* that you send into a command (stdin) with **<<**. The syntax that you use, **command << stopword**, tells Unix to prompt you for input until you enter **stopword**. With a *here document*, you effectively append text, line by line, at the prompt into stdin. To end the input and run **command** with your input text, you must enter **stopword** only once with no spaces or other characters on the current line. Note that the input sent into **command** does not include **stopword**. For example, you can use **more** (or **less**) to output text that you enter at the prompt:

Step 8.22: Create a *here document*

```
unix> more << SToP                           Append input into more.
? Hello. I am now typing.                    Type something.
? I am typing something else.                Type something else.
? SToP                                       Enter the "magic word" that quits input.
Hello. I am now typing.                      more now acts on all the lines of
I am typing something else.                  stdin that you created with <<.
unix>                                        The unix prompt returns.
```

Did you notice my weird **SToP**? When picking **stopword**, pick something odd or misspelled, so that you do not accidentally choose a word that belongs to your input. You can include other features in *here documents*, such as variables (**$USER**, **$SHELL**, ...) and command substitution (**`command`**).

PRACTICE!

20. Use **cat** and a *here document* to create a text file.

21. Write a *here document* for **more** that shows the date and your username in a friendly fashion, as thus:

```
Hello, dis. (Display your username.)
The date is currentdate. (Display the current date.)
```

8.2.12 Prompting for Input

When writing your own scripts, you may occasionally want to prompt the user to enter data interactively just as you do at the prompt. You can even make your own prompt! Each shell offers different forms of syntax. I will show you two basic forms:

- **csh/tcsh**: `set var = $<`.
- **sh** and descendents: `read var`.

To store the input after reading it, you must use variables. (`$<` is a *special parameter* in **csh/tcsh**: Section 8.4.13). For now, recall that `$NAME` extracts the value of variable `NAME`. For **csh/tcsh**, I demonstrate `echo -n` to display a prompt without a terminating newline character. The semicolon (`;`) forms a *compound statement* (Sections 2.7.1 and 8.3). Unix will first print the prompt and then await your text entry:

Step 8.23: Read user input (`csh, tcsh`)

```
unix> echo -n "enter something> " ; set tmp = $<        Prompt the user.
enter something> hello                        Enter a string. tmp stores the input.
unix> echo $tmp                                     Show value stored in tmp.
hello                                          This is what you entered. Hooray!
```

When using **sh** and its descendents, you have less cryptic syntax and more options. Below, I demonstrate `read -p prompt variable` for **bash**:

Step 8.24: Read user input (`bash`)

```
unix> bash                                                Use bash.
$ read -p "enter something> " tmp             Prompt the user to enter something.
enter something> 10                              This time enter a value.
$ echo $tmp                                    Show the value stored in tmp.
10                                           Unix got it right again. Go Unix!
```

You can learn more about user input from **man read** and each shell's manpage.

8.2.13 Piping

As introduced in Section 2.8, pipes provide another useful form of redirection, which is called *piping*. Rather than sending `stdout` into a file, you can redirect the output of one command as the `stdin` of the next command, just as fluid flows from one pipe to the next. To pipe the output of **command1** into **command2**, use the syntax **command1 | command2**. Try pretending that the bar (`|`) resembles a pipe, rotated from an *em*-dash (–). A common use of piping is paging through output. For example, a recursive listing might inundate you with text, but with a pipe, you can leisurely step through the pages:

Step 8.25: Using a pipe for paging

```
unix> ls -R / | less                            List everything on your system.
Ridiculously long output not shown.              Use ^C or q to quit from less.
```

Piping through **wc** (*word count*) also helps to count lines:

Step 8.26:   Count items in a file

> *Count how many words in your system dictionary start with the letter z. I use* **egrep** *with regex* **$z**. *I pipe the*
> *results into* **wc -l**, *which counts the number of lines. You could also count the number of words with option* **-w**:
>
> ```
> unix> egrep '$z' /usr/dict/words | wc -1          Display number of words starting with z.
> 39                                      Actually, you could simply use egrep -c for the same answer!
> ```

Pipes allow you to chain multiple programs together: **cmd1 | cmd2 | cmd3 | ....**
Not only do pipes allow you to chain programs together, pipes cause each program to
run as *pseudo-simultaneous* processes. A small amount of data from the first process ini-
tiates the second process, and so forth down the chain, causing rapid execution. Also,
keep investigating the shell manpages—you can do some funky operations, like **|&**,
which pipes both stdout and stderr (**csh**, **tcsh**, **zsh**).

PRACTICE!

22. Write a command line that shows a listing of active users in ascending alpha-
betical order.
23. Write a command line that displays a count of the number of active users.

8.2.14 **tee**

The output from a command resembles fluid flow through a pipe, but the flow is of bits,
not water.[8] Real plumbing pipes have all sorts of shapes. The T-pipe forms a junction
that splits flow into vertical and horizontal flows. With Unix, you can use **tee** for a similar purpose: **tee file** stores the current stdout in file while also allowing the
stdout to continue through the command "pipeline." So, **tee file** stores intermediate results, depending on where you place the command. I demonstrate a common use in Figure 8.4, where I pipe the output of **cmd1** into both an output file
(out.txt) and another command (**cmd2**). For example, you could save a copy of the
current users before sorting it.

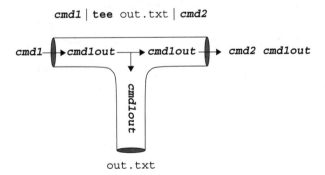

Figure 8.4   Using **tee**

---

[8]Three engineering students were gathered together discussing the possible designers of the human body. One said: "It
was a mechanical engineer. Just look at all the joints." Another said: "No, it was an electrical engineer. The nervous system has many thousands of electrical connections." The last said, "Actually it was a Civil Engineer. Who else would run
toxic waste pipeline through a recreational area?" For more laughs see *www.thecivilengineer.org/laugh.htm.*

Step 8.27: Use **tee** to store intermediate results

```
unix> who | tee users.txt | sort          See and store active users.
Sorted list is displayed.                   sort acts on output of who.
unix> less users.txt                    See intermediate results that tee created.
Unsorted list of active users is displayed.  users.txt was created before sort activated.
```

You could be even fancier and enter **who | tee users.txt | sort > sorted.txt**, which would store the output resulting from **sort** as sorted text without interfering with the unsorted list **users.txt**. Note that **tee -a** is handy too—you can append output to a file. See **man tee** for more information.

PRACTICE!

24. Using Step 8.27, store the results of the sorted users in a different file.
25. In Step 8.27, explain what happens if you rearrange the command line, as thus: **who | sort | tee currentusers.txt**.

8.3   COMMAND SEQUENCES AND GROUPING

Besides redirection and piping, you can group commands together at the command line to perform or select multiple operations. I have occasionally used sequence (**;**) and grouping (**()**) syntax throughout this book. This section formalizes and extends the discussion of these features.

8.3.1   Exit Status

When you run a Unix process, it returns a numerical value that indicates its success or failure. This numeric status value is called the **exit status** or *exit value*. Upon completion, the child process "reports" the exit status to the parent process. Process yield the following values:

- 0 if the command succeeds.
- non-zero if the command fails.

You can see a process's exit status with **$?** (**sh** and descendents, **tcsh**) or **$status** (**csh**, **tcsh**, **zsh**). I explain the syntax of **$?** later in Section 8.4.13.

Step 8.28: View exit status

```
unix> cowabunga dude                     Make a mistake.
cowabunga: Command not found.            Don't have a cow, man!
unix> echo $?                            See exit status.
1                                        cowabunga failed!
```

Other than your love of Unix and the joy it brings, why do you need to know about all of this? When writing scripts, you may wish to test if a particular command fails and what to do, if so. You will have a small taste of *conditional execution* in Section 8.3.3.

8.3.2   Compound Sequences

Entering individual command lines becomes tedious, especially when you wish to perform a sequence of tasks. To combat this tedium, you can separate independent command lines with the semicolon (**;**), as thus: **cmd1 ; cmd2 ; ....** Your shell works left to right, processing **cmd1**, then **cmd2**, and so forth. Each command will completely finish before the next one starts:

Step 8.29: Enter sequence of commands

```
unix> cd ~/Unix_work ; pwd                          Change CWD, then print CWD.
/home/dis/Unix_work                                 Result of multiple commands.
```

Actually, my shell (**tcsh**) already has a special *alias* (customized command, Step 2.15) that redefines **cd** as **cd \!*;echo $cwd**. In this command, **!*** is a special **csh/tcsh** command for *all command-line arguments*. The semicolon (**;**) combines both **cd !*** and **echo $cwd**, which causes the shell to process *both* commands sequentially whenever I enter **cd**. See Section 8.8.2. for an explanation of **\!***.

8.3.3   Conditional Sequences

Suppose you wish to connect multiple commands, but you are not sure if all of the commands will work. Why would you not be sure? A file might be missing, or a user enters the wrong information. You will encounter this scenario in script programming, whereby you need to test if different commands will work. To test if a command succeeds, you can check its exit status, which indicates success or failure. When writing shell languages for testing process success/failure, programmers used mathematical logic.[9] But instead of truth, we test process exit values: 0 means success and non-zero means failure. To operate on exit values of two commands, **A** and **B**, use **&&** (*and*) and **||** (*exclusive or*), which have the following syntax and semantics:

- **A && B**: If **A** succeeds, do **B**. If **A** fails, stop the execution.
- **A || B**: If **A** succeeds, stop the execution. Otherwise, do **B**.

You can see these operators in action by listing directories that may or may not exist.

Step 8.30: Try conditional sequences

```
unix> ls Scum && ls $HOME              List Scum and list HOME. If no Scum, stop.
Scum: No such file or directory        Scum wasn't found, so Unix stopped.
unix> ls Scum || ls $HOME              List Scum or list HOME. If no Scum, list HOME.
Scum: No such file or directory        No Scum, so Unix tries to list HOME, which works.
Unix lists HOME.                       Then again, perhaps you do have Scum.
```

If you begin to write scripts, you will find the **if**, **while**, and other commands quite useful for handling exit values. See **man shell_builtins** and individual shell manpages for more information.

8.3.4   Subshells

When constructing command lines, you might wish to group commands together before doing another operation. Refer to Step 8.19 for an example, where you direct stdout and stderr to different places with **csh/tcsh**. Because these shells lack file descriptors, you need to group the commands together with parentheses (**()**). Commands grouped together, as **(commands)**, form a *subshell*. Unix processes a command inside a subshell as a child process. The parent process is the process that spawns the subshell.

---

[9]You can test the truth of statement *A* and *B* by checking the truth of "*A* and *B*." For example, let *A* = *My last name has only one vowel*, and let *B* = *June is my friend*. Because both of these statements are true, then *A and B* is also true. Welcome to the world of logic!

Subshell commands all share the same `stdin`, `stdout`, and `stderr`, which means you can redirect information as a group. For example, suppose you would like to output the listing of two directories into the same file. You might be tempted to enter **ls A ; ls B > out.txt**, but this command will send only **B**'s listing. Why? The shell parses the command line from left to right, processing **ls A** first. So, to convince the shell to list *both* **A** and **B** before sending output, group them together with a subshell:

Step 8.31: Form a subshell

```
unix> mkdir TestSub ; cd TestSub          Create a directory in which to work.
unix> mkdir A B                                   Create two subdirectories.
unix> cat > A/test1.txt                            Create a text file inside A.
Type something. Enter ^D on a new line to finish.
unix> cat > B/test2.txt                            Create a text file inside B.
Type something. Enter ^D on a new line to finish.
unix> (ls A ; ls B) > lists.txt       Send listing of A and B into lists.txt.
unix> more lists.txt                                    View what you sent.
test1.txt                              Your subshell sent both listings. Cool.
test2.txt
```

Although **sh** and descendents permit grouping in the current shell with **{ cmds; }**, I recommend getting used to subshells first.

PRACTICE!

26. Why does viewing an empty file (size of 0) return an exit status of 0?
27. Write a command line that lists A or B if C cannot be listed.

8.4   VARIABLES

Throughout this text, I have needed to jump around in the discussion because learning Unix is a bit circular. You have seen some variables already (**HOME**, **SHELL**, **USER**, and others). What is a *variable*? A variable is a symbol that represents something else. In Unix, besides setting up and customizing your environment, programmers use variables in scripts. This section develops variables in further detail so that you will have the background to explore Unix further.

8.4.1   Mathematical Variables

You have likely used many mathematical variables. The formula for a line, $y = mx + b$, has four variables. Each of these variables requires values of a particular type that belong to a particular set. Likely you have used the set of all real numbers. Besides relying on a particular number system, science and engineering variables usually include units! Although this concept may seem obvious, the idea that you can attach specific values to a variable, including meaning (remember semantics?), has tremendous applications in programming.[10]

8.4.2   Variables in Programming

Programmers use variables to represent values, which provides the ability to recall a value. To remember a value for reuse, the programmer allocates a portion of computer

---

[10]I am only scratching the surface in this section. *Object-oriented programming* (OOP) allows you to describe behaviors and attributes of *objects* with a single description called a *class*. You can create objects—like virtual birds, eyeballs, meatloaf—and label them with variable names. Check out Java and C++, which are common OOP languages.

memory at a specific location and stores a value there. Many programming languages simplify this process by allowing you to use variable names instead of numerical addresses. As shown in Figure 8.5, a programmer using Java (or related languages with C-like syntax) can allocate space for a variable **x**. Later in the program, the programmer can put a value **10** inside the space for **x**. The process of associating a variable with a particular value is called *assigning*. You can think of **x = 10** as $x \leftarrow 10$, meaning, "assign the value 10 to x." After assigning **x**, the program will replace **x** with **10** in other statements until you give **x** a new value or this "chunk" of code terminates. So, if I write the Java command **System.out.println(x);** somewhere after **x=10;**, Java will output 10 to the user.

PRACTICE!

28. Write a Java program that uses variables **x** and **y** to store **1** and **2**, respectively. Output the sum of **x+y**. Refer to Section 3.6 for a Java template and the commands to use.

8.4.3 Unix Parameters and Variables

Recall that the shell has two purposes: provide an interactive (and customizable) environment and supply a language for writing scripts. Unix shells supply variables to help with these tasks. As you investigate shells, you will find unfamiliar terminology. I clarify general terms in this section using many explanations culled from the shell manpages, especially DEFINITIONS and PARAMETERS in **man bash**:

- *Word* or *token*: A sequence of characters considered as a single unit.

- *Name* or *identifier*: A word consisting only of alphanumeric characters and underscores. I state the complete set of rules in Section 8.4.5.

- *Parameter*: A token that represents something else. Parameters include names and other characters, which shells use to make variables, *special parameters* (also called *special variables*), and *positional parameters* (also called *positional variables*). For example, **$$** is a special parameter that represents the PID of the current shell, and **$1** is a positional parameter that represents the first command-line argument. I explain these terms in Section 8.4.13.

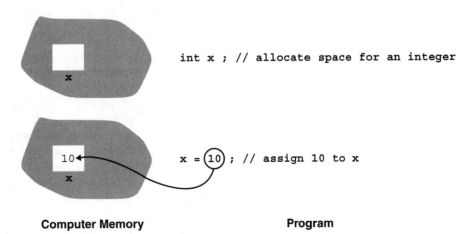

Computer Memory   Program

Figure 8.5 Basic memory model for variable allocation and assignment.

So, which of the above character clumps is a variable? A *Unix variable* refers to a name. When talking about storing values, **sh** (and it descendents) tend to focus on *parameter*, whereas **csh** and **tcsh** use *variable* most often.

8.4.4   Unix Variables

If you write scripts, you will use parameters (special and positional) to interact with the command line. Given our focus on the interactive shell, I concentrate on variables to show you how to understand and modify your environment. Unix has two kinds of variables:

- **Shell variables** (also called **local variables**): These variables affect the current shell. Their values exist only during the life of the shell process in which they were assigned.

- **Environment variables** (also called **global variables**): These variables can affect multiple shells. Once assigned in a parent shell, new child shells spawned from the parent share the parent's environment variable values.

If you would like to get feel for the difference, enter **set** and **env** to display local and global variables, respectively. I demonstrate these (and other) commands that will help you learn about the distinction in the subsequent sections.

8.4.5   Variable Names

Throughout this book I have shown you some predefined variables, like **HOME**, **SHELL**, and **USER**, but I have not explained how to make your own. Unix variable names follow common programming language convention:

- You can use letters, digits, or underscores. (See **ksh93** for use of the dot (**.**).)
- Shells differ in a maximum length, but if your name exceeds 20 characters, it's too long anyway.
- Names can begin only with a letter or an underscore (_). Be glad about this rule. Imagine having a variable called **1** to which you assign the value **2**.
- Variables are case sensitive.

When it comes to case convention, shells differ, which I explain below:

- **sh** (and its descendants) use *UPPERCASE* variable names.
- **csh** and **tcsh** use *lowercase* for shell variables and *UPPERCASE* for environment variables.

Shells do not require these conventions when you crate your own variables, but you must reproduce the names of predefined and built-in variables. For example, **User** does not refer to **USER**.

8.4.6   Viewing Variable Values

Variables store strings, which are collections of characters. For example, if you use **sh** (or its descendants) to set a variable value, you enter *var=string*, like **COLOR=blue**. For now, I want you to focus on seeing a variable's value. As demonstrated many times throughout this book, you can display a specific variable value with **echo $name**. Note that **$** is an operator that extracts the value inside the memory location of **name**.[11]

---

[11]In Figure 8.5, Java and other programming languages extract a variable's value without the **$** operator. When you use a variable in an expression or on the right side of an assignment statement, many languages automatically extract the value.

Step 8.32: Display one variable's value

```
unix> echo $HOME                                    Display your home directory.
/usr/u/dis                                          Note that HOME stores a string.
```

To see all local variables and their values for the current shell process, use **set** with no arguments. Depending on how extensively your system administrator (and soon to be you) customized your start-up files, you might have a lengthy display. If you do not use **tcsh**, your output might have a different look:

Step 8.33: Display all local variables

```
unix> set | less                                    Page through the display of
cwd      /usr/u/dis                                 local variables and their values.
noclobber                                           I show only a partial listing.
```

To display environment variables, use **env** or **printenv**. If you use **csh** or **tcsh**, you can also use **setenv**. Later I demonstrate how to set environment variables by supplying options and arguments to **env** and **setenv**.

Step 8.34: Display all global variables

```
unix> env | less                                    Page through the display of
HOME=/usr/u/dis                                     global variables and their values.
SHELL=/usr/local/bin/tcsh                           I show only a partial listing.
```

PRACTICE!

> 29. Display the value of your **HOME** using **printf**.
> 30. Compare the results of both **env** and **printenv** using redirection and **diff**.

8.4.7 Null Value

When viewing all local or global variables, if you see the output name= (no value on the right), you've got a variable with a *null value*. The null value (or just *null*)[12] is really an *empty string*–two double quotes with no space between them (**""**). For example, in **sh** (and it's descendents) you could enter **X=""**.[13] When you display **X**'s value, nothing appears because an empty string contains nothing!

Step 8.35: Display null variable

```
unix> bash                                          Run sh or descendent shell.
$ X=""                                              Assign null to X.
$ echo $X                                           View null variable.
$                                                   Nothing to display.
```

---

[12]Depending on the language, *null* might refer to a completely different token! For example, Java has a value called **null** and a separate *null string* (**""**).

[13]Why would you bother? As demonstrated in Figure 8.5, sometimes you need to allocate space for a variable before you actually need it. When variables have types, you often need to say *type name* to allocate space for name to hold the specific type, like **int x** in Java. Moreover, having all your variables *declared* early in your code helps you and others read it.

8.4.8 Errors

Variables with null values have nothing to display, but the values still exist. But what happens if you attempt to display a variable that doesn't exist? Depending on your shell, you will get different responses for a variable **var** that does not exist:

- **csh** or **tcsh**: echo $var produces an error message.
- **sh** (and descendents): echo $var produces a blank line, which bugs me. You need to use echo ${var:?}, which will produce an error if **var** is null or not set.

Below, I demonstrate both kinds of responses:

Step 8.36: Non-existent variables and null values

```
unix> tcsh                              Run csh or tcsh.
% echo $FUNGUS                          Is FUNGUS among us?
FUNGUS: Undefined variable.             Not this one!
% exit                                  Exit shell.
unix> bash                              Run sh or descendent.
$ echo ${JimmyHoffa:?}                  Whatever happened to JimmyHoffa?
JimmyHoffa: parameter null or not set   Sleeping with the fishes.
```

When writing scripts, you could redirect stderr for cases when a variable doesn't exist. All shells have multiple forms of syntax to access variable values, which shell manpages state in sections such as PARAMETER SUBSTITUTION and PARAMETER EXPANSION. You may also see VARIABLE instead of PARAMETER.

8.4.9 Variable Values Are Strings!

As introduced in Section 8.4.6, variable values are strings. Even if you use a number, the shell treats the number as a string of digits.[14] When entering a value, you do not need to surround your string with quotes, except if you want to include whitespace or metacharacters. I discuss rules for choosing double (" ") or single (' ') in conjunction with other quoting rules in Section 8.7.

8.4.10 Setting Local/Shell Variables

Local, or shell variables affect shell behavior. For instance, the shell variable **noclobber** prevents overwriting of files, as in copying, redirecting, and other operations that create files. **noclobber** is local, or specific, to the login shell—so, within the same session, you could spawn shells with variables set to permit clobbering.

- **sh** (and descendents): You might have .profile that contains the statement **set -o noclobber**.
- **csh** and **tcsh**: You might have .cshrc that contains the statement **set noclobber**.

The syntax for setting a variable value differs depending on the type of shell:

- **sh** (and descendants): Use **name=value**. Do not surround = with whitespace! Sometimes you can use **set**.

---

[14]You can do arithmetic operations with variables. Shells convert number strings to their numerical values. Some shells, like **bash** and **tcsh**, even treat the null string as 0 in an arithmetic operation. See **man expr**, **man let**, and the shell manpages for more information.

- **csh** and **tcsh**: Use **set** *name* = *value*. You may surround = with whitespace.

The shell will assign **value** to **name**. The **value** will remain until you change it or exit from the shell. I demonstrate two examples below:

Step 8.37: Set a local variable

```
unix> tcsh                                                    Run tcsh.
% set test1 = Pungent                  Assign Pungent to local variable test1.
% echo $test1                                     Access the value of test1.
Pungent                                                  Value of test1.
% exit                                               Quit the current shell.
unix> bash                                                    Run bash.
$ test2=Putrid                          Assign Putrid to local variable test2.
$ echo $test2                                     Access the value of test2.
Putrid                                                   Value of test2.
% exit                                               Quit the current shell.
```

Below, I demonstrate how a local variable is not inherited (passed along) to child shells.

Step 8.38: Demonstrate that local variables do not inherit

As depicted in Figure 8.6, create a local variable **society** *(I am using* **tcsh***) and give it a depressing value. Then, enter* **xterm** *to run a child process, which now exists without* **society** *(which is worse: social anarchy or dystopia?).*

Once you set a shell variable, it will be included in the listing of **set**. Shells provide even more ways to set values with lists, arrays, and more, as described in **man set** and the shell manpages.

Figure 8.6 Local variables not inherited by child shells.

PRACTICE!

31. Set a local variable called **test3** to the value of **test2** in Step 8.37. If you change the **test2** afterwards, does **test3**'s value change? Explain your answer.

32. Use **typeset** to set a variable with **ksh**. Do other shells "know" about **typeset**?

33. In Step 8.37, can your **bash** session access **test1**? Why or why not?

8.4.11 Setting Global/Environment Variables

Global, or environment, variables affect your entire session and different programs requiring the same environment variables. As shown in Section 8.4.6, you can view all your current environment variable settings with **env** or **printenv** (**csh** and **tcsh** also have **setenv**). Depending on your shell, system, and start-up files, you might see the variables that I describe in Table 8.4 (and likely more!).[15] See also **man -s5 environ** for several system environment variables that I did not include. To learn about more variables to set, look for sections called ENVIRONMENT VARIABLES in a command's manpage. For example, **man less** explains how **less** can automatically call options you store as a string in variable **LESS**. After you learn how to edit your start-up files (Section 8.9), you can add, remove, and change variables.

Setting environment variables gets a bit more complicated than setting shell variables. Both types of shells have different commands, which I explain below:

- **csh** and **tcsh**: To assign a value to a environment variable **VAR**, use **setenv VAR value**. If you do not supply **value**, the shell will assign the null value to **VAR**.

- **sh** (and descendents): Surprise! You cannot distinguish a variable as global or local—a variable is effectively local unless you inform the shell otherwise. So, you first use **VAR=value**. Then, to make the shell treat **VAR** as global, you must *export* it–enter **export VAR**. Except for **sh**, you can abbreviate these two steps with **export VAR=value** (no whitespace around **=**).

Note that by convention (though not mandatory), you should specify **VAR** as *UPPER-CASE*. I demonstrate both approaches in the following steps. Because I will spawn child shells from parent shells, I recommend using the predefined environment variable **SHLVL** (*shell level*, Table 8.4). **SHLVL** keeps track of the shell depth—each time I spawn a child shell from a parent shell, the shell depth increases by 1.

Step 8.39: Setting global/environment variable (**csh**, **tcsh**)

As depicted in Figure 8.7, enter **setenv WARMING bad** *to assign* **bad** *to global* **WARMING**. *Next, spawn another shell with* **xterm** *(placed in background). Since* **WARMING** *is global, you can view it's value in the child shell.*

---

[15]Few books seem to agree on what each shell actually supports, and of course, the shell manpages on Solaris do not always agree with my references, so I tried to merge several sources. Your actual system and set-up might have some discrepancies. The shell manpages do have more complete descriptions of each variable, so start there.

TABLE 8.4 Common Environment Variables

Environment Variable	Description	Shells*
_ (underscore)	Last argument of previous command.	K, B, Z
CDPATH	Search path for **cd**.	S, K
COLUMNS	Screen width.	S, K, B, Z, T
DIRSTACK	Directory stack.	B
DISPLAY	Server for X Window display. Set by GUI or user.	N/A
EDITOR	Pathname for built-in text editor.	K, B, T
ENV	Name of configuration file to invoke when shell invoked.	K, B
EUID	User ID.	B, Z
FIGNORE	Suffixes to ignore for filename completion.	B, Z
GROUP	User's group name	T
HISTFILE	File to store command history.	K, B, Z
HOME	Login directory. Set by **login**.	S, K, B, Z, C, T
HOST	Current host. Set by system.	Z, T
IFS	Token separators. Default set by shell.	S, K, B, Z
LOGNAME	Your username. Set by system.	Z
MAIL	File that receives mail. Set by **login**.	S, K, B, Z
MAILCHECK	Interval to check for new mail. Default set by shell.	S, B
MAILPATH	Files to receive mail.	S, B
MANPATH	Directories in which to search for man. Typically default set by system.	Z
OLDPWD	Previous working directory.	K, B, Z
PATH	Directories to search commands. Default set by shell.	S, K, B, Z, C, T
PPID	PID of parent process.	K, B, Z
PRINTER	Default printer. Typically set by system.	N/A
PS1	Primary prompt. Default set by shell.	S, K, B, Z
PS2	Secondary prompt. Default set by shell.	S, K, B, Z
PS3	Program for **select**. Default set by shell.	K, B, Z
PS4	Debug prompt for tracing. Default set by shell.	K, B, Z
PWD	Present working directory.	S, K, B, Z, T
RANDOM	Randomly generated number.	K, B, Z
SHACCT	File to store executed commands.	S, K, B
SHELL	Default login shell. Set by **login**.	S, K, B
SHELLOPTS	List of shell options.	B
SHLVL	Current depth of shell process (e.g., call **ksh** from **ksh** from **ksh** …).	K, B, Z, T
TERM	Terminal type.	S, K, B, C, T
TMOUT	Amount of time to logout after waiting for next command. Default set by shell.	K, B, Z
USER	Your username. Set by system.	C, T
VISUAL	Editor for command-line editing.	K, B, T

*. S = **sh**, K = **ksh**, B = **bash**, Z = **zsh**, C = **csh**, T = **tcsh**

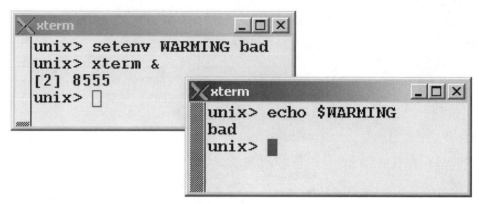

Figure 8.7 Set global variable with **csh/tcsh**.

Step 8.40: Setting global/environment variable (**sh** and descendents)

```
unix> bash                    Spawn a child shell process with bash.
$ export OIL=crisis           Assign crisis to OIL and export it.
$ bash                        Spawn yet another child process.
$ echo $SHLVL                 Check the shell depth.
3                             The depth of child shells you've spawned.
$ echo $OIL                   Display OIL's value.
crisis                        Yes, OIL's crisis is global.
$ exit; exit                  Return to top-level parent shell.
```

Be careful concerning the notion of how global a global variable really is. Below, I present two principles to which you must adhere:

- Parent processes do not inherit from their children.
- Children inherit from their parents at the time the processes spawn.

So, if you spawn child shells and *then* set a global variable in the *parent* of the children, the children do not know about that variable! Why? All of their variables were already inherited from the parent when you originally spawned the children. Likewise, if you set a global variable in a child shell, the parent does not know about that variable because inheritance does not work backwards.

Step 8.41: Parent does not inherit from child

```
unix> tcsh                          Spawn a new child shell.
% setenv POLITICS quagmire          Set global POLITICS to quagmire.
% exit                              Exit the child shell.
unix> echo $POLITICS                Does the parent shell know about POLITICS?
POLITICS: Undefined variable.       No, POLITICS did not inherit.
```

The shell manpages describe much more about setting variables. For example, you prevent changing a variable value by making the variable *read-only*. You can also expand and control expansion with a variety of forms of syntax. If you begin to write shell scripts, I strongly recommend that you explore these other features.

34. Spawn a **bash** process. Predict the output of the command line **(export GOODS=profit)** ; echo **$GOODS** and then test it. Explain the result.

35. Spawn an **xterm** as a background process. Inside that **xterm**, run **tcsh** and enter **setenv COOLNESS waycool**. Does the **xterm**'s parent have **COOLNESS**? Explain your answer.

8.4.12 Removing Variable Settings

Besides setting a variable's value to null (which doesn't actually erase the variable), you can obliterate a variable (deallocate its memory), depending on the variable type:

- local/shell (all shells): Use **unset VAR**.
- global/environment (**sh** and descendents): Use **unset VAR**.
- global/environment (**csh** and **tcsh**): Use **unsetenv VAR**.

When you deallocate a variable, the system reclaims the memory, which means that any stored value is also erased. I demonstrate the process for **tcsh**, below:

Step 8.42: Destroy a variable (**csh** and **tcsh**)

```
unix> set confusion = true          Set a local variable confusion.
unix> unset confusion               Deallocate your confusion.
unix> echo $confusion               Do you still have confusion?
confusion: Undefined variable.      No more confusion!
```

36. Set a global variable called **METAL** to value `false` in **bash**. Then, destroy the variable.

37. Can you retrieve a value from a deallocated variable? Explain your answer.

8.4.13 Parameters

Shells support **parameters** that help you to extract information about processes and the command line. As introduced in Section 8.4.3, Unix parameters are tokens that store strings, but unlike variables, parameter names may use nonalphanumeric characters, like *****, **?**, **!**, and others. **bash**'s manpage clearly distinguishes variables from two other kinds of parameters:

- *Positional parameters*: Parameters that store specific elements of a command line, depending each elements position from left-to-right.
- *Special parameters*: Parameters that store other kinds of information about a command line or process.

I provide a list of common parameters in Table 8.5. (See also Section 8.2.12.) You should consult your shell's manpage to see which parameters it supports. Newer shells, like **tcsh**, **bash**, and **zsh** support quite a few. Unfortunately, not all shell manpages follow **bash**'s terminology. For both kinds of parameters, **sh** lumps them under `Parameter Substitution`, and **csh/tcsh** list them under `Variable Substitution`.

TABLE 8.5 Common Positional and Special Parameters

Parameter Type	Parameter ($param)	Description
Positional	$1, $2, ..., $9	The 1st, 2nd, ..., 9th argument of the command line.
	$#	Number of positional parameters.
	$*	All positional parameters.
	$$	Process ID.
Special	$?	Exit status.
	$!	Previous background PID.

I hope that you are curious why I list the variables in Table 8.5 with the **$** operator. The shell disallows manually setting their values, as in **?=10**. If you could set **$?** to arbitrary exit status, then your shell could report an erroneous value. So, you will see these parameters only in the context of their *use*. I demonstrate some examples, below.

Step 8.43: Set and access positional parameters

Although you cannot manually use = to set a positional parameter, **sh** *and its descendents provide* **set p1 p2** *.... You can then use positional parameters to extract* **set**'s *arguments:*

```
unix> bash                          Use sh or a descendent. zsh also works.
$ set A B C                         Set positional parameters.
$ echo $1 $2 $3                     Display 1st, 2nd, and 3rd parameters.
A B C                               These values are the arguments that were set by set.
$ exit                              Return to your default shell.
```

Step 8.44: Access process IDs

While writing this step, I discovered that I had two zombie shell processes lingering because I had only one open window after losing remote access. So, instead of using my original example (which I moved to a practice problem), I demonstrate how I knew which shells I could remove:

```
unix> ps -fu dis                                    Display my processes.
   UID   PID  PPID  C    STIME  TTY      TIME CMD     Standard listing.
   dis 12354 12353  0 23:57:54  pts/18   0:00 tcsh      Is this my shell?
   dis 18862 18861  0 16:54:05  pts/19   0:00 tcsh      Is this my shell?
   dis 27842 27841  0 00:38:05  pts/12   0:00 tcsh      Is this my shell?
```
Other processes not listed.
```
unix> echo $$              Display my the PID of my current process (my shell).
18862                               So, I now know which tcsh is alive.
unix> kill -9 12354                          Destroy a zombie.
unix> kill -9 27842                          Destroy another zombie.
unix>                              I am still logged on! Hooray!
```

PRACTICE!

38. Does your shell support **$0**? If so, explain the parameter's type (positional or special) and its use.

39. Assuming that you are using a GUI, spawn a window from your current window (e.g., **xterm**) and place it in the background. Show your current PID and most recent background PID.

8.5 COMMAND LOOKUP

Now and then, when you enter a Unix command, your shell might complain that the command does not exist. Or perhaps the command's behavior differs from your expectation, including what I have instructed in this book! When do these situations arise? By default, shells include many useful commands, and your shell variables search a certain number of places in the Unix file system for executable files (*everything is file!*). You can also define custom commands. This section explains the basics of *command lookup* and associated operations every time you enter a command line.

8.5.1 Command Types

I summarize the five types of commands in Table 8.6. For now, I focus on aliases, built-in commands (called *builtins* by some shells), and utilities, which are most common for new Unix users. You have seen the basics of aliases in Step 2.15—I demonstrate further concepts in Section 8.8. In terms of built-in commands, you can see a complete list for **sh**, **csh**, and **ksh** with **man shell_builtins**. For **bash**, **tcsh**, and **zsh** and more information about each built-in and/or keyword, see the shell manpages. I use *utility* to describe all other commands, which are composed of system and user commands. You can find these commands in directories, like /usr/bin, /util/bin, and other locations in the Unix file system, including your own scripts.

TABLE 8.6 Command Types

Type	Description	Example	Shells
Alias	Customized command.	`alias rm rm -i`	all but **sh**
Built-in	Command provided as part of shell's program.	`cd`	all
Function	Name for group of commands.	`test() { echo A; echo B; }`	sh, ksh, bash, zsh
Keyword	Word that belongs to shell's language.	`if`	all (many shells consider keywords as built-in commands)
Utility	Executable program (binary, script) on system.	`mkdir`	N/A

8.5.2 Order of Execution

If you specify a full pathname, the shell does not search for your command. But when encountering a command with a relative pathname, all shells have a predefined order by which they search for the program to run. If you do not consider functions, the shell first checks the command name in this order: alias, keyword, built-in, utility.

8.5.3 Command Path

All shells have an environment variable **PATH** that contains the directories to search for the utilities. Your system administrator has likely set up default paths for you: a system default and your start-up files. To see your current **PATH**, use **echo $PATH**. You will see that a collection of directories separated by colons, like the following:

Step 8.45: See your **PATH**

```
unix> echo $PATH                                          Display your shell PATH.
/usr/bin:/usr/ccs/bin:/usr/ucb:/usr/bin/X11:.             This is just a snippet of my PATH.
```

To find a command, the shell checks **PATH** from left-to-right, looking in each directory for a file that matches the command name. If the shell cannot find the command, you have two choices:

- Enter the full pathname, which I expect will irritate you.
- Go to the file's directory and enter **./***name*, which means "in the CWD, look for a file called *name*, see if it has x permission, and if so, run it."

In time, you will discover more Unix commands in directories not in **PATH** (see Section 8.5.6). You may also wish to use different versions of some commands (GNU vs. system, for example).

So, how do you change **PATH**? You can modify **PATH**, just like other variables. The two types of shells treat **PATH** differently:

- **sh** (and descendents): To set **PATH**, enter **PATH=***dir1***:***dir2***:**... Then, enter **export PATH** to make it global.
- **csh** and **tcsh**: You have two choices. The standard method is **set path = (***dir1 dir2*** ...)**. **csh** and **tcsh** will automatically export **path** to a global equivalent called **PATH**. If you prefer to work directly with **PATH**, use **setenv PATH** *dir1***:***dir2***:**..., whereby the shell will automatically create an equivalent local **path**.

At first, I recommend testing how to modify **PATH** at the prompt—if you make a mistake, you can always close the window and try again. Once you feel comfortable, I recommend modifying your **PATH** (or **path**) variable in your start-up files (see Section 8.9).

8.5.4 Protecting Your Path

Below, I describe two common issues with modifying your **PATH**:

- **HOME**: If you ever write or copy shell scripts into your account, you will likely create a directory called $HOME/bin. Place ~/bin near the end of **PATH,** not the beginning. Otherwise, you may access a malicious program you have copied or accidentally alter the meaning of a command that you frequently use.
- CWD (**.**): Do not place **.** as the first directory in your path, like **.:/usr/bin:/**.... Why? Suppose you are inside another user's directory. That person may have created a malicious program with a common name, like **ls**, that deletes all of your files. To avoid these *trojan horses* (malicious programs that masquerade with benign names), put the **.** only at the end of your **PATH**, if at all.

8.5.5 Execute Permission

Remember that to run a file as a program, it must have *execute* (x) permission. In general, utilities have user, group, and world execute permission. See **man chmod** and Sections 4.10 and 5.10.5 for more information.

8.5.6 Finding a Command (and Help)

I use **apropos** *word* quite often to search for commands with descriptions that contain *word*. But, as Table 8.7 shows, Unix has many ways to discover commands and their locations. Simply looking inside **man whereis** can give you an idea of which directories you might wish to include in **PATH**. The Free Software Foundation (*www.gnu.org*) supports **info**, which is sometimes more informative than **man**. Your system might also have a "home-grown" **learn** or **help** program. I describe *file completion* as a useful trick to finding out about commands in Section 8.5.7.

TABLE 8.7 Ways to Find Commands and Help

Command	Description	Example/Reference
apropos	Locate commands that contain a word. Equivalent to `man -k`.	`apropos game`
find	Look for a file.	See Section 5.12.2.
man	Find help on a command.	`man -s1 Intro`
type	Display description of command.	`type ls`
whatis	Display one-line command descriptions. Equivalent to `man -f`.	`whatis twm`
whence	Display how a command line interprets the command (`ksh`, `zsh`).	`whence -v ls`
whereis	Look for commands. See `man whereis` for directories that it searches.	`whereis ls`
which	Check **PATH** and aliases in .cshrc (`csh`, `tcsh`; see also `type`).	`which ls`
woman	Browse manpages inside **emacs**.	Enter **M-x woman** in **emacs**.
xman	GUI browser for **man**.	`xman &`

8.5.7   File Completion

File completion is a process in which a shell attempts to complete a pathname using the CWD, your **PATH**, and your aliases. All you need to do is type a few characters and then press a key, which depends on your shell:

- **csh**: **Esc**. You must have shell variable **filec** set.
- **tcsh**, **bash**, and **zsh**: **Tab**. Then, you may enter **^D** (**tcsh**, **zsh**) or **Tab** (**bash**) to see a list of potential matches without completing the name.

You might be curious why I bring up file completion here. By trying to complete just one or two letters, you can learn about many commands (and other files). For example, in the following example, type **z** and then **Tab** with no space after the **z**.

Step 8.46:   File Completion (**bash**, **tcsh**, **zsh**)

```
Type z and then press Tab
unix> zTab                              Typing z and pressing Tab will display everything beginning with z.
zcat    zenger   zic2xpm   zipcloak   zipnote   zippy3    zmore    zsh
zcmp    zforce   zinger    zipgrep    zippy1    zippy4    znew
zdiff   zgrep    zip       zipinfo    zippy2    zipsplit  zot
```

The shell manpages have lot more information on completion, especially **man zshcompctl**, which explains *programmable completion*.

8.5.8   Running Shell Built-in from Other Shell

I like **ksh**'s **whence**, but **tcsh** does not support it. You can actually run another shell's built-in command from another shell with ***shell command***:

Step 8.47:   Run command from another shell

```
unix> ksh whence ls                              Describe ls with ksh's whence.
/usr/bin/ls                                      whence resembles which.
```

See the shell manpages for options when running shells this way.

PRACTICE!

40. Does globbing work with filename completion at your command line?
41. Does the GNU command directory belong to your **PATH**? If not, find the GNU directory and include it somewhere in your **PATH**.
42. Find one command beginning with the letter **y** that I have not used in this book.

8.6   HISTORY

When you edit a command line, you might move the cursor left and right to edit the tokens. Have you tried the up and down arrow keys, too? In newer shells these keys access your command *history*, which is a record of command lines that you enter. Below I explain what happens when you press these keys:

- *Up* (↑): The shell moves backward in your history, displaying progressively older commands.
- *Down* (↓): The shell moves forward in your history, displaying progressively more recent commands.

Besides these nifty shortcuts, what else can you do? This section introduces history capabilities for **csh/tcsh**, **bash**, and **zsh**. I do not spend much time on other shells: **sh** lacks history, and **ksh** has limited features. I recommend investigating shell manpages, which provide a blizzard of details.

8.6.1   History Files and Variables

To see if how your account is configured, see **$history** (**csh/tcsh**) or **$HISTORY** (**ksh**, **bash**, **zsh**). Assuming your shell enables history, the shell records your command lines in memory (the *history list*). When you exit the shell it appends the list to a text file called .history or something similar. In your variable listings, look for names that contain hist or HIST to see your current settings. These variables toggle history, determine the history filename, and more.

8.6.2   Accessing History

Steps 2.13 and 2.14 demonstrate how to access your command history with **history**. Note that **ksh**, **bash**, and **zsh** also support **fc** (*fix command*)–the command **fc -l** provides a basic history listing, but you can do much more—e.g., **fc -e** allows you to edit your history.

PRACTICE!

43. List your five most recent command lines with **csh/tcsh/bash**.
44. List your five most recent command lines with **ksh/zsh**. Hint: Use a hyphen.

8.6.3   Event Substitution

Some shell manpages refer to a command line that you have entered as an *event*, regardless of how glorious or mundane it was. Shells that support history assign a number to each event, starting from 1 (the earliest event). As shown in Step 2.14, you can use an event number to re-enter a command line. For example, entering **!10** causes the shell to re-execute event 10. Shells with history typically use **!** and **^** as *history* *metacharacters* to signal an *event substitution* (sometimes called *expansion*) in another command.[16] Table 8.8 summarizes many common history substitutions (called *event specifications* or *event designators*) for **tcsh**, **bash**, and **zsh**.

Step 8.48:   History substitutions

```
unix> grep tort /usr/dict/words                    Search for lines containing tort.
Lines containing tort.                   For more fun, try part of shitepoke (a small green heron).
unix> ^tort^tortu                     Replace tort with tortu in the most recent event containing tort.
tortuous                              The shell accesses the event grep tort /usr/dict/words
torture                                      and enters grep tortu /usr/dict/words.
unix> !?tort?                                  Run the most recent event containing tort.
grep tortu /usr/dict/words              The shell finds a matching command line (this output)
tortuous                                   and runs it, which gives the same result as before.
torture
```

History designators tend to focus on an event's command name, though a few operate on other words in the command line like options and arguments. Sections 8.6.4 and 8.6.5 demonstrate additional features to access such tokens, which Table 8.8 also summarizes. You will see that you can specify and modify an event using the syntax **!e:d:m:m...**, where **e** = event designator, **d** = word designator (Section 8.6.4), and **m** = word modifier (Section 8.6.5). You can place a history command of this form anywhere in a command line–the shell will substitute the appropriate tokens before executing the commands.

TABLE 8.8   Some History Designators and Modifiers

Event Designators	
!n	Event **n**.
!-n	Current event minus **n**.
!!	Previous event. Same as **!-1**.
!s	Most recent event starting with **s**.
!?s?	Most recent event containing **s**.
^old^new	Previous event, substituting each instance of **old** with **new**.

Word Designators	
0	The first token (usually the command name).
n	**n**th argument.
^	First argument. Same as 1.
$	Last argument.
%	Word matched by **?s?** search.
x-y	Range of words between **x** and **y** (inclusive) from left to right.
*	Abbreviates **^-$**. Returns no output if event has only one word.

Word Modifiers	
h	Remove all but the head from a pathname.
t	Remove all but the tail from a pathname.
r	Remove a file extension (**.string**) from a pathname.
e	Remove all but the file extension.
p	Display the event but do not enter it.

---

[16]See your shell's **histchars** variable if you wish to create potential havoc by changing these symbols. Modern shells are very customizable!

PRACTICE!

8.6.4   Word Designators

To access and manipulate command-line tokens (e.g., arguments, operators, and options—all separated by whitespace), enter an event designator followed by **:** followed by a *word designator*. A word designator is another collection of symbols that matches a variety of types of words, as summarized in Table 8.8. The shell numbers each token from left-to-right, starting with 0 for the command name. For example, if event 58 is **grep   tortu   /usr/dict/words**, I could feasibly (and pointlessly) enter **!58:0 !58:1 !58:2** in one command line to rebuild and execute the same event. In the following step, I access the first argument of two previous commands to use in a new command line:

Step 8.49:   Use word designators to extract event arguments

```
unix> pico a.txt                                        Edit a file.
Uriah                                                   Enter something.
unix> pico b.txt                                        Edit another file.
Heep                                                    Type something else.
```
Below, use **cat** *to append these files.* **pico a.txt** *is the previous event (*!-1*), and* **pico b.txt** *is previous to that event (*!-2*). The filenames are first arguments (*:1*) in each event:*
```
unix> cat !-1:1 !-2:1 > c.txt          Append b.txt to a.txt and store in c.txt.
cat b.txt a.txt > c.txt                    The shell echoes the command line.
unix> less c.txt                                        View your results.
Uriah                                                Did your command work?
Heep                                                   Yes, history worked!
```

Note that if your word designator is **^**, **$**, *****, **-** or **%**, you do not need to specify the colon (**:**). Consequently, if you do not specify an event designator, the word designator refers to the previous command. For example, you can abbreviate **!!:*** as **!***.

PRACTICE!

8.6.5   Word Modifiers

You can modify the tokens extracted by the word extracted by with *word modifiers*. To use a word modifier, enter a colon after a word designator (or another word modifier) and another sequence of letters, some of which I show in Table 8.8. Although **bash**, **tcsh**, and **zsh** share syntax for event and word designators, they differ for word modifiers (see the manpages). Below I demonstrate a simpler application–suppose you want to repeat a command on a file because you typed the wrong extension. You can use **r**:

Step 8.50: Remove a file extension with a word modifier

```
unix> less a.text                    Attempt to view a non-existent file.
a.text: No such file or directory    Whoops! (Assuming you don't own a.text.)
```
Rather than recalling the command with Up ($\uparrow$) and then using **Backspace***, you will use a history substitution of the form* !e:d:m. *Use* ! *(for* e*) to recall the previous event,* 1 *(for* d*) to access its first argument, and* r *(for* m*) to remove the extension.*
```
unix> less !!:1:r.txt                Redo the previous command with a new file extension.
Uriah                                                                    Hooray!
```

In the above example, you can type .txt directly after :r because the shell substitutes (or, *expands*) the meaning of !!:1:r before processing the rest of the command (Section 8.1.5).

PRACTICE!

50. Write a command line that *displays* the previous event.
51. Using **zsh**, write a command line in all uppercase to generate an error message. Next, fix your mistake by using an appropriate word modifier.

8.7   QUOTES AND QUOTING

Throughout the manpages, this book, and your configuration files, you will see many kinds of quotes in action: *forward quotes* (also called *single quotes*) (´,`, '), *backquotes* (`,`), *double quotes* (", ", "), and even the *backslash* (\), which counts as a quote in Unix. (I list the variety of names in Appendix A.) Depending on the syntax, quotes alter or protect the meaning of tokens (or groups of tokens) in the command line, which helps you define variables and generate output with non-alphanumeric characters. Common applications of quoted text include variable values and output statements. The process of protecting characters is called ***quoting***, which is essentially using single quotes, double quotes, and the backslash. Backquotes involve a different process. Dealing with quotes poses several challenges for new students—as always, try lots of small examples. As usual, you should review your shell's manpage.

8.7.1   Backquotes (Command Substitution)

Although some references place this section outside of quoting, I worry that Unix newbies may confuse backquotes (`) with forward quotes ('). Backquotes trigger ***command substitution***, which does not protect other tokens. In fact, command substitution differs entirely from quoting. The shell treats text surrounded by backquotes as an independent command line. The shell substitutes the output of the *backquoted command line* directly inside the current command line. For example, suppose that you wish to create a directory with the current date as part of the name. Why not use **date** to assist you?

Step 8.51: Use command substitution to create a directory

```
unix> date +%m_%d_%Y                 Remind you about how date works.
06_20_2005                           %m is month (mm), %d is day (dd), %Y is year (YYYY).
unix> mkdir `date +%m_%d_%Y`         Make a directory with the current date in its name.
unix> ls -F                          List CWD's contents.
06_20_2005/  and other output        Here's your new directory!
```

If your backquoted command produces vertical output (**who**, for instance), have no fear! Backquotes treat newline characters as whitespace that separate arguments. If you are particularly adventurous, investigate **$(...)** for nesting command substitutions.

PRACTICE!

> 52. Write a command line that tells a user how many files they have in their CWD in a friendly fashion.

8.7.2   Single Quotes (Strong Quotes)

To prevent the shell from interpreting any character, use single quotes to surround the text—you will often see the terminology for *matching* quotes, as in **'text'**. Single quotes protect metacharacters with only two exceptions:

- You cannot include forward quotes; i.e., **'''** gives an error.
- **csh/tcsh** will interpret the shell history (**!** or its equivalent in **$histchars**). To interpret **!** literally, use **\!** (Section 8.7.3).[17]

Why should you care? Occasionally you might wish to use a shell metacharacter as plain text as output or a character to search for in a file. Without forward quotes, the shell will interpret a metacharacter, triggering the substitution of other text. In the following example, I demonstrate ways single quotes can assist **set** and **echo**.[18]

Step 8.52:   Single quote examples

```
unix> set hello=')('                Set hello to a bizarre string.
unix> echo $hello                   Did it work?
)(                                  Yes, because forward quotes disable ) and (.
unix> echo 'x*y'                    Echo some text.
x*y                                 Single quotes disable *.
unix> echo '''                      Can you echo just one forward quote?
Unmatched '.                        No. You must match forward quotes.
```

Step 8.53:   Trickier single quote examples

```
unix> echo 'a'b'c'        echo parses the input text as 'a', then b, and then 'c'. Why?
abc                       A single quote matches with the next single quote in each pair.
unix> echo '\\'                           Does this command output just \?
\\                          No! Backslashes are just another kind of metacharacter.
```

Step 8.54:   Including newline characters

```
unix> sh                                    Use sh or descendent.
$ echo 'x ↵                Start quoted text and press Enter (↵) before matching the '.
> y' ↵                             Type more text, the final quote, and Enter.
```

---

[17]Actually, **csh** and **tcsh** exhibit different behaviors. An unprotected **!** always triggers **csh** to attempt a history substitution. But **tcsh** ignores the **!** if it is alone, has no subsequent character, or the subsequent character lacks a history interpretation. For example, try **echo '!-'**: **csh** will complain, and **tcsh** won't.

[18]Given **echo**'s prevalence for demonstrating examples, I recommend that you check your system's configuration. My system's **tcsh** automatically sets **echo_style** as both, which causes my **echo '\\'** to display just one \. Figuring that out took over an hour—and all we get is a lousy footnote ☺. Step 8.53 works for **csh/tcsh**, assuming you for set **echo_style** to bsd or none. See **man -s1 echo** and **echo**'s descriptions inside the shell manpages. Other shells have variables that affect **echo**: xpg_echo (**bash**) and BSD_ECHO (**zsh**). Try also **alias echo** to see if it is modified. If all of this disgusts you, use **printf**.

```
x
y                                          sh and descendents allow you to include newlines
$ exit                                     until you enter the second forward quote.
                                           Return to previous parent shell.
```

Step 8.54 will not work for **csh/tcsh**. See the *Practice!* problems in Section 8.7.3 for a demonstration.

PRACTICE!

> 53. Write a command line that outputs `I want my two dollars!`.
> 54. Explain what `echo '!!'` does, using **csh** or **tcsh**.

8.7.3 Backslash (Strong Quote)

Backslashes have various roles in Unix shells and other programs:

- *Protection of a single character*: To interpret a metacharacter *m* literally, use *****m*. Recall that forward quotes do not interpret (or as sometimes called, *escape*) backslashes (except for **csh/tcsh**'s **\\!**).

- *Removal of a command alias* (i.e., protection of an entire word): References rarely mention the syntax **\\command**, which instructs the shell to disable any alias defined for **command**. The disabling occurs only for the duration of the command line. Life becomes more complicated if you attempt to include a backslash as part of the alias, as discussed in **man zshall**.

- *Indication of an escape character*: Many applications use backslash notation to indicate escape characters, like **\n** (*newline*), **\t** (*tab*), and more. See **man -s5 formats**, **man echo**, and **man printf**.

- *Line continuation*: When you type a \\ and then press **Enter** at the end of a command line, a shell prompts you to continue typing on a new line. The second line will have a new prompt. For **csh/tcsh**, see variable **prompt2**; for **sh** and descendents, see variable **PS2**. The shell will process the entire command line as if you entered it on one line.

Below, I demonstrate these uses of \\:

Step 8.55: Protect a single character

```
unix> echo *                                            Can you echo just a * ?
You will get a list of your CWD's files and directories. Why? The * matches every file and directory in your CWD
due to command-line globbing.
unix> echo \*                                           Protect your metacharacter.
*                                                       The \ makes echo display just the *.
```

Step 8.56: Remove command alias

First, create an alias for s. For ksh, bash, or zsh, use alias name=value (Section 8.8). After you enter the alias command, the customized command will persist for the current shell until you exit or remove the alias:

```
unix> alias ls 'ls -F'                                  Define ls to mean ls -F.
unix> ls                                                Run the customized version of ls.
You will see a list of your CWD's contents and their types. See Section 5.10.3 for details.
unix> \ls                    Disable your definition of ls for the duration of this command line.
Normal listing with no file types shown. To use your customized version again, (until you exit the shell) enter ls.
```

Step 8.57:   Indicate an escape character

```
unix> printf "%s" Bananas!                          Print Bananas!.
Bananas!unix>                            Whoops! We need a newline character.
unix> printf "%s\n" Bananas!             Try again, but use a newline (\n) this time.
Bananas!                              printf prints Bananas! and then newline.
unix>                                               All is well in the land of output.
```

Step 8.58:   Continue a command line

*When continuing a line, your shell's second prompt appears. Below, I use **tcsh**:*
```
unix> pico \↵              Feel free to enter any command. After typing \, press Enter (↵).
? something.txt↵           Continue typing at the second prompt. When done, press Enter.
```
Depending on your command line, Unix now executes the complete command. Actually, as long as you keep terminating a line with a \, your shell will continue to prompt you before processing the command line.

PRACTICE!

55. Demonstrate how you can output the line \ \ \ \ with **echo**.
56. Using **csh/tcsh**, demonstrate how you can use a backslash to continue a line with **echo** and single quotes.

8.7.4   Double Quotes (Weak Quotes)

You may surround a group of characters with double quotes. Some people call double quotes *weak*. But don't prejudice yourself against **"** for fear of lame command lines! The "weakness" derives from the ability to allow interpretation of the following meta-characters–I perceive that feature as a strength!

- **$**: *variable/parameter substitutions*. The **$** tells the shell not to interpret other characters that belong to the substitution, like { and }.
- **`**: *command substitution*. Inside the double quotes, shell will replace the text of the command substitution (including the backquotes) with the output of the command.
- **!**: *command history*. A lone or terminating single **!** does not trigger history. If you change the history character (e.g., **$histchars** in **csh/tcsh**), the double quotes will interpret that character instead of **!**.

Double quotes also allow \ in some cases:

- **sh** and descendents: \ disables **'**, **"**, **$**, and another \.
- **csh** and **tcsh**: \ can only disable **!**. To include **$** and **'** without interpretation, you need to use a combination of single and double quotes. See also the **backslash_quote** shell variable.[19]
- All shells: your shell might have variable or alias settings that cause **echo** (and other commands) to accept escape characters, like **\n**.[20]

---

[19] Do you see the q.v. in **man tcsh**? It represents *quod vide*, or *which see*, which effectively means *look around for more information*, as I did to figure out what *q.v.* means.

[20] See Footnote 18. Can you believe it—a footnote that refers to *another* footnote? I still blame **echo** for the confusion.

As with single quotes, you can also continue a line:

- **sh** and descendents: Press **Enter** (↵) before the matching **"**.
- **csh** and **tcsh**: Use **\↵** to terminate a line that you wish to continue.

Hopefully your head isn't spinning at this point. I demonstrate some of the rules, below:

Step 8.59: Allow variable substitution with double quotes

```
unix> echo "My shell is ${SHELL}!"          Double quotes allow variable expansion.
My shell is /usr/local/bin/tcsh!            The $ signals the shell not to interpret {}.
```

Step 8.60: Allow command substitution with double quotes

```
unix> echo "I have `ls | wc -l` files in `pwd`."    Command substitution inside text.
I have    37 files in /home/dis.                    If you get an error, see if you swapped ' for `.
```

Step 8.61: Mix quotes

```
unix> echo "Doesn't Doug doodle?"           Double quotes permit single quotes.
Doesn't Doug doodle?                        The ? is also protected from interpretation.
```

PRACTICE!

57. Using **bash**, use a parameter expansion to test and return the value of a variable called **BLAH**. Use **echo** or **printf** to report either **BLAH**'s value or Not set!.
58. Using **csh/tcsh**, enter **ls**. Then, use command substitution, history, and double quotes to display the number of files and directories that **ls** reports.

8.8 ALIASES

As shown in Steps 2.15 and 8.5.5, Unix allows you to create your own commands using *aliases*, which helps you to abbreviate long command lines and automatically set command options. An alias is a command name that you create—sometimes even reusing a predefined name—that represents a command line. For example, if **rm** prompts you with yes/no, then you have (perhaps unknowingly) aliased **rm** to mean **rm -i** (*interactive remove*). This section introduces aliases for all shells but **sh**, which lacks the facility. As usual, the shell manpages contain complete details: see listings under Aliases (**bash** and **csh**), Alias Substitution (**tcsh**), Aliasing (**ksh**), and ALIASING (**zsh**).

8.8.1 Viewing Aliases

I bet that your system administrators have set some aliases for you already. For all shells, enter **alias** (no arguments) to see aliases from the system and user configuration files. Below, I show some of my own:

Step 8.62: View aliases

```
unix> alias                                 View current aliases.
..    set dot=$cwd;cd ..                     I have a number of aliases
all   more -ec *                            that I store in a file called .aliases in Home.
ll    ls -la |less                          Some of these linger from my first Unix account!
and many others
```

Where are configuration files that contain aliases? For now, look inside your dot files inside **HOME**. I explain these files in further detail in Section 8.9.

You can change aliases by editing their definitions, as explained in the subsequent sections. Until you learn how to edit your configuration files I recommend using your interactive shell for changing, setting, and removing aliases, which means that changes persist until you exit the shell. Since subprocesses do not inherit aliases, you will ultimately want to modify your configuration files. For more information, see **man alias**.

PRACTICE!

59. How do you view a particular alias?
60. Show a command line that pages through all your aliases.

8.8.2   Setting Aliases with `csh` and `tcsh`

To create an alias, **csh** and **tcsh** require **alias   name   commandline**. The **commandline** is a string composed of a command line that you wish to assign to **name**. Do you see how the **alias** statement resembles a variable assignment, where you associate a name with a value? For **name**, you may select your own name or even a predefined name–you must follow Unix filename rules. If **commandline** lacks metacharacters, then you do not need to use quotes, as demonstrated below:

Step 8.63:   Set an alias with `csh/tcsh`

```
unix> alias ls ls -F                          I want ls to mean ls -F.
unix> ls                                      Try the new and improved ls.
You will see a listing of your files along with types.       Do you agree with me?
unix> alias ll ls -l              I'm sick of entering ls -l. I want ll, instead.
Listing along with file types in CWD.         Another useful alias is ls -al | less.
```

You may find it disconcerting that **ls -F** does not necessitate quotes:[21] **csh/tcsh** aliases do not interpret the command modifier (**-**) and path separator (**/**). However, I still recommend that you surround your definition with single quotes to protect all characters and clarify the **alias** statement.

If you use metacharacters in an **alias** definition, you do need quotes, depending on the particular characters (Section 8.7). Why? During the processing of the **alias** *assignment* statement, the shell replaces unprotected metacharacters with their expansions inside the alias. But we want an alias to store *literal character names*, not their expansions, inside the definition—we want an alias to interpret its metacharacters when it runs, not beforehand. For instance, suppose you wish to define **ll** to mean "page through a long listing of everything." Below, I demonstrate **ll**'s **alias** statement with and without quotes:

Step 8.64:   Aliases and metacharacters with `csh/tcsh`

```
unix> alias ll ls -al | less             Attempt to define ll, which includes a pipe.
Your shell will pipe the result of alias ls ls -al  (which is empty) into less. So, you will view nothing.
unix> alias ll 'ls -al | less'                Use single quotes to protect the pipe.
unix> ll                                            Try your new alias.
Long listing of all files in the CWD.                  Try also ll dir.
```

[21]In Step 8.63, when I redefine **ls**, the shell does *not* recursively process the alias of **ls** as (**ls -F**) **-F** (and so forth). Otherwise, the shell would never cease executing the **alias** statement.

With **ll** in Step 8.64, you can use **ll** *dir*, like **ll** **/usr/bin**. When entering *myalias args*, the shell will pass *args* directly to the original command line that the alias represents.

To insert an argument anywhere inside an alias, you need to use history, which makes things trickier. **csh** and **tcsh** treat an aliased command line's arguments as if they belonged to the previous event. When I first learned this feature, I had to scratch my head—understanding how it works will reinforce your other Unix skills. Using an alias for **cd**, I explain the processing rules, which I list below:

- *Quoting* (Section 8.7.3): To protect **!** from interpretation during the definition of an alias, use **\!**. You can now define aliases that look like **alias cd 'cd \!* ; echo $cwd'**. Keeping reading to understand the rest of **\!***.

- *Aliasing* (**man tcsh**–see Aliases): If an alias contains a history substitution (**\!***stuff*), the shell treats the defined command line as the *previous event*, including the arguments that you supply when running the aliased command. For example, my shell expands **cd blah** internally as **cd blah ; echo blah**.

- *History* (Section 8.6): To refer to arguments of a previous command, you can use **\!!:***d*, where **\!!** refers to the previous event, and *d* access arguments from that event.

- *History shortcuts* (Section 8.6.4): You can abbreviate **\!!:*** (*all previous arguments*) and **\!!:^** (*first argument*) as **\!*** and **\!^**, respectively.

So, given that the alias for **cd** contains a history command, the shell "pushes" the current arguments into the previous event. Thus, you need to use the syntax for previous history (**\!***) to extract those arguments when writing your alias.

Step 8.65: Alias with middle argument (csh/tcsh)

```
unix> alias cd 'cd \!* ; echo $cwd'          Define cd to echo the CWD.
unix> cd /usr/bin                            Set CWD to /usr/bin.
/usr/bin                          My aliased cd goes to /usr/bin and echoes it.
```

PRACTICE!

> 61. Create an alias called **bf** that creates a backup of *file*. **bf** should always use the name **Backup.***file*.
>
> 62. Why do I use **\!*** instead of **\!^** in Step 8.65?

8.8.3   Setting Aliases with **ksh**, **bash**, and **zsh**

Descendents of **sh**[22] have a slightly different syntax than that of **csh/tcsh**.

> **alias** *name1=commandline1 name2=commandline2* …

which has the following rules:

- You must *not* surround the **=** with whitespace.

---

[22]**man -s1 sh** explains that the **/usr/xpg4/bin/sh** (*Open Group compliant*) version of **sh** has **ksh** functionality, which means that your **sh** likely supports aliases, too. See also **man -s5 standards** for an explanation of *XPG*.

- You must surround each command line with single quotes to include spaces, the hyphen (**-**), and metacharacters. With **zsh**, you can sometimes skip the quotes.

- You cannot use history inside an alias. Instead, you need to use functions (Section 8.8.5).

- Your alias name follows Unix filename conventions.

Regardless of the differences, these kinds of aliases strongly relate to those of **csh** and **tcsh**. I demonstrate some "**sh**-type" aliases in the following step:

Step 8.66: Bourne shell-type aliases (**ksh**, **bash**, **zsh**)

```
unix> bash                                  Pick ksh, bash, or zsh.
$ alias l=ls                                Define a simple alias for listing.
$ alias ll='ls -al | less'                  ll: page through everything in the CWD.
$ alias dir=ls lf='ls -F'                   Assign multiple aliases in the same command line.
```

You can do some funky things with **sh**-type aliases. See **ksh**'s *tracked aliases* and **zsh**'s *global aliases* under **alias** in each of these shell's manpages.

PRACTICE!

63. Create an alias called **purge** that removes any filename that terminates in **~** or **#**.

8.8.4 Removing an Alias

To remove an alias, you have three options, which I list in order of increasing severity:

- Disable the alias with **\name**. As explained in Section 8.7.3, using **\name** disables **name** for the duration of the command line and does not affect the alias's definition.

- Enter **unalias name**. Your shell will cease associating **name** with your definition for the duration of the shell in which you entered **unalias**. If **name** is defined in a shell configuration file, other shells will use the alias, including any new shell process that you start. But if you entered the alias at the command line, the alias vanishes when you exit your shell.

- Delete the alias from the configuration file. Obviously, this option does not work for command-line definitions. Actually, I prefer commenting old definitions (placing a **#** in front of the statements) in case I wish to reuse them one day.

For more information, see **man unalias** and the shell manpages.

PRACTICE!

64. Set an alias for **ls -x** called **lx** at the command line. Remove the alias temporarily and then permanently.
65. How can you remove all aliases for the current shell process (but not permanently) for **csh**, **tcsh**, **ksh**, **bash**, and **zsh**?

8.8.5   Going Beyond Aliases: Functions and Scripts

If you want to make a complex alias, I recommend that you investigate making a function (**sh** and descendents) or a script (all). I leave scripts for later study. For a brief function example see Table 8.6. Below I show common forms of syntax:

- `name () { commands; }`
- `function name { commands; }`
- `function name () { commands; }`

When creating functions, you must follow these rules:

- Follow Unix filename conventions for function names. Avoid renaming a current command or alias.
- Surround the first brace with whitespace. Actually, surround both **{** and **}** to be safe.
- Separate each command line with an appropriate separator (Section 8.3).
- Terminate the last command with a semicolon.
- Arguments that you pass to the function become positional parameters (Section 8.4.13).

You might be curious how to define an alias for **cd** akin to the version for **csh/tcsh** in 8.65:

Step 8.67:   Create and use a function

```
unix> bash                                                    Use sh or descendent.
In my definition of cdp, I want bash to change the CWD to my supplied argument ($1) and then echo the CWD:
$ function cdp () { cd $1; echo $PWD; }                       Define a bash function.
$ cdp Unix_work                                              Change to my Unix_work directory.
/home/dis/Unix_work                                          bash echoes the new CWD.
```

Of course, I ignored a whirlwind of details in the shell manpages. If writing functions appeals to you, you will love programming!

PRACTICE!

66.   Create a function called **cdl** that changes a directory and lists its contents.

8.9   SHELL CONFIGURATION

Although I have focused on the interactive shell, a tremendous advantage with Unix is its capacity for customizing, especially with configuration files. Each shell's manpage contains a wealth of information, which helps you to create your own files. Eventually, you might learn about scripts, too. Unfortunately, the amount of time needed to describe every customizable feature of every shell would require another book, maybe more. Instead, I explain how to begin customizing your account.

8.9.1   General Advice

Each system administrator sets up your account differently. I can't even predict which shell you use, though I suspect a majority of you use **tcsh** or **bash** by default. (Any **zsh**ers out there?) Regardless of your shell, changing configuration files could be dangerous: changing file permissions, losing important work, preventing access to your own account, etc. To work on your account, you will need this advice:

- Create a backup directory that contains all your dot files inside **HOME**. These files have names like `.profile`, `.cshrc`, `.zshrc`, and so forth. You may even want to print or archive the key files. (You will need to read some more to learn about which files you actually need. I show typical names later in Table 8.9.)

- Check your current settings. See **set**, **setenv** or **env**, and **alias**, perhaps redirecting the output to a file or printer so that you have a reference copy.

- Test variables, aliases, and (in some cases) functions at the command line in an interactive session. If you make a mistake you could always kill the shell. If you use a GUI, kill the window and open a new one.

- Try to use your own files for customizing. For instance, I created my own `.aliases`, in which I have my `.cshrc` run. See Section 8.9.4.

- Attempt ideas incrementally. For example, if you want to test a new alias, edit the proper configuration file for just *this* alias, not 20 more. Most newer shells use **source *file*** to execute ***file***. I explain this process more in Section 8.9.4.

- Use comments when editing statements in configuration files, which are lines that start with **#**. The shell ignores comments. Why bother? You might not remember the role of a complex function a couple years from now.

- Keep a separate login process running with the original configuration files. Run multiple windows, log into multiple machines, or perhaps even remote login (**ssh**) to your own account. You can also use **su** (*super user*) as **su - *you*** (see **man su**).

- Refer to public websites, like *www.dotfiles.com*. People love to post their configuration files, and the other users will certainly appreciate inspiring you!

PRACTICE!

67. Create a backup directory for your configuration files.
68. Review the manpage for your default shell. Which configuration files does it use? Backup the files in your **HOME** that relate to the files listed in the manpages.

8.9.2 Command-Line Login

Depending on your system, you should see a login screen, which is usually a GUI. Regardless of the setup, you need to enter your username and password to access your account. Most books focus on "non-GUI" logins, which are called *command-line logins* (also *text* or *character*). In this section, I explain this traditional process that you will frequently encounter, especially if you run your own version of Unix, like Linux.

As shown in Figure 8.8, my computer starts with a GUI program that lets me select window manager options or a command-login screen before I enter my username and password. If you have a similar initial login screen, select the command-line option. Unix will run **login** as a single terminal, which fills the entire screen (in some cases, a single window). You should see a `login` prompt, as shown in Section 2.3. After logging in, a program called **login** performs a variety of security checks (like checking for stale passwords), which I leave for later studies. After identifying you, **login** does the following:

- Extracts information about you, often from /etc/passwd.

- Sets default values to certain environment variables. For example, my system sets **HOME**, **LOGNAME**, **PATH** (using default /usr/bin), **SHELL** (your default shell from /etc/passwd), **MAIL**, and **TZ** (*time zone*).

- Starts an interactive shell using the default **SHELL**. The interactive shell is a *login shell* (Section 8.1.2), which typically sets terminal information and global variables.

- Executes system configuration files, if configured to do so. Look inside /etc or /etc/skel to see if you have files that contain profile, cshrc, or even just rc in their names.

- Execute *your* configuration files. I explain the order and typical names in a later section, because it gets a bit weird. For example, **login** typically processes $HOME/.cshrc *before* $HOME/.login for **tcsh** users.

I provide an extensive list of shell configuration files in Section 8.9.5. To learn more about the details and processes, see **man login**.

8.9.3   Login with GUIs

If you see a login window like the one depicted in Figure 8.8, you see **dtlogin**, which differs from **login**. Traditional Unix books do not discuss this process, which is unfortunate, because of two fundamental questions[23] to consider when configuring your account:

- Which configuration files does the GUI login program use?

- When you run a window program from the window manager, does the window access your configuration files?

The answers differ depending on which window system you choose.

If you select X Windows[24] or a command line terminal to start X Windows, your login program will access another program called **xinit**, **xstart**, or a customized version on your system. **xinit** (or equivalent) uses your $HOME/.xinitrc to spawn specific windows (typically **xterm**) and a window manager (see *xwinman.org*). The windows spawn shell processes, which access shell configuration files. However, if your

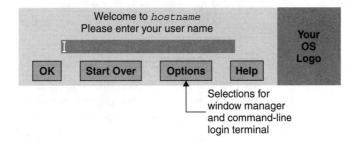

Figure 8.8   Typical GUI login screen (**dtlogin**).

---

[23]I had a third question when writing this book. How do you take a screen capture of the login screen? The program is called **dtgreet**. Because you have to login to use screen capture tools (like **xwd**), you're got a problem....

[24]For purists, it's really the *X Window System*.

.xinitrc does not modify an **xterm** with -ls (*login shell*), the **xterm** does not access login configuration files. (See also the value of xterm*loginShell inside $HOME/.Xdefaults.) Note that the filenames for login configuration files contain either profile (**sh** and descendents) or login (**csh** and **tcsh**). See **man xinit**, **man X11**, and Appendix B for more information.

dtlogin (*desktop login*) and similar programs follow an order of processing akin to **login** but use different configuration files. If you use **dtlogin**, snoop around /usr/dt/config, /var/dt, and /usr/dt/bin. See also the login configuration file $HOME/.dtprofile, which gives lengthy explanations (it uses **sh**-type syntax). So, instead of your shell's start-up files, CDE looks for a saved configuration of your desktop and $HOME/.dtprofile for other user commands. Just as with X Windows, terminals that you spawn from the desktop might not run login shells. Fortunately, CDE and other systems offer extreme flexibility and robust configuration tools, allowing you to set many features via GUI programs. See **man dtlogin**, **man dtterm**, and **man dtwm** for more information.

PRACTICE!

> 69. Start a command-line login. Start X Windows and determine if your initial **xterm**s are login shells.
> 70. How do you start a login shell with **dtterm**?

8.9.4 Implementing Configuration Files

To implement the changes you make inside a configuration file, you could log in and out, which wastes time. Moreover, if you make a mistake inside the file, you might screw up your account. Instead, spawn a backup shell process (in case you still screw up) and use **source filename** to process each statement inside **filename**. (For **sh**, you might see references to the "dot command," or **. filename**.) **source** works because the configuration files are scripts! Each statement (alias, variable setting, ...) is something you can enter at the command line. When finished, your shell will now use the settings of **filename**. If you make a mistake inside **filename**, the shell will lose its settings while sourcing the files, which provides more motivation to run backup shells! For more information, see **man source**. To learn about related material (commands that run other commands), see **man exec** and **man eval**.

PRACTICE!

> 71. What happens if you source one of your original, unmodified configuration files? What does your shell do? Is this test dangerous?

8.9.5 Shell Configuration Files

In Table 8.9, I summarize the majority of shell configuration files that affect your session (*system files*) and those that you can edit (*user files*).[25] The system files may have different names, and you may discover that your system configuration departs from the descriptions in manpages. You can often alter the names and include additional files inside HOME by setting certain shell/environment variables. For now, I just want you to realize that your system may do some work before your shell sees your configurations. Regardless of the names, bear in mind two key principles.

---

[25]Many files have rc in their name. Although some say *run command*, I prefer *run control*.

- An interactive, login shell processes login and nonlogin configuration files. I provide conventional sequences in Table 8.9.

- An interactive, nonlogin shell processes certain shell configuration files, which I indicate in Table 8.9.

Below, I provide further notes about each shell:

- **sh**: Your version might support **ENV**, where you have **ENV=$HOME/ .shrc ; export ENV** inside your `.profile`. Note that nonlogin shells do not source $HOME/`.profile`. But these shells inherit any variable that you export.

- **ksh**: Only login shells read $HOME/`.profile`. If your is **ENV** set (usually to `.kshrc`), **ksh** will source that file next. Nonlogin shells source **ENV**, so it typically contains shell variables and aliases (recall that aliases do not inherit).

- **bash**: The shell looks for one of these files in this order: $HOME/ `.bash_profile`, $HOME/`.bash_login`, and $HOME/`.profile`. Like **ksh**, **bash** sources **ENV**, which is usually $HOME/`.bashrc`. Nonlogin shells use **ENV**, too. Some systems might also have /etc/bashrc, which executes before **ENV**. See also $HOME/`.inputrc` for key bindings that **bash** sets.

- **zsh**: At first, the list may seem bewildering. If you do not believe me, see **man zshall**. **zsh** encourages you to organize settings according to purpose. If your system does not set **ZDOTDIR**, then **zsh** uses **HOME**. Note also that **zsh** lets you customize pretty much everything.

TABLE 8.9 Common Shell Configuration Files

Shell	Login Configuration	Nonlogin Configuration	Login Order	Other Files
sh	/etc/profile $HOME/.profile	N/A	/etc/profile $HOME/.profile	possibly $ENV
ksh	/etc/profile $HOME/.profile	$HOME/.kshrc	/etc/profile $HOME/.profile $HOME/.kshrc	$HOME/.sh_history
bash	/etc/profile $HOME/.bash_profile (or, $HOME/.bash_login, or $HOME/.profile)	$HOME/.bashrc	/etc/profile $HOME/.bash_profile $HOME/.bashrc	/etc/inputrc $HOME/.inputrc /etc/bashrc $HOME/bash_history
zsh	/etc/zshenv $ZDOTDIR/.zshenv /etc/zprofile $ZDOTDIR/.zprofile /etc/zlogin $ZDOTDIR/.zlogin	/etc/zshrc $ZDOTDIR/.zshrc	/etc/zshenv $ZDOTDIR/.zshenv /etc/zprofile $ZDOTDIR/.zprofile /etc/zshrc $ZDOTDIR/.zshrc /etc/zlogin $ZDOTDIR/.zlogin	$HOME/.zlogout
csh	/etc/.login (or /etc/csh.login) $HOME/.login	$HOME/.cshrc	$HOME/.cshrc $HOME/.login	$HOME/.history $HOME/.logout
tcsh	/etc/csh.login $HOME/.login HOME/.cshdirs	/etc/csh.cshrc $HOME/.tcshrc (or $HOME/.cshrc)	/etc/csh.cshrc /etc/csh.login $HOME/.tcshrc $HOME/.login HOME/.cshdirs	$HOME/.history $HOME/.logout

- **csh**: The system filenames may appear quite different on your system. Dig around /etc. Don't forget to list hidden files and see what's in /etc/skel.

- **tcsh**: The configuration order is modeled after that of **csh**. In fact, you can use .cshrc instead of .tcshrc. Although I list the typical order of processing, the manpage warns that **tcsh** might swap the order of (t)cshrc and login for the system and for your account. I recommend that you experiment or simply check with a system administrator.

As usual, you can find out more details, in the shell manpages.

PRACTICE!

72. What are the file permissions on system configuration files? Can you edit these files?

73. Explain various ways to separate system aliases and other settings from those that your system administrator provided with configuration files in **HOME**.

8.9.6   Modifying Your Configuration Files

I wish had the space to properly demonstrate a variety of shell configuration files. Unfortunately, I have only enough space to point you in the right direction. I strongly recommend you follow the advice that I list in Section 8.9.1—otherwise you could totally screw up your account. Once you have prepared your account for modification, you need to address the major issue of what goes where. I recommend that you split configurations roughly into two places:

- For login files (.login, .profile, ...), I recommend that you follow the conventions that I list in Table 8.10. Global variables (which affect your entire session), and programs that you need to run only once are good candidates for login files.

- For nonlogin files (.cshrc, .bashrc, ...), I recommend that you set local variables and aliases/functions, though I prefer putting aliases in a separate file. The shell manpages contain descriptions of the many kinds of shell variables that you can set.

Note that **csh/tcsh** automatically export some local variables, like **home**, **path**, and **user** (and vice versa). See **man csh** or **man tcsh** for more information.

TABLE 8.10   Login Shell Settings

Feature	Example	Reference
Search Path	`PATH=$PATH:$HOME/bin` `set path=($path ~/bin)`	Section 8.5.3
Terminal Type	`setenv TERM vt100` `TERM=vt100; export TERM`	`man tset`, `man tty`, `man stty`, **TERM** inside shell manpages
Control Keys	`stty erase ^h` `stty erase ^\?`	`man stty`, `man xmodmap`
Environment Variables	`setenv LESS 'QiaMcw'` `PRINTER=jaded; export PRINTER`	Section 8.4.11
System Communication	`news` `uptime`	Chapter 6 (system and local communication)

Unix is a fascinating subject that can draw you in and never let you go. Unix exudes mystery! At first, you experiment with simple commands. After all, what other choice do you have? But scientists and engineers are an inquisitive lot. I hope that you wonder how other students have all those wild screen backgrounds and wonderful shell prompts.

Unix was designed to be discovered, and many people founded careers delving into its depths. To begin your own exploration, copy the dot files from adept and knowledgeable users and decipher each line of code. Also, study your site's literature, and maybe buy a few computer books—they're relatively cheap and incredibly informative. Select books that discuss shells and shell programming. From shells, all else follows.

Manual pages also provide a wealth of knowledge. (Granted, manual pages are rather circular—**man man**!) Try various command options described in the manual pages; then try customizing commands to automatically select options, as discussed in this chapter. Investigate related commands listed at the bottom of most manual pages—perhaps an unfamiliar command might ease your work.

Many will still choose Unix strictly out of necessity. But computer-skill development, including competence with Unix, enhances your development as an engineer or scientist. Software is always in flux–you must learn new applications and techniques as technology improves. Knowing Unix will sharpen your ability to learn new innovations and help you succeed throughout your career.

CHAPTER SUMMARY

- A Unix shell forms your interface to the internal Unix operating system. There are two primary branches of the shell family tree: Bourne Shell (**sh**) and C Shell (**csh**).

- Your command line environment uses an interactive shell. A shell in which you use **login** is a special kind of interactive shell. A login shell processes certain configuration files. A "regular" (or nonlogin) interactive shell processes fewer files.

- The shell parses the command line into individual tokens. Depending on the shell, the shell performs a variety of expansions following a predetermined order (see each shell's manpage).

- You can customize command-line editing keys for modern shells.

- You can redirect (**>**) and/or append (**>>**) output from a command to another source, like a file or printer.

- Standard error resembles standard output. You can direct error messages to the same or different location as output.

- You can redirect input (**<**) or make a *here document* (**<<**) into a command. This form of redirection is less common.

- Piping commands together (**|**) sends the output of a command into another as input. The **tee** command sends a copy of the output to a file during the piping.

- To process a sequence of commands in a single command line, separate each "sub-command-line" with a semicolon.

- Commands return exit values, which you can use to selectively process command sequences: **&&** (*and*) and **| |** (*or*).

- When you group commands together in a subshell (**( )**), the subshell becomes a child process. The parent process (the process in which you write the command line) waits until the child finishes.

- A variable stores a value for reuse. Unix shells have two kinds of variables: local/shell and global/environment. Some shells refer to *parameter* as a general kind of variable, which includes positional and special types.

- Variables store strings. Shells have special commands to convert strings that represent numbers. A variable with no value differs from a variable set to the null value (the empty string `' '` or `" "`).

- Local variables do not inherit in child shells. Global variables inherit, but only to processes that you spawn after setting the global values.

- Parameters have special roles: You can access elements of a command line with positional parameters. You can access process information with special parameters.

- When parsing the command line, the shell must resolve the location of the commands. If you do not specify a full pathname, and if the command is not a shell built in, the shell searches **PATH**. The global variable **PATH** contains a list of directories in which to search.

- Unix supports many programs to find commands. You can use file completion as a way to look.

- Except for **sh**, shells support command history, which is a mechanism that stores previously entered commands (*events*). You can identify an event with `!e:d:m:m`.... *e* is an event designator (pick an event), *d* is a word designator (extract a word or words from the event), and *m* is a word modifier (modify the words). You can supply a sequence of word modifiers.

- Backquotes (`` ` ` ``) are used for command substitution and are not considered part of Unix quoting. `` `cmd` `` substitutes the result of **cmd** inside the command line that calls `` `cmd` ``.

- Single (or forward) quotes (`' '`) protect all metacharacters from interpretation, except for **csh/tcsh**'s history character (`!`). Some applications, like **echo**, can be set to accept backslash sequences inside single quotes.

- Backslashes (`\`) protect the next character, disable an alias, form escape characters, and continue lines.

- Double quotes (`" "`) are weaker than single quotes, permitting the shell to interpret some metacharacters: `$`, `` ` ``, `!`, and sometimes `\`.

- You can name a command line with an alias, which allows you to abbreviate commands. **alias** statements work at the command line, though you should eventually store your favorites in a configuration file. Aliases do not inherit.

- **csh/tcsh** aliases can include history characters, which allows you to generalize arguments anywhere inside a command line.

- **sh** and descendents have functions, which are mini-programs in which you can write sequences of command lines. Functions allow you to include metacharacters.

- When configuring your account, you need to save your current files and set up multiple logins. You should also test each change one at a time. Window managers typically use their own configuration files.

- Non-GUI login shells implement a larger set of files than non-login shells. Each kind of shell uses its own files, which might be configured differently on your system.

- Login configuration files typically contain global settings and programs that you run only once. Nonlogin files tend to contain shell variables and aliases.

- Every interactive shell or window that you open accesses the nonlogin configuration files.
- Unix is cool. Have fun exploring it!

KEY TERMS

alias	here document	quoting
command substitution	history	redirection
environment variable	I/O	script
event	interactive shell	shell variable
exit status	local variable	subshell
file completion	login shell	trojan horse
file descriptor	parameter	variable
global variable	piping	

COMMAND SUMMARY

`alias`	Abbreviate a command line.
`apropos`	Search for a string in manpages.
`bash`	Run Bourne Again Shell.
`bind`	Assign key binding.
`bindkey`	Assign key binding.
`csh`	Run C Shell.
`dtlogin`	Run CDE login (only `root` may do so).
`dtterm`	Run CDE window.
`echo`	Output a string.
`env`	Display environment variables.
`exit`	Logout from shell.
`export`	Convert a local variable to a global variable.
`fc`	Process event list
`find`	Look for a file.
`function`	Define a function.
`info`	Find information on a command; might extract manpage.
`ksh`	Run Korn Shell.
`login`	Run login process.
`man`	Find information on a program.
`printenv`	Output global/environment variables.
`printf`	Report output; eventual replacement of **echo**.
`set`	Display all local/shell variables; assign local/shell variable.
`setenv`	Display global/environment variables; assign global/environment variable.
`sh`	Run Bourne Shell.
`source`	Execute a shell script.
`su`	Login as another user or yourself.
`tee`	Send output to a file during a pipe.
`type`	Describe command type.
`typeset`	Get/set shell variables and functions.
`unalias`	Remove command alias.
`unset`	Remove local/shell variable assignment.
`unsetenv`	Remove global/environment variable assignment.
`whatis`	Display one-line summary of command.
`whence`	Get/set shell variables and functions.
`whereis`	Find binary, source, and manpage files for a command.
`which`	Find pathname for a command.

woman	**man** browser in **emacs**.
xinit	Run X Window System.
xman	Run X Window manpage browser.
xstart	Run X Window System.
xterm	Run X Window terminal.
zsh	Run Z Shell.

Problems

1. What is a Unix shell?

2. What family does **ash** belong to? Does your system support it?

3. When someone says that they have installed Linux, do they mean that they use **bash**? Explain your answer.

4. Find at least two Unix shells not included in Table 8.1—no, you can't use **ash**. Hint: Look for the *Unix FAQ* on the World Wide Web.

5. Explain the difference between these two kinds of interactive shells: *login* and *nonlogin*.

6. Why do many system administrators and Unix programmers still write shell scripts in **sh**?

7. Describe the process of parsing in terms of a shell command line.

8. What is whitespace? What kinds of characters does the shell consider as whitespace?

9. How do you change the shell's whitespace characters? For even more fun, see if you can find a programming language called *Whitespace*.

10. Explain the relationship between non-printing ASCII characters and escape characters. Give some examples.

11. How do you remove a filename that includes a blank space?

12. What happens if you kill your login shell process?

13. Describe the order of expansions that your default shell performs on the command line.

14. Does your shell support a logout configuration file? If so, create a file that displays *Buh-bye!* in huge ASCII-graphics letters. Hint: See **banner**.

15. Explain the difference between a function and a script.

16. Using your system dictionary, create a list of words beginning with z, and store the results in a file called zwords.txt.

17. Write a command line that stores a complete, long listing of your **HOME** while you page through the output.

18. Write a command line that sends the CWD as redirected input to **ls**. Does the result of this command line differ from conventional use of **ls**? Explain your answer.

19. Explain the difference between **ls > dirlist 2>&1** and **ls 2>&1 > dirlist**.

20. Distinguish between the command lines **ls -R > list.txt** and **ls -R | more**.

21. Create a text file that contains a list of your favorite bands on each line. Show a command line that removes any duplicate entry, sorts the remaining names, and stores the result in `sortedbands.txt`.

22. Write a command line (or sequence) that stores an alphabetized list of current users logged on with no duplicate names. Hint: See **man cut**.

23. Write a command line that demonstrates how to use **cat** as a rudimentary text editor.

24. Write a command line that copies a file called A to file B, but if that operation fails, the shell attempts to copy to file C.

25. Using the command line from Problem 24, direct standard error to E.

26. Why doesn't the command line **(test71=10) ; echo $test71** produce 10?

27. Demonstrate a sequence of command lines that reads in values for variables **A** and **B**. Then, write command lines that swap the values of two variables. For example, if **A** is 1 and **B** is 2, then **A** is 2 and **B** is 1 after the swap. You may use only one additional variable to assist with the swap.

28. If you assign a global variable **BORKNAGAR** at the command line and then log into your account from a different computer, does that new session recognize **BORKNAGAR**? Explain your answer.

29. Can you set a null value with just **var=**? Explain why this statement does/doesn't work.

30. Demonstrate **bash**'s parameter expansion `${parameter:+word}`.

31. When configuring **csh** or **tcsh** for your account, do you need to set **PATH**? If you do set your command path, should you set **path** or **PATH**? Does the choice matter to the shell?

32. When you enter a full pathname for a command, like **/usr/bin/ls**, does the shell search for **ls**?

33. When does **info** not read manpages?

34. Explain the role of `$(command)` for **bash**.

35. Echo the line !@#$%^&*()_+ with **tcsh**, using **printf**.

36. Echo the line "Hello, I'm using ', ' and \ in my output.".

37. I often enter the wrong command for a given task and pathname. For example, perhaps I enter **cd /home/jre/hrmonitor.txt**. But I really meant to *view* that file. Write a command line using history that you can enter immediately after making such a mistake.

38. Using command substitution, write a command line that reports your username and number of files in your account (yep, all of them).

39. If you use a history command to refer to **ls -aF** and **ls -a -F**, the word designators differ. Since these command lines are effectively identical, why does history treat them differently?

40. Demonstrate how to include events in your primary shell prompt.

41. Find help on **man** using only one "**man**" and one history substitution in the command line.

42. Using **tcsh**, demonstrate a history command that will convert the previous command line to all lowercase letters. You will need to look up word modifiers from **man tcsh**.

43. Explain why **zsh** handles Problem 42 in a much simpler fashion.

44. Sometimes Unix users make aliases for MSDOS commands. Do you agree with this idea? Explain some advantages and disadvantages.

45. Write an alias called **rerun** that mimics **!!** in **csh** and **tcsh**.

46. What are the name conventions for aliases? For example, can you make an alias called **666** that echoes something? Can you make an alias called ****** that prints a file? If you can indeed make these aliases, should you? Explain your answer.

47. When configuring **TERM**, you will often see vt100 as a value. What is a vt100? Why is it common?

48. Write a command line that enables **emacs**-style editing for your command line.

49. Configure your $HOME/.xinitrc such that it opens an **xterm** that runs a login shell.

50. Project 1: Draw analogies between file management and process management. Discuss parallels between parent-child relationships. Relate similarities and differences. Be sure to include several examples. Edit your report with a text editor.

51. Project 2: Define all shell and environment variables inside your current shell configuration files. Present your report in three columns: variable name, assigned value, and description/role.

52. Project 3: Find ten commands not described in this text and write a synopsis for each. Include at least one example of usage.

53. Project 4: Modify your configuration file(s) for your default shell–you should include at least 10 new aliases and 10 variable settings.

54. Project 5: Write a crontab that copies all text files in a particular directory to a backup directory whose name depends on the date. The copying will occur at 4 A.M. daily.

55. Project 6: Define a function called **swap** that swaps filenames for two supplied files. You must not create other files. (See Problem 27.)

56. Project 7: Write a shell script called **aboutme.sh** that prompts a user to enter their name, age, and height. The script should create a file called me.txt that contains this information. Write a command line that demonstrates how to input the data into your program and output the results to me2.txt.

Online Resources

Index

A

a, 39
A, 39
Absolute pathname, 91–92
    changing directories, 91–92
    copying by using, 108–109
Abstraction, 88
acroread, 75
alias, 23, 25, 99, 103, 184, 197, 209, 214, 217–224, 230–231
Aliases, 184, 219–223, 230
    and editing, 185
    and functions/scripts, 223
    global, 222
    removing, 222
    setting with `csh` and `tcsh`, 220–221
    setting with `ksh`, `bash` and `zsh`, 221–222
    tracked, 222
    viewing, 219–220
American Standard Code for Information Interchange (ASCII), 13, 17, 22, 27–28, 30, 46, 55, 57, 64, 69, 74–75, 129, 145
    ASCII table, 28
    text files, 27–28
Application software, 4
apropos, 211, 231
Archiving/storage, 28, 75, 107, 118–121, 224
    disk resources and usage, 118–119
    external archiving, 121
    file compression, 119
    file sizes, 118
    procedure for, 119–120
ARPANET, 129
Arrow keys, 14
    `pico`, 32
ASCII NULL characters, and Unix, 30
Assembler program text, 28
Assigning, 199
Asterisk (*), 114–115
AT&T, and Unix, 5

B

Background, *See* & (ampersand); `bg`; Process background
Backquoted command line, 215
Backquotes, 215–216, 230
Backslash (\), 115, 217–218, 230
Backspace key, 16
    in emacs, 52
    in `pico`, 32–34
    swapping with the Delete key, 17
Backup, 103
"Bad" command lines, 20
banner, 22, 25
basename, 91
bash, 180–181, 187, 194, 201, 202, 212, 214, 231
    configuration, 227
BASH_ENV, 204
Berkeley Software Distribution (BSD), 5
bg, 169, 177–178
biff, 135
Binary files, 28
bind, 231
bindkey, 231
Bits, 4

Booting, 20, 164
Bourne shell (`sh`), 16, 180–181, 187, 189, 192, 194, 197–198, 200, 202, 205, 207
Bourne-again shell (`bash`), 180–181, 187, 194, 201, 202, 212, 214
Branches, 87
Browsers, 152–154
Buffer:
    defined, 32
    emacs, 45
    writing out, 32
Built-ins, 184, 209
Bytes, 4

C

C, 5
C-/, 53
C shell (`csh`), 16, 19, 99, 180–181, 188, 191, 194, 195, 197, 200, 202–203, 205, 207
C-@, 53
C-_, 53
C++, 18, 198
C-a, 53
cal, 22, 25, 131
cancel, 82–83
cancer, 74
Caps Lock key, 16
    avoiding use of, 13
Carpal tunnel syndrome (CTS), 22
Case sensitivity, 13
C-b, 53
cat, 61–62, 187, 189
cd, 97–100, 124
C-d, 46, 53
CDPATH, 204
C-e, 53
Central processing unit (CPU), 3, 107
C-f, 53
C-g, 53
C-h, 46
C-h b, 52
C-h C-h, 52
Change directory, *See* cd
Change mode, *See* chmod
Change permission, *See* chmod; File permissions; Permissions
Changing directories:
    absolute pathname, 91–92
    to HOME, 99
    relative pathname, 91–92
    to root, 99
    by using shortcuts, 99
Chatting, 133–134
    blocking messages, 134
    Inter Relay Chat (IRC), 134
    talking with others, 133
chdir, 99
Checking file type, 28
Child directory, 87–88
chmod, 76, 79, 83, 117, 124
Chottiner, Jeffrey, 8
chsh, 182–183
C-k, 53
Class:
    getting the most out of, 59
    in OOP, 199
Cleaning house, 111
Clipboard, 34
C-M-/, 53
C-n, 53
COLUMNS, 204
comm, 67, 83